THE TROUBLE WITH WALL STREET

THE TROUBLE WITH WALL STREET

•

Lewis A. Bracker

and

Walter Wagner

PRENTICE-HALL, Inc.
Englewood Cliffs, N.J.

Printed in the United States of America T
Prentice-Hall International, Inc., London
Prentice-Hall of Australia, Pty. Ltd., North Sydney
Prentice-Hall of Canada, Ltd., Toronto
Prentice-Hall of India Private Ltd., New Delhi
Prentice-Hall of Japan, Inc., Tokyo

●

Library of Congress Cataloging in Publication Data
Bracker, Lewis A.,   date
    The Trouble with Wall Street.
    1. Stocks—U. S. I. Wagner, Walter, date
joint author. II. Title.
HG4910.B7   332.6'2   71-158491
ISBN 0-13-930834-2

For
Phyllis
who invested the most

CONTENTS

The stock market is one of the most written about, most discussed subjects in the world, yet it is one of the least understood.
—*Lewis A. Bracker*

THE TROUBLE WITH WALL STREET

ONE

PORTRAIT OF AN UNLIKELY
MULTIMILLIONAIRE

Ambition should be made of sterner stuff.

SHAKESPEARE

"Superbroker!"

I winced slightly as the razzle-dazzle word—an alleged description of me—flashed up from the front page of the Los Angeles *Times* on the Friday morning of January 24, 1969.

"Superbroker"—a semantic conglomerate that wasn't even in the dictionary. It was pure newspaperese, a catchy tag in the headline above the column-one story detailing my career as a successful securities salesman, investment broker, underwriter, corporate financial counselor and, most importantly, discoverer of buried treasure in the stock market jungle—young, unknown, promising companies which, with a judicious creative touch, had been built into little-known blue chips, blue chips more blue than such gray-bearded, wounded colossi as General Motors, AT&T, IBM and U.S. Steel.

The story carried the bromidic overline RAGS TO RICHES, but the text of the piece was factual despite its hoary Horatio Alger slant. It told, accurately, that I had started as just another broker eight years before, and gone on to acquire personal assets of several million dollars.

However, I wasn't a "superbroker," whatever that meant. There was nothing mystical about my rise. My good fortune was due in large measure to the circumstance that among the overwhelming majority of my fellow brokers, there wasn't much competition. It hadn't been all that difficult to soar above most of them.

I had no secret, no magic formula, no never-wrong tout sheet. I did not, as in a story I once read somewhere, have a copy of tomorrow's newspaper, replete with stock quotations twenty-four hours ahead of anyone else.

1

I had, in short, no infallible system. Those with an "infallible system" go broke as quickly in Wall Street as they do in Las Vegas.

My bonanza had been acquired by a simple principle—Methuselahan in age—that the bulk of brokers have either forgotten, neglected, never learned or heartlessly ignored.

My principle was *to make money for my clients,* a revolutionary idea among brokers. Yet it is an idea as old as the stock market. To borrow a phrase from Psalms 83:16, I fed my clients "the finest of the wheat." I left the chaff of the fast buck to others.

What I had accomplished could have been achieved by any broker. And a conscientious broker in Omaha or Orlando, New York or Los Angeles, can begin tomorrow to travel the same golden highway. I am delighted to share my road map with fellow brokers and individual investors.

What I did and what I am doing is also being done by other diligent brokers throughout the nation. Unfortunately and tragically for the investment public as well as the securities industry, there are all too few brokers who serve themselves well by serving clients well. The brokers who do so are rich, as are many of their clients.

RAGS TO RICHES, as the *Times* had put it, wasn't quite accurate. There had never been rags before I became a broker, although there certainly had been hardscrabble times.

I came to the broker's profession without a dream of acquiring great riches for myself. Taking into account my somewhat listless and indifferent background and lack of success in previous attempts at making money, nobody, least of all myself, could foresee that I would become that comparatively rare American—one in every thousand who is a millionaire.

I also came to the broker's profession completely untutored in the world of stocks and finance. Perhaps this was fortunate, for I had little to unlearn once I entered the rough-and-tumble of the market. My ignorance undoubtedly helped me find a clear-eyed, better way of serving clients, a method no one else around, to my everlasting astonishment, seemed to be using when I initially stumbled across it.

About the only thing I had going for me when I obtained my first broker's job was a desire to be in on the decision-making process of big business. Some money, I assumed, but never in seven figures, would come as a by-product if I applied myself and was lucky.

The Los Angeles high school I attended in the early 1940s didn't offer a course in economics. That subject in those unsophisticated days was lumped into a catch-all course in math. And I hated math. I mastered the fundamentals, but that was it. I flunked algebra and thus never got the opportunity to flunk geometry. (Nobody, I've discovered, needs algebra or geometry in the market. No one even needs math beyond the routine ability to add, subtract, multiply and divide. The market doesn't need mathematical wizards. Conceivably, Einstein would have been a lousy broker.)

I breezed through the subjects that I enjoyed, particularly English, history and civics. In my spare time I played trumpet in the band.

My first ambition was to become a newspaper reporter, and I planned to apply to the school of journalism at the University of Missouri. Then I found out what reporters earned. Although I wasn't thinking in terms of great wealth, my hope for remuneration exceeded a newsman's $50-a-week starting salary with prospects of only small, turtle-paced increases.

I waited for something with greater potential to turn up after my graduation from high school. It didn't. Therefore, because I had nothing else to do, I enrolled at California State Polytechnic College in San Luis Obispo.

I was an indifferent student. The school, in the summer of 1946, was flooded with ex-GI's, most in their middle or late twenties, some in their thirties. All of them seemed terribly ambitious. I was seventeen and totally devoid of ambition.

I attended my English classes but didn't trouble to turn up for my math course. The most intelligent thing I could have done at that questing, restless, unsure stage of my life would have been to bum around the country for two years or so, gaining experience, maturing, learning about people, ingesting a sense of what the world was all about, becoming equipped as a man—a quest far more important than earning money.

Instead I bummed through college, a confused kid without a compass to provide any direction. I piled up a covey of incompletes, which meant I had to repeat some courses. I hadn't failed them, I just hadn't bothered to show up for lectures. I much preferred spending my time at the student union playing Ping-Pong.

After two years I dropped out, with only a couple of credits in English, economics and elementary accounting. In none of my classes had the stock market once been mentioned.

Next I entered a private business school, the tuition underwritten by my father. With the exceptions of English and business law, I found the courses flat and dull. Again I dropped out.

With somewhat more desperation than optimism, my father put me to work for him. He was in the produce business, specializing in financing Mexican farmers. He would then handle the sales of their tomato and vegetable crops and distribute them in carload lots across the country.

As in the stock market, very hot markets sometimes occur in the produce business. On one occasion we projected a two-month shortage in tomatoes. We went to El Centro, in the Imperial Valley, and bought an eighty-acre crop. It proved an extremely profitable venture, showing a profit in only six weeks of more than $100,000.

But it had been my father's deal and my father's money. However, working for him had whetted my appetite for business. I liked the action and the excitement.

When the Korean hostilities broke out I enlisted in the Army, spending eighteen months stationed at Fort Ord, California, where I did little but play trumpet in the band. I spent another eighteen months in Japan, most of it as manager of the band.

After my discharge I still had a desire to become a businessman. But what business? All I knew for certain was that I didn't want to join my father in produce. Those pulse-racing $100,000 short-range profit deals were few and far between, and I had no particular desire to spend my life maneuvering amid tomatoes and watermelons.

I returned to Cal Poly and immediately found myself in the same rut. I took a few more courses in economics, but most of my "education" was in sports. I made the varsity basketball squad, was number-one man on the tennis team and became ever more proficient at Ping-Pong. If I had a hero then, it wasn't Bernard Baruch, but football great Elroy Hirsch. I had far more admiration for a man who could score a touchdown than a man who could score a financial coup. Shortly I fled school once more. I was now a three-time loser in the halls of academe.

The necessity for somehow filling my time and earning a living stared at me. My lone opportunity came through a friend of my father who had an insurance brokerage. He offered me a job and I accepted. Insurance was certainly part of the business world. Perhaps I had found my niche.

For the first time in my life I developed some semblance of enthusiasm for what I was doing. I set out to learn the insurance business as thoroughly as possible, even taking time to unearth some fascinating minutiae. From reading the history of the Prudential Insurance Company, world's largest insurer, I learned that it was founded in 1873 under the name—are you ready?—"The Widows and Orphans' Friendly Society." (The term "widows and orphans" survives today in the lexicon of Wall Street as the traditional designation for "surefire" blue chips.) In further pursuit of useless but bewitching trivia, I shuddered at the tale of one I. F. A. Studdart, who owes his footnote in history to the circumstance that he, perhaps too ambitiously, sold policies for the West and New York Life Insurance Company to General George Armstrong Custer and five of his officers, all of whom soon afterwards were massacred by the Sioux at the Battle of the Little Big Horn. The company paid $40,000 in death claims to the heirs of Custer and his officers.

Charging into the insurance business myself, I sold life and casualty policies and went after the firm's slow-pay accounts. Some premiums were in arrears as much as $2,000. I collected a great deal of this overdue money and was bringing in new business at the same time. For my efforts I was earning $75 a week.

After a year and a half I asked for a raise. "You're not worth it," my boss said. "I don't think you're worth what you're getting."

I went straight out the door and opened my own insurance

brokerage. My boss had done me quite a favor in turning down my request for a raise. Had I received it, I might still be there.

In the first year of operating my own business I didn't clear $3,000. I married in 1957 and became a father the following year. With responsibilities, the need to earn more money became more urgent. I went into partnership with several real estate agents. I felt it would be a good situation—they had five offices and were selling a great number of homes on which I hoped to write a great amount of coverage.

But the Bracker Insurance Company did not thrive. The real estate tie-up failed to generate the income I had anticipated. I began going into debt, and I only managed to buy a two-bed-room crackerbox $19,000 house with a down payment loaned by a relative.

Soon our second child was born, my wife was ill for a time and it became necessary to hire a housekeeper. My expenses were increasing tremendously while my insurance business was running at a loss.

My income was nil, my cash flow decidedly negative. I wasn't even paying income taxes.

By now I detested the insurance business, and not just because I wasn't making money. Under the right conditions the business could have been profitable. But the right conditions could not materialize because the big companies were putting the squeeze on independent agents. I'd work my tail off finding new, legiti-mate clients, only to discover that the major insurers wouldn't cover them for what seemed to me unsatisfactory reasons. The large outfits also began cutting commissions for independent brokers, so I had to do twice the amount of business to earn even the small amount of money on which I found it impossible to live.

I sold out and was tickled to death to get $3,000 for my brokerage.

A washout in school and in the insurance business, I now had nothing to fall back on except my latent interest in jour-nalism. I was destined to wash out again. I spent the next six months trying to be a free-lance writer, my urge to participate in business dormant. I wrote a number of teleplays and articles.

The only thing that sold was a fan magazine story, which informed the publication's readers that actress Connie Stevens had a constant problem fighting weight.

The story brought $100 into the household.

The $3,000 from the sale of my business disappeared rapidly. While I still had the brokerage I had borrowed $9,000 from a bank, although it is an enduring mystery to me why it would lend that much to a green businessman. When I couldn't meet the payments on the loan, I borrowed $5,000 from a "shylock," who charged one point and interest of 10 percent a month. I used his loan to pay the balance I owed the bank.

One night at dinner, a friend who worked for a securities firm said my insurance background was "perfect" training for me to become a broker. He urged me to try it. I couldn't have been less interested. I pictured myself calling on my old clients and telling them I was no longer selling insurance, this year I was selling stocks, and maybe in another year I would be back pitching the same clients aluminum siding.

It didn't make sense. But soon it began making more sense because it was the only option I had.

Financial pressure on me was mounting alarmingly. I was now $11,000 in debt, thirty-two years old, a husband and a father of two—and I had no prospects whatever for a solvent future.

I wasn't neurotic about the fact that I was approaching the middle point of life as what the world would consider a failure. I didn't consider myself a failure, yet I realized I wasn't exactly J. Paul Getty.

And so I was delighted when the brokerage firm of Stern, Frank, Myer & Fox agreed to take me on as a trainee at $420 a month.

That wouldn't cover my expenses, but it was $420 more a month than I was earning.

TWO

NOBODY EVER TALKED ABOUT PROTECTING YOUR CLIENTS' MONEY

The happiest time in any man's life is when he is in red-hot pursuit of a dollar with a reasonable prospect of overtaking it.

JOSH BILLINGS

Instead of the tastefully subdued lettering outside the offices of Stern, Frank, Myer & Fox (and every other brokerage house), there should be a sign with the irresistible clarion call of the circus ringmaster, "Children of all ages, welcome to the greatest show on earth."

I found that the atmosphere in the board room was not without parallel to the circus. Most of the performers who darted across the stage of the quotation board were the staid, sometimes fading stars who'd been around a long while—the oils, rails, automobiles, utilities. The stage, however, was enlivened by exciting new stars—electronics, computers, copying machines, among others. One especially dazzling act at that time was Edward Land's sensational Polaroid, the biggest thing to hit the consumer camera market since the Brownie. Polaroid brought ferocious, healthy competition to an essentially moribund and unexciting industry.

In the jammed board room, stocks rising or dipping as little as a quarter of a point galvanized everyone's attention. The raptly attentive audience of tape watchers included high-flyers, wire-walkers, bears, bulls, lions, lambs and the inevitable clowns, not to mention an occasional freak.

But there was an essential difference between the circus and the market. The big top was show business—rehearsed, staged, artificial and, except for rare occasions, predictable. The market was unrehearsed and always unpredictable. And I never saw a circus crowd exhibit the intensity of emotion displayed in the board room.

Men's fortunes and day-to-day circumstances were dictated

by the quotations hurrying by. Depending on how the tape read that day, a man would enjoy a zestful dinner or pick disconsolately at his food; a new car would be bought or the old clunker cleaved to; children's teeth would or would not be straightened; there would be the thrill of making a killing and then trying for the next killing, or there would be the hangdog gloom of defeat and discouragement. The market watchers lived their lives by the numbers, participants in a second-to-second drama.

My baptism as a trainee began at a testing center where I underwent five hours of psychological probing, a puzzling experience. (These aptitude tests are still in vogue among many houses hiring new men.) But I couldn't determine how tearing through my psyche would reveal whether or not I could sell stocks—much less make money for investors. The only profit from what to me was an extremely tenuous and doubtful procedure accrued to the testing center, which had a good, fancy-fee operation going. The professional probers have obviously convinced the houses their tests can spot men capable or incapable of becoming successful brokers. It would be fascinating if the securities industry underwrote, say, a two-year follow-up to test the judgments of the testers. Given the heady turnover of brokers and the large number who fail or malfunction in the job, the mind investigators might properly be asked to explain why so many aspiring brokers destined to be poor performers slip through the psychological net. And given the incredibly poor performances of Wall Street sachems, the tests might better be applied to the managing partners of most brokerage houses.

Whatever the probers were looking for, they apparently found it in me, much to my honest surprise. I was told that I was in the top one percent in the nation so far as sales ability was concerned. How the tests determined that defied my understanding. My previous foray into business certainly didn't seem to sustain such an encouraging, flattering verdict.

The ennui of the six-month training period demanded by the New York Stock Exchange before I could be licensed was a sharp contrast to the adrenalin-racing activity in the board room among brokers and investors during trading hours.

The training passed as lugubriously as the pages of a bad Russian novel, but I began to feel I had found my niche. I was on the threshold of big business. I was going to be a decision-maker, at least on a freshman level. This was what I had been searching for, and Connie Stevens would have to find herself a new Boswell.

However, training gave me no key to Fort Knox. I participated in no brain-bursting bouts with experienced giants of the securities industry. As a fledgling in the world of high finance, I did not sit at the feet of all-knowing gurus who imparted nuggets of wisdom I could then pass on to clients so that everybody would become rich. Rather, as in the Army, I did little but put in time. This is still true of broker training today.

The "learning" process to which I was exposed consisted of a few weeks of observation in the research department, several weeks learning the ins and outs of the mechanics of trading—spending some time in the cashier's cage, absorbing the trivial details of office routine and instruction in how a transaction is processed through the exchanges when a client gave a buy or sell order. I also attended a short, turgid market extension course at UCLA.

It soon became evident that what the training program omitted was far more germane than what it included.

The most important omission—and this hit me like a sledgehammer—was that throughout my training, never once, even by implication, did anybody talk to me about protecting the money of clients!

The entire thrust was on salesmanship and sales technique. Hustle! Sell! Push! Promise! Plead! Cajole! Sock-it-to-'em! Make the sale! Keep your volume up!

The focus was solely on earning money for the house and the broker, not the client. If the client happened to make money, wonderful. If the client didn't make money, well, too bad. If clients became disenchanted, find new ones. Or give disappointed investors cliché explanations—the market is undergoing a temporary reversal, earnings unfortunately are below expectations, Dow Jones is down, a technical correction followed by an upswing is expected, the market is a two-way street, and with patience everyone always comes out ahead. Those are the platitudes a broker usually hands clients, none of which really pacifies a client who is taking a beating.

Such cynicism and total disregard for the interests of clients was never stated that crudely or in so many words. The message was oblique, always strongly implied but never said out loud. That's the way the game was played.

The type of training I received—and what still passes for broker training—doesn't make anyone a qualified broker. Not only wasn't I cautioned about protecting the money of the people I would be selling stock to, but I wasn't educated in such nitty-gritty essentials as what to look for in a stock, what to guard against, what the factors are that will tend to make an issue rise or fall, how to analyze a situation.

And the majestic New York Stock Exchange accepted this mountain of superficiality as bona fide preparation to award me my broker's license, which I received in July, 1961.

Credentials in hand, my so-called training period completed, knowing as much about the market as my canary, I was now unleashed, tigerlike, to sell stocks—and the public was fair game.

I was given a desk, a telephone and the commandment to sell, sell, sell to an unsuspecting public. Naturally, the first problem I faced as a new broker was what stocks to sell.

It didn't remain a problem for five minutes.

Down from the ivory tower of the research department (and that ivory tower atmosphere is the fundamental trouble with most research departments) came a flood of recommendations, lofty pronunciamentos from what I was told were seasoned observers. What it really amounted to was that I was handed printed pages on various companies and urged to talk up and sell these particular stocks to clients. How research arrived at its decisions as to which stocks clients should buy was a process already suspect in my mind.

I went along with the system and became as guilty as anyone else in uncritically pushing on unwary customers whatever stocks research recommended.

In fact, I was so hot to go that I set a precedent. Stern, Frank wanted my training to continue for another six months. But I didn't look forward to another half year of Russian novels. Moreover, the terms of the proposed extended training were impossible, unfair and unrealistic. I was told I could sell stocks during the additional training period, but I wouldn't receive the commissions on my sales! I would remain chained to my $420 a month salary. When I said forget the salary and that I wanted to go on straight commission, I was informed that it had never been done before. I declared, however, that I intended to make much more than $420 a month.

If the lengthened training was of value and I had been offered a decent salary, I would have been delighted to move more slowly and learn more. It was all too true that in my case I was being pressed to the wall with personal debts and I needed income. But fair compensation, perhaps $200 a week, would have allowed me to make ends meet while allowing me to gain more training, bad as it was.

Reluctantly, the house agreed to let me go on commission.

In my first ten days as a broker I earned $1,700 for myself. I earned it by selling stocks that I knew absolutely nothing about, stocks whose real value was completely unknown to me. I had no idea of whether I was putting my clients on the road to riches or ruin. I sold the stuff recommended by research and I also sold stocks my father happened to favor. The recommendations of research were no better or worse for the profit picture in the portfolios of my clients than those of my father, who did not even have my presumed expertise as a trained broker backed by the presumed expertise of trained research analysts.

As long as the orders kept coming in, the house didn't much care what I peddled or where I got my information.

Electronics were the glamour stocks of that period and I sold a great deal of two sister companies, Electronics Capital and Electronics International Capital. Both were so fantastically overpriced that it was nonsense. Yet my clients bought on my say-so. These two stocks were my father's recommendations. He knew the people involved in the companies and liked them as individuals, although he didn't know much about their qualifications as management men.

I also sold a number of new issues that the house wanted pushed, mostly secondary offerings—additional shares put on the market by a company that was already public and wanted to raise more capital. I already had enough knowledge to realize that secondaries were a bad deal for clients. They not only diluted the value of the original common, but the new buyers were paying a higher price going in for already eroded shares. If a company wants to raise money the second time around, it should give the public a break. Why issue more common? Why not instead issue convertible bonds or warrants so that the individual investor has more leverage, more chance of making money. There aren't too many secondary offerings around to-day. Burned so badly so often, the public is generally too wise to go near them. Now it would have to be a very attractive secondary for me to touch it with a ten-foot tickertape. Nor would I now touch any stock—not one—that I sold as a beginning broker.

After ten months in the business I ran into the first bad market I had experienced. In May, 1962, the market collapsed, sweeping away $107 billion in the paper value of stocks.

In the six months it took for the market to recover, I watched and learned. The downswing was the result of a long speculative boom, and almost everybody got hurt—those holding blue chips and those clinging to the glamour stuff. Blue chips were selling at wild prices in relation to earnings, so there was plenty of room for them to tumble. Many of these blue chips have never regained the sky-high prices they commanded in 1960. Those who held the glamour issues fared even worse. The balloon of one hot-air issue after another was punctured. Even though they had no intrinsic value, investors had dived into these issues recommended by brokers—and the brokers hawking them knew it.

I learned that for people who gamble in overvalued blue chips or ballooned stocks there is always a day of reckoning. I also learned that if a stock has a realistic relationship between price and earnings, the investor will survive a down market because it is virtually certain the company will bounce back. ˙

It was bad enough to be clobbered in blue chips, but those

who were really hurt in 1962 were buyers who got caught in
promotions, rank speculations, stocks that were discounted into
infinity. Anytime the price of a stock is way out of proportion
to its earnings, the buyer is living on borrowed time and playing a very dangerous game.

The downswing edged me along, gropingly, toward a discovery of paramount importance, a discovery that was to shape
my entire future and my philosophy of investing clients' funds.

My point of reference began to change from stocks to companies, a distinction that makes all the difference between a
winner and a dog.

I cast a close eye around the board room and it occurred to
me that something was very wrong. Every broker was doing the
same thing. We were crisscrossing each other's paths, bumping
heads, often soliciting the same clients with the same pitch for
the same stocks. It was an idiotic rat race that invariably ended
in the broker and the house taking their commissions, but flog-
ging the hapless investor.

The research department of the house had not, of course,
anticipated the 1962 drop, and my clients suffered. It hardly
took a genius to realize that there must be a better way of protecting clients.

The core of the decision-making process concerning which
stocks to buy or sell was obviously research. But the house
analysts were only handing me puff sheets. It became crystal
clear that the only way I could offer my clients a realistic chance
at a profit, and the only way to attract more and larger clients,
was to do my own research. Then, and now, this was an almost
sacrilegious procedure for a broker since the house analysts are
hired precisely for that job. The house research men, however,
were underpaid and invariably preferred the comfort of their
cushioned swivel chairs to the more difficult, time-consuming
process of field research. And, from the analysts' point of view,
what difference did it make? Clients were buying and that made
the house happy. If current clients were being fed cats and
dogs, so what? There was always a new supply of investors who
could be gulled.

Gingerly, I began for the first time to get out of the board
room, personally visiting a number of small companies and

ferreting out my own research information. On days when it was impractical for me to leave the office, I used the telephone as an arm for research. It amazed me how flattered most executives were to be visited or phoned by a broker genuinely interested in their companies.

I started writing my own research reports to clients, hammering them out on a typewriter I brought to the office myself. If the research department resented my doing my own footwork and analysis, I never heard about it. Not that my research was worth much at this point. Despite my on-the-spot investigations, I was too ignorant to know what questions to ask management. One of my first trips was to San Diego to visit the Electronics Capital plant. The executives I met were charming and cooperative, but I gained no particular insight because I was simply at a loss to intelligently discuss their business, to elicit the crucial information about such vital matters as their prospects, what share of the market they controlled in their industry, new technological developments, and so on. Most of all, I had not yet learned to judge the men who made the judgments by which their companies rose or fell.

But however naive and primitive my first-person research was, I at least had a toe in the water, one more toe than any other broker in the house.

The beginning of the end of my tenure at Stern, Frank came when I got involved with one memorable client, an attorney with a small practice. He was also a small investor who had designed a perfect and brilliant system of beating the market. His system was as perfect and brilliant as it was unethical and tawdry.

I had recommended that he purchase what appeared to be a promising electronics stock. I hadn't investigated this particular company. I took the word of another broker that it was a good situation based on a sizable projected increase in earnings.

The lawyer invested about $5,000, buying in at 5. The stock shortly went to 7½. Beneficiary of a quick 50 percent profit, I phoned and asked him if he wanted to take his gain. His answer was a resounding no. He believed he was riding a comet, that the price would skyrocket.

The company's shares did stay up for a while, but in the

1962 toboggan they went down like everything else, although not too badly. They settled around 4.

When the lawyer found himself in the position of being some $700 in the hole, he phoned me, choleric, demanding his money back! He accused me of giving him misinformation and said if his money wasn't returned he was going to sue the house, sue me, and for all I knew he might sue the men who ran the company for having the audacity to issue shares whose price was vulnerable to a decrease as well as an increase.

I reminded the client that the projected earnings had come in around the figure I had quoted and that I had offered him an opportunity to take a considerable profit while the taking was good.

The man would not be pacified.

He swept into the office and barked at the head men of Stern, Frank, threatening a storm of legal action if his money wasn't returned forthwith.

The house was terrified and it buckled like the knees of a repentant sinner, although the attorney's gambit was sheer blackmail. I couldn't believe it when I was told that the man's money was going to be given back. I explained there had been no misrepresentation and he had been given the chance to get out with a 50 percent profit.

Not only was the house authorizing repayment, but *I* was going to be forced to repay the client.

From the point of view of the house, this made perfect sense. The house could afford to be cavalier and generous with my money.

The practice at Stern, Frank was to put the first $750 a broker earned in commissions into an error fund. This money not only earned no interest, but it indicated that the house did not trust the stability and responsibility of its own brokers.

The client thus was going to be reimbursed with $700 from my error fund; a client, incidentally, who had no clout, a shyster with more brass than anyone I have ever encountered, a man simply trying to get out from a bad market, a client to whom a fifty-cent gain on every dollar invested hadn't been enough.

The incident was ludicrous. If every loser in the market demanded and received his money back, the securities industry would vanish overnight.

I refused to believe that the house would go through with it. How could a brokerage firm trading in millions of dollars a year be cowed by a sore-loser con man? Perhaps the house feared damage to its image because of the attorney's threatened litigation, but given the circumstances he would certainly be laughed out of court. Perhaps the house didn't believe or trust my side of the story. In this instance the house was displaying a rare sensitivity for the client, but then it was costing them nothing to maintain the doubtful goodwill of the attorney.

When the dust cleared it was July, 1962, the end of my first year as a broker. The unthinkable did happen—$700 was removed from my error account and paid to the client, proving, among other things, that the wheel that squeaked the loudest still got the oil.

The client had accomplished what only law-breaking insiders in the market have managed. He had reduced his risk to zero. With such a ploy—assuming it could be worked repeatedly—the man was certain to become a millionaire, taking his profit when the price of his shares went up, whittling down his losses when shares declined. This client had rigged the only infallible system for beating the market I have run across.

The incident ended my association with Stern, Frank.

Through bull and bear markets I had cleared $12,000 for myself in twelve months—my net minus the $700 rape of my error fund.

I had never before seen that kind of money. And although I wasn't out of personal debt, my situation was improving. I was able to buy a slightly larger house and provide a few luxuries for my family.

Now I was hooked on the brokerage business. It *was* the greatest show on earth.

THREE

THE DEAL MAN

A man is known by the company he organizes.

AMBROSE BIERCE

I needed another umbrella, another house that would give me a desk, a telephone and above all else the freedom to go my own way.

I went to see John Berl, the perceptive, pleasant resident partner of a larger firm, Sutro & Company, which had flagship offices in Beverly Hills and San Francisco.

I told Berl about myself, my plans, how I intended to proceed; and told him as well the incident concerning the refund to the attorney. "You're kidding," he said with undisguised shock. "We would never have paid it."

A few top brokers earn 40 percent of the total commission income that results from their sales. But most earn one-third, and that's the split I agreed to at Sutro (the same as I'd been receiving at Stern, Frank) when Berl welcomed me into the firm.

At Sutro my education continued, and I really learned fundamentals: how to chart a stock, how to interpret the action on the tape, the psychology of the market—the traditional mixed bag of reality and myth by which the securities business has operated since the founding of the New York Stock Exchange. "A little more than 175 years ago," says *The New York Times Encyclopedic Almanac,* "a group of men gathered beneath the sheltering limbs of a buttonwood tree to buy and sell securities that were remarkably similar to the ones being traded today. Indeed, the current process, though refined and institutionalized, is not too different from what it was in 1792."

Therein lies much of the trouble with Wall Street. In a fast-changing world, its technology as well as its thinking is still lashed to nearly two centuries of outmoded, no longer valid assumptions and widely held beliefs. Most contemporary brokers—and this is the reason so many are second-rate—would feel perfectly comfortable, could they be sped back in time, under the sheltering limbs of that storied buttonwood tree.

Most brokers today are noncreative in a dynamic profession that demands creativity. It is not entirely the fault of the brokers. They are already obsolete, troglodytes in business suits, when they emerge from their training. But most do not adjust or extemporize. They fail to realize their approach is outmoded, even when they find in everyday experience that their training contradicts reality.

Older and more pertinent than the gibberish taught to brokers is the idea I had culled from the Bible—giving my clients only "the finest of the wheat." And such a harvest can be gathered only by living with a company and its people; only through dogged, untiring research girded by judgment. There nested the sheaves of stability and sense in the market, there could be found the keys to the kingdom of profit.

My schooling in fundamentals did not satisfy me at all. There was no question in my mind now that I wanted to keep marching in the Wall Street parade, but to the beat of a different drummer.

A broker works primarily as an independent agent. He is in business both for the house and himself. Although his income in most houses depends solely on commissions, as an unsalaried man he has unparalleled opportunities. He isn't locked into the normally hidebound corporate salary structure, which may or may not reward his efforts as the years pass. And few salaried men ever get a shot at really big money. Thus a broker has a lot going for him. The choice is pretty much his own as to how well he will fare. He can make it big, near-big, average, below average or not at all.

Once the daily tape ripples to a close, the broker is free to spend his afternoons any way he chooses. He can, as many do, use the telephone to scout clients, calling his barber or a Dallas millionaire. He can, as some others do, spend his afternoon digesting routine information, reading statistics and trying to sift clarity and pattern from the conflicting interpretations of his own research department and the stuff that everybody else is reading in the *Wall Street Journal, Forbes, Barron's* and other financial publications. (Some brokers prefer idling their time away reading *Playboy,* which is also a publication that has more than a passing interest in statistics.) And there are those brokers who do nothing with their afternoons. They prefer to let clients seek them out. While waiting for the phone to ring they play cards or twist paper clips. Too, there are brokers who spend their afternoons on the golf course or in hotel room trysts.

I began spending my afternoons visiting more small companies, picking up additional insight and knowledge every time I talked to an executive. I was beginning to smarten up, sharpening my judgment, learning what questions to ask, what to look for in a company. And, primarily, I was learning how to evaluate management. Above every other factor, proper evaluation of the men running a company is the cornucopia from which all blessings flow in the market. Good management can run a garage business into a blue chip. Bad management could run General Motors into a garage business.

By the first quarter of 1963, I was the biggest producing broker at Sutro's Beverly Hills office. I had told Berl I could rack up a $60,000 annual volume, and my business was in fact running at $5,000 a month.

Gradually I began moving in more rarified circles. I met a few wealthy men who would come in on a first-class situation with large orders, and I fortified my client list with many not-so-wealthy investors, but whose wealth together exceeded that of any one client I had.

Both large and small clients are crucial to a broker's business, although the fashion these days on Wall Street is to ignore the small client. That makes as much sense as Sears or Woolworth's catering solely to millionaires. It is only natural for any broker to husband rich clients, but the broker who disdains the modest investor is a fool.

I have never had one or a few favored clients. I offer the same opportunities in the same stocks to all, no matter how much or how little they have to invest. A broker who spreads a good situation around is going to prosper. It's common sense and common arithmetic. The broker who relies on his *"A* list" of customers, no matter how wealthy, eventually finds himself operating from a smaller base. In some ways it is preferable for a broker to have ten clients with $10,000 accounts each than one client who can invest $100,000. A broker operating in this fashion may have to work a little harder, make a few more telephone calls, go the last mile rounding up the last client and perhaps miss his usual commuter train or freeway run and be late for dinner. But it is a valid presumption borne out by my experience that if ten $10,000 clients make money they will eventually ignite more business than the $100,000 client. This is enlightened self-interest, to say nothing of the moral obligation every broker has to give every client a slice of the profits from a winning situation. The time is over, or should be, when all the cream goes to all the fat cats.

A client is a client is a client—and he should not be judged by the size of his pocketbook.

Wealthy clients have played an important role in my career. But I would have had no career worth mentioning had I not put my less wealthy clients into promising situations and made money for them.

At Sutro I was becoming more convinced than ever that companies were more important than stocks.

If a broker could somehow tunnel inside a company, learn the picture accurately and assess it intelligently, it seemed to me he would have a money-making machine for his clients and himself.

I hasten to add that I wasn't seeking or thinking in terms of acquiring "insider" information of the type that is outlawed, and rightly so, by the regulations of the Securities and Exchange Commission and all the exchanges. Participating in illegal and forbidden insider deals has murdered the careers of many brokers and company officials.

A good broker doesn't have to go that route. The kind of inside information I was hunting for was pure research, available to any broker or investor who cared to take the trouble to ferret it out.

Thus my "secret" for making money in the market adds up to two interlocking factors, as close as yin and yang: gathering and appraising information about an individual company; and once gathered and appraised, putting everybody in.

My method of selecting companies for investment is not 100 percent foolproof. I have had losers. I will have more losers. I have made mistakes in judgment and evaluation and there have been those agonizing, inexplicable occasions where certain stocks had everything going for them, yet the market did not respond to their latent promise.

No broker is going to be right every time. But if a broker can be right 60 to 70 percent of the time—and this is my record— he is going to make an awful lot of money for his clients and himself.

I was earning a good living under Sutro's umbrella, but it was small potatoes compared to the possibilities I could not only sense, but see. The nuggets were waiting to be picked up if I could find the Mother Lode.

I now thought I had reached the point where I was ready to move "inside" in a big way.

But inside where?

In 1963 I read a newspaper story about a New York financier named Jack Wilder who was leading a proxy fight against U.S. Smelting, an old-line company that had been run by the same family since its founding. From the story it appeared that Wilder had considerable backing in his attempt to take over U.S. Smelting.

The situation interested me. If Wilder indeed had the money, the know-how, the management team and the votes to acquire control, the profits to those on his bandwagon could be enormous.

But how could I find out? How could I get on the inside of this situation? I didn't know Wilder from Adam. And he certainly had never heard of an anonymous broker a continent away.

The black telephone on my desk glistened and beckoned. Why not?

I called Wilder. I easily got him on the line and, unashamedly exaggerating my importance as a "big Los Angeles broker," told him of my interest in his proxy battle.

To my surprise, Wilder cordially invited me to meet him in Chicago where he was planning a strategy session with a number of his backers.

It was as easy as that.

Now all I had to do was get to Chicago.

But that was a major problem—I didn't have the price of the plane ticket.

I had just begun to earn decent money, but my personal debts were still inhibiting me. My cash flowed out as fast as it came in, and I was living on hope and hustle, the wolf of insolvency with his paws not at my door but under my bed.

The problem reduced itself to naked simplicity. No trip to Chicago meant being shut out of a door-knocking opportunity.

With some embarrassment and reluctance, I called one of my wealthy clients and explained the budding potential in the U.S. Smelting situation. He was intrigued. For the price of a plane ticket, he could possibly earn a fortune.

He agreed to grubstake me.

I flew to Chicago literally on a wing and a prayer. It was true, as I had told Wilder on the phone, that I had a number of clients who would buy into U.S. Smelting and undoubtedly vote their proxies for him—if the deal was right. Yet I was operating for the most part on sheer guts and bluff. I didn't belong in Wilder's league, but here I was at lunch with him and Harold Brady, one of his principal backers.

They told me they believed they already had enough shares to win control of U.S. Smelting, which was rich in assets—oil reserves, gas and copper. Feelers had already been placed with Kerr-McGee, Occidental Petroleum and Kennecott All three companies were interested in purchasing U.S. Smelting, if Wilder came out on top.

As Wilder and Brady talked to me without condescension, I was mentally pinching myself. This was heady stuff. Merger! Takeover! At last, the big business action I had hungered after.

Wilder and Brady invited me to Boston to sit in on a series of meetings with their attorneys. I spent two days saying little, listening much. Wilder, Brady and their lawyers talked for hours about the pending proxy fight. I got a good feeling from these men. Unquestionably they knew what they were doing, and they were betting millions on their judgment. They were whip-smart, whip-tough, impressively formidable. Not only the quality of the men impressed me, but the thoroughness of their planned strategy. In so far as it was possible in such a fluid, dynamic situation as a proxy fight, they were leaving nothing to chance, crossing every *t* and dotting every *i*. They were men with microscopes, leaving no part of the detailed snowflake that was U.S. Smelting uninspected, unconsidered or unevaluated.

I next moved on with Wilder and Brady to New York for two more days of talks with more attorneys and several other important backers.

It all added up to a fantastically exciting situation. With only small change in my pocket, I returned to Los Angeles totally convinced that Wilder and his people knew precisely what they were doing and that they would successfully acquire control of U.S. Smelting. At the very least, the large blocs they were buying would continue to force up the price of the stock.

Back at my desk I made an ocean of phone calls. I put every client I had into the situation, including, of course, the client who had paid my plane fare. Everyone got in between 55 and 65.

By this time my thinking had gone well beyond the point of ignoring house research in favor of doing my own. A modern broker could do much more. He could be a seminal force. Beyond personal legwork, he could suggest acquisitions to companies, help put mergers together, advise and consent, advise and not consent. He could participate directly in the future growth of a promising company by aiding in arranging bank loans and underwritings.

These were all legitimate, ethical ways to get inside a company, with consequent benefits for clients and myself.

Shortly after urging everyone on my client list to get in on the U.S. Smelting action, I ran across another situation that seemed promising. I felt that one of the companies I had investigated first-hand would make an excellent acquisition for Technicolor. Although I didn't know him, I phoned Technicolor President Mel Jacobs and briefly outlined my proposal. He wanted to hear more, and a meeting was arranged.

I arrived early at Technicolor headquarters on the appointed day, and so did a man named Victor Nemeroff. A secretary put us into a room and served coffee while we waited. Nemeroff, I learned, was a wealthy Chicagoan who coincidentally was a large stockholder in the company I was suggesting Technicolor acquire.

"Anything else you're interested in?" Nemeroff asked.

I told him about U.S. Smelting.

He opened an account with me and his buy of 5,000 shares of U.S. Smelting was the largest order I had taken to that time. Nemeroff and I became friendly, and he subsequently became one of my biggest clients.

The meeting with the Technicolor management was instructive. At the table of power, a few properly phrased questions can be translated into incredible results for clients. Frequently, questions need not even be asked. The men who oversee a company are invariably proud of their firm, and are particularly proud and anxious to convey information, especially if their business is going well.

To a man, the Technicolor executives thought their company was underpriced and underestimated by the market. They felt expected earnings, as soon as they were confirmed and publicly announced, would quickly bounce their stock. Jacobs and his team rejected my acquisition suggestion. But my time had not been wasted. In addition to the chance acquaintanceship with Victor Nemeroff (Mel Jacobs also became a valued friend and client), I had gained an "inside" appraisal of Technicolor's future. I agreed that the stock was underpriced.

I also put my clients—no exceptions—into Technicolor.

Soon the blood-tingling rises began flashing across the tape.

Wilder did acquire control of U.S. Smelting. He and Brady had given me their estimate that the company, while selling in the 55–65 range, was worth 200 a share.

They were badly mistaken.

U.S. Smelting rocketed to the equivalent of 325 after it split four for one!

Every client who had bought on my recommendation made a killing. Some rode it all the way to the top. Virtually everyone increased his investment five or six times based on information that flowed my way as a result of a single phone call. There wasn't a broker in the nation who couldn't have called Wilder and followed up as I did.

I had put everybody into Technicolor at 11. It soared to 36. Again many clients went for the full ride, more than tripling their investment.

I didn't get into a position to buy a single share of anything for my own account until 1965. But my rewards from the U.S. Smelting and Technicolor recommendations were many—sizable commissions, a fast-growing client list, the satisfaction of making money for clients and growing confidence in myself. Beyond all, there was a pearl without price: the self-assurance that my *modus operandi* worked, a method so simple yet so transcendently important. I knew from the start that it wouldn't, couldn't, be surefire in every instance. But it was more surefire than anything else I saw any other broker doing.

U.S. Smelting was the turning point in my career. Technicolor solidified my reputation.

Wilder and Brady would have talked to any interested observer, as would the Technicolor management. There was nothing privileged about the information they gave me.

Admittedly, there is self-interest on the part of men enmeshed in a proxy fight or in the management of any company in propagandizing their own situations. It is perfectly possible a broker will get nothing more than a snowjob. Management men seldom, if ever, downgrade their own company. But it is the task of the broker to discern and distinguish between puff and substance. A broker can walk away, as I have many, many times, from a deal that isn't snug, clean and rich in potential. Critical assessment of the factors involved is all-important—how the broker interprets, measures and weighs the information he has gathered from the high lamas of a company. A doctor friend of mine, a cancerologist, says that one of the shocking realities of American medicine, a fact little known and little publicized, is that thousands of lives are lost each year because even reputable cancer specialists fail to detect the symptoms of the disease when they examine patients. These doctors are faulty diagnosticians. Most brokers are also faulty diagnosticians, unable to discern whether a company is healthy or cancerous.

As my career has peaked, so has criticism of me. My critics are many, their charges legion, although I receive no rebukes from brokers who operate as I do or who have surpassed my performance using the same methods. I also receive no criticism from clients for whom I have made money.

I've been accused, for example, of touting stocks, of overestimating earnings of companies I know well. Since I am as close to my situations as Abelard to Heloise, the charge of touting is mere mudslinging. I act only on my informed judgment, and when the risk to clients has been minimized as much as possible. A tout may occasionally guess right, but he will never correctly call six or seven out of ten.

Projecting earnings can be a risky matter. But all analysts bank on projected earnings as part of the reports they write on individual companies. Most companies project, however, on the upside. I project conservatively, on the downside, always allowing room for the explosion of undetected grenades that can turn a company's financial statement into a casualty report.

In that Los Angeles *Times* story, what I accepted as a compliment was hurled at me as an indictment.

An unnamed critic said I was too forthright in my comments about the ailments afflicting the securities industry. He added, "Lew Bracker's too apt to say what he thinks."

He's damn right.

FOUR

THE DEAL MAN (CONTINUED)

> *October is one of the peculiarly dangerous months to speculate in stocks. The other dangerous months are July, January, September, April, November, May, March, June, December, August and February.*

> *MARK TWAIN*

Samuel Langhorne Clemens dropped more in stocks than he could earn even as a prodigiously successful author. In 1891 he was more than $100,000 in debt, and despite urging by friends, he refused to declare bankruptcy. He recouped, paying off every dime, by exiling himself and family to Europe for nine years where expenses were cheaper, and by a grueling worldwide lecture tour he undertook at the age of sixty despite failing health.

Had Mark Twain had a good broker, he would have been free to produce who knows how many more works of genius. He perhaps would also have died a less embittered man (among his final bon mots: "Each person is born to one possession which outvalues all his others—his last breath").

But Twain also wrote, and it's as contemporary as tomorrow: "Let us be thankful for the fools. But for them the rest of us could not succeed."

Harsh as it sounds, Mark Twain might as well have been writing about the structure of the brokerage business. Immodest as it sounds, this left me in the pole position as I made the run for the roses—my first million, remembering always Twain's advice about speculation.

The fortuitous meeting with Victor Nemeroff, whose profits in U.S. Smelting had been handsome, led to his recommending other clients to me. He also led me into a valley of velvet in the Greer Hydraulics situation. Knowing the way I operated, Nemeroff called me one evening from Chicago and urged me to look into Greer, which he described as an extremely interesting small company. "Visit them and see what it's all about."

The next morning I hightailed it out to Culver City, a half-hour's drive from my office, and met the president, Edward Greer. He greeted me heartily and was delighted with my interest in his company. There had been no trouble arranging the appointment, although he had never heard of me until I called him.

Greer's unglamourous primary business was manufacturing a hydraulic product for both the government and private sectors, something called "Greerolators." I toured the plant and spent several hours talking to Greer in his office. On the day of that first of several meetings, Greer's car happened to be in the shop for repairs. I gave him a lift home, and during the drive he loosened up and became even more friendly.

Greer was as completely candid as he was hypnotically enthusiastic about the future of his firm. He said he had been operating at a loss, but I had arrived at a propitious moment, a moment when he was beginning to see daylight. Sales were jumping and his earnings picture was extremely bullish.

A raft of textbooks have been written on the subject of management. I haven't read one of them. There's no point in wasting the time. Those who live by such books invariably die by them. I've found that making a judgment about a man is in the final analysis an intangible decision. It boils down to a smell, intuition, a feeling, instinct. And there is no existing yardstick for measuring the unmeasurable. In this sense my business is management, too—a management-oriented broker judging the management capabilities of executives who will help or hinder the financial condition of my clients.

The basic qualities that will propel a given man and his company to the forefront defy precise analysis and definition. All the books in the world won't supply the key; neither will aptitude and IQ tests. If this is by-the-seat-of-the-pants judgment, unfashionable and iconoclastic in a society where the psychologists' tests have assumed the aura of Scripture, so be it. I remain totally unconvinced that psychology, books or a battery of tests can indicate success, much less predict it.

It is much easier to spot a failure. In evaluating a man headed for the top, certain traits are, of course, measurable—his capacity for hard work, dedication to his company, intimate knowledge of his own firm and his competition. Without the presence of these factors, the failure-prone executive can be spotted as easily as a red barn in Indiana.

The businessman who has a predisposition for success need not be a man for all seasons. He has to be brilliant within only a relatively narrow range.

Henry Ford was a curmudgeon, but he patched together a pretty good thing called the assembly line.

Who could have predicted that a poker-playing drifter named H. L. Hunt would emerge as a businessman brontosaurus?

Who would have singled out one-time computer salesman H. Ross Perot as a man who would leave the financial world gasping at his billion-dollar empire?

There are hundreds of stories of lesser-known men who became wealthy despite heavy odds.

With capital of only $17,000, a thirty-three-year-old businessman named Frederic V. Malek emerged as a millionaire in only eighteen months. He's from Orangeburg, South Carolina, a cotton and lumber backwater, population about 13,000. After researching investment opportunities for two years, Malek and two associates bought a local tool-making company that was losing money. They quickly ran it into a mini-conglomerate. Malek went on to become a key aide to Richard Nixon as Deputy Under Secretary of the U.S. Department of Health, Education, and Welfare. His real job? Soldering sound management into the cast-iron, cumbersome, elephantine HEW, which spends $15 billion a year. Malek's specialty is cutting red tape, dispensing with unnecessary paper-shuffling, and trying to bring order out of the chaos of 260 separate programs administered by HEW, programs which in dollar volume account for almost one-half of all Federal grants.

Of his success before going to Washington, Malek said, "It didn't take any genius, just sound management principles."

The roll call of men who have worshipped at the shrine of sound management principles is a roll call of millionaires.

I have never run a private check on anyone, as do an alarm-

ing number of people in the business world. Such an investigation would undoubtedly turn up a skeleton or two in any man's
closet. But that has nothing to do with whether or not a man
has that peculiar genius to build a winning company. Conversely, a praiseworthy private investigative report wouldn't
show me if a man was a talented executive.

Ed Greer impressed me as a winner. He knew his operation
inside out, he was thorough, had the good of his company at
the core of his being, had the ability to attract top-notch people
to his team and had an eye for profit. He was one of those men
who would have prospered with an Edsel dealership.

I not only liked Greer but I believed every word he told me.
There was also the right smell, intuition, feeling, instinct. And
above all—the timing was right. It was time for Greer Hydraulics.

I gave Nemeroff a glowing report about Greer. Nemeroff
promptly placed an order for 15,000 shares and soon increased
his holdings to 35,000 shares.

As usual, I put all my other clients into the new find.
("Money is like muck, not good unless it be spread," said
Francis Bacon.) In all, I placed more than 100,000 shares,
most of it between 2 and 2½.

It was my largest deal thus far. My own managerial capacity
for assessing the managerial capacity of Ed Greer was now on
the line to the tune of more than $1.2 million of my clients'
funds.

I had often seen and known brokers who drummed up five
times that amount of business with situations plucked from thin
air. They hadn't a thing to go on except a silver tongue. And
their clients had nothing to go on except faith in their brokers,
whom they trusted like their doctors and ministers. I was completely confident about Greer since I was going on far, far more.

The stock galloped gorgeously to 6 shortly after I bought.
And the situation was a bullet with a trajectory still on an upward
curve. Six weeks after my first buys in the 2–2½ range, Greer
bumped merrily along to 11, then 12, then 14.

When it hit the high teens a few months later, most of my
clients sold. I took everyone out when Greer settled in the low

20s. No client failed to make more than five times his money; in less than a year some made back ten or eleven dollars for every dollar invested.

Nemeroff's tip, a tour of a plant, discussions with a gifted company president and careful judgment of all the real and instinctive factors involved in the situation had put everybody in the winner's circle.

By this time Sutro had given me a secretary. I was very happy there. The firm was filled with lovely people. But Sutro was a regional house and not active in the deal business. I was getting restless. I felt ready for a bigger ball game. I was earning more than $40,000 a year, and it seemed likely I could do better, much better. (I had at last paid off the shylock and was almost clear of debt for the first time.)

Nemeroff arranged for me to meet the people at Hentz & Company, a national house with headquarters in New York.

Hentz made what sounded like an extremely attractive offer —I was to be their head of western corporate finance. The title was to mean absolutely nothing, although it looked good on my business card.

I moved to Hentz in November, 1964, with the same one-third commission split. But I was to receive 40 percent of the net total fee to the house of any merger, acquisition or underwriting I put together.

In my first year at Hentz I increased my earnings to almost $70,000.

One afternoon I got a call from Ed Greer. He suggested I take a look at a company called Electrada, located near his plant in Culver City.

Electrada's president was Dan Burns, alert, competent and ready for mushrooming growth. This was another firm with an essentially mundane, unglamorous product mix, its vital business the manufacture of pump and oil-drilling equipment (it had a respectable chunk of the market) plus a small line of aerospace components. There was little in Burns' operation to set the pulse of the average investor racing. But what was not mundane and what was extremely exciting was that here again was a company on the threshold of a turnaround. Somewhat frightening was Burns' offer to me to take 25 percent of a private placement, which amounted to $375,000 of the $1.5 million he wanted to raise so that he could acquire the Sargent division of A. J. Industries, which would give him a much broader base in producing parts for the aerospace industry, and greater earnings.

Participating in a private placement is not for every investor. It is venture capital usually placed by sophisticated people who in return for their money receive shares that are not registered with the SEC. Putting money in a private placement means that the investment in unregistered shares is locked up and non-liquid for a minimum of two years, probably more. Such procedure contrasts sharply with buying shares on the open market, which are immediately negotiable since they can be sold at any time. As an inducement for squirreling money into an investment for at least two years, those participating in a private placement are given a sizable discount—they can purchase their shares as low as 70–80 percent under the public market price. Unfortunately, the average man in the market seldom gets into a private placement situation because he doesn't have the capital and usually can't afford to tie up his money. For those who can afford to wait, the bargain stock is a potential mint, if it's the right situation. They cash in when the company is on sound financial footing and decides to register the shares, which then can be sold immediately or held.

With some trepidation I accepted Burns' proposal to participate in the private placement. For the first time I wasn't selling stock in the conventional retail manner, and I wasn't at all certain I could meet a $375,000 commitment. As it turned out, I had to sweat the deal down to the wire.

The market price of Electrada, for those who wanted liquidity, was 6. For those willing to invest in the unregistered, not-immediately-liquid shares, the price was only 3½.

Close to the deadline, I placed my last share. Others also taking part in the financing placed their shares. Burns had his $1.5 million and he made his acquisition, changing the name of his company to Sargent Industries.

My participation not only brought me 40 percent of the house commission, but a bonus of 2,160 of the unregistered shares. The shares were registered in 1969, and I sold them for $30,000.

Sargent soon rose to 20. I had also put a great many liquidity-minded clients profitably into the stock on the open market.

Everyone who came into the Sargent situation, either with registered or unregistered shares, made a substantial gain. The company is still a thriving enterprise.

In 1965 the House of Fabrics entered my life. I got wind of it through a financial consultant who had been an adviser to Dan Burns on his private placement. The adviser was also a small underwriter, and when I met him in his office he told me he had an underwriting that was in trouble. It simply wasn't selling. Seemingly, nobody wanted to touch it. The adviser himself had come into the underwriting reluctantly, taking part only because a few of his clients had loaned money to the House of Fabrics. He asked me to field-check the House of Fabrics operation.

The firm's headquarters was located fifteen miles from my office in Sun Valley, for the most part a lower-middle-class community of modest homes and thrusting freeways bordered by endless vistas of supermarkets and pizza parlors.

But in Sun Valley there reposed a man with a Midas touch.

House of Fabrics Chairman David Sofro told me he had a chain of fifty-one stores that retailed yard goods. Most were located in California, a few in Oregon; many were in cities too small for giants like Sears or Montgomery Ward, who could only offer their materials to shoppers through catalogs. Sofro's stores had the big advantages of accessibility, on-the-premises display of a wide range of yard goods, comparison of materials which could be felt and seen, and immediate purchase. He thus had much of the market for himself.

Now he had big plans. He wanted to open thirty-five to fifty new stores a year throughout the United States. To finance his national expansion he was trying to place shares of his privately-held company on the public market.

He couldn't understand why the underwriting had become a

touch-and-go proposition. Sofro, indefatigably, had told his plans and expectations to anyone who would listen, but he had not convinced anybody on Wall Street that a chain of stores selling material to the home seamstress had much of a future. Two important houses couldn't make up their minds whether or not to take the plunge on the underwriting. They were on the verge of coming in, yet they kept holding back, seesawing, stalling, playing it close to the chest before making up their minds.

I was more taken with Sofro than I had been with Wilder, Greer and Burns. To me he was another winner. Sofro had explained to me in detail what the addition of each new store would do for his profits. His projections seemed not only rational and reasonable—they seemed sensational. The House of Fabrics, if it could be funded through an underwriting, would, in my view, become another little giant. It was in fact a gold mine, and I hadn't the slightest hesitation in urging it on my clients.

The total underwriting was 250,000 shares at 5, which would raise $1.25 million. Sofro's small underwriter offered me, and I accepted, 45,000 shares of the package, a large commitment for my first underwriting.

Hentz did not share my enthusiasm for House of Fabrics. They hemmed and hawed, and finally said they didn't like the deal at all and weren't going along. Not until I assured the powers at Hentz that I would guarantee placing every share of our participation would they agree to come in.

I was pledged to sell $225,000 worth of stock. Theoretically, if the issue didn't move I could be wiped clean of my personal assets and end up in debt.

Add to the charges against me the one that I hear quite frequently—I'm a lucky gambler who one day is going to destroy himself. But those who thus charge me are more often than not the selfsame brokers who push on unsuspecting clients stocks they know nothing about. The more investigating a broker does, the more he increases his chance for success. The more information he accumulates side by side with his sixth sense for spotting a winner, the greater is the chance that his clients will benefit. And if he is unwilling to rely on his own judgment and ability, he should get out of the business.

Finding little-known companies and helping them grow is my specialty. It takes no talent, insight or research for a broker to recommend an alleged blue chip, although millions of shareholders have taken a beating in companies with household names. More on that later.

David Sofro has said many times that without my participation there wouldn't have been an underwriting for House of Fabrics. If I had not come in, Sofro, at that juncture, would have been checkmated and his consummate talent for creating a money-making business would have been thwarted.

Selling my 45,000 shares of the underwriting proved no problem whatever. I placed without difficulty—my clients now trusted me wholeheartedly—25,000 shares. I gave 20,000 shares to other brokers at Hentz for their clients. And because Hentz finally came in, Sutro and a couple of other good houses decided to take a piece of the underwriting.

Sofro had his expansion financing and House of Fabrics was now publicly held.

Then there was a setback.

Right after the underwriting money was raised, the price dropped to 4½, then to 3½. House of Fabrics was caught in a bad market.

But my faith in Sofro and his company never wavered because I knew the situation backwards and forwards. I bought hell out of the stock at its lower price, considering it a bargain and putting every client who would listen into it. My clients ended up with approximately 10 percent of the company.

One reason I could act with such confidence was that by now I had spent a great deal of time with Sofro. I went on the road with him to Denver, elsewhere in the Middle West, and to New York as he searched for new sites for his stores. I didn't know a thing about the yard goods business, but every move Sofro made seemed exactly right. I watched him closely, and observed him with his own personnel. He, too, had a knack for hiring the right people. And he had his business down to a science.

Almost to the dollar, he could estimate what each new location would produce in profits. It was akin to watching Joe Namath in action, except Sofro had no trick knee, no handicap whatever, and every time out he scored a touchdown.

During this time, through the recommendation of a mutual friend, I picked up three of the legendary Marx Brothers as clients.

I immediately put Gummo into House of Fabrics at 5, where the stock had resettled after its dip.

Zeppo was another problem. His portfolio was a disaster. He was a gambler, and as is invariably true of high rollers in the market, he'd had terrible luck. I immediately sold off a lot of his junk, and it was junk. I urged him to buy as much as possible of House of Fabrics. He also got in at 5, purchasing 10,000 shares.

Groucho followed suit, buying 5,000 shares at the same price.

House of Fabrics stock, as Sofro built quietly and efficiently, didn't do much for the balance of 1965.

But in the first quarter of 1966, as the clutch of new stores opened in 1965 were established, earnings grew. House of Fabrics began moving—to 7, to 10, to 12.

Now it zoomed up like an Apollo spacecraft, lunging into the 20s, splitting 3-for-2, hitting the low 30s and splitting again. In 1969 it reached 36, and this after two splits. It was a phenomenal success story, and House of Fabrics is a stock I recommend to this day. Its future is unlimited.

David Sofro had pleaded with the investment community to listen to him, to give him a chance. He had told everyone his plans and projections. I was the only one in the beginning who believed him, and the results were incredible for my clients.

Since I first heard of House of Fabrics it hasn't reported less than a 50 percent growth rate in any year. It is presently a chain of more than 200 stores, and still expanding. Sofro now has to fend off Wall Street analysts wanting to know more about his company.

Behind it all was the brain of a single man, supremely equipped to captain his company through the tumultuous shoals of retail competition with a product almost as old as civilization.

Everybody who invested in House of Fabrics did extremely well. Zeppo Marx, after the two splits, ended up with 18,000 shares. And even in the tough market of 1969, the company closed the year at 27¼. In 1970, it traded at a low of 21¾, and a high of 46¼.

No broker sitting at his desk, relying on in-house research, could possibly have uncovered this situation for his clients. The real action for the broker is outside the office, in quiet restaurants in Chicago, Boston and New York, in conferences with management in Culver City and North Hollywood, in sometimes offbeat places in big and small cities of a giant country. A broker's office is only a place to make phone calls and pick up mail.

Tips about potentially exciting new companies now floated into me like computer orders to IBM. Hundreds of people in the financial community—from Los Angeles to Wall Street itself—were aware of what I was doing, what I was interested in. It amazed me that no one else I knew personally was operating in the same fashion.

I had reached the point where I could paint the potential price of a stock I was interested in with considerable accuracy. If anything, I habitually found that I was estimating earnings and the eventual market price of a stock too conservatively. If I thought a company at 20 would go to 50, it unfailingly shot to 75.

I was now taking home more than $100,000 a year from my brokerage business and deal income. I hadn't yet reached or joined the million-dollar club, but it seemed apparent that never again would I have to hock myself to a shylock.

FIVE

GOLD IN CHEMICAL TOILETS—FROM 8 TO 240

*. . . And yet the true creator is necessity,
which is the mother of our invention.*

PLATO

I chafed at the Hentz operation. As head of western corporate finance, I was in actuality a eunuchlike member of the Hentz harem. I was serving but not really participating, for Hentz did no corporate financing of any consequence. I wanted more than a business card with a title. I wanted big action and a new house, the best available.

I made no hasty decision in finding yet another new umbrella. I looked around carefully. I didn't want to become a perpetual house-hopper. I planned carefully because this was to be my final move, or so I thought.

In searching for the house that would best suit my needs, I received a number of flattering offers, and I weighed them all.

I not only intended to sell stocks, but I wanted to plunge into the heart-racing world of investment banking in a big way, and what I was seeking was an arena in which I could so function. I wanted a house that had imagination and daring, a solid reputation; a house that would also allow me complete freedom to create my own situations.

My final choice was McDonnell & Company, a fat, happy, old-line firm (or so I thought) with twenty-six offices. It was a privately held family brokerage with close ties to some of the richest and most influential people in the country. McDonnell oozed prosperity and prestige, first cabin all the way.

I joined McDonnell on January 17, 1967, as head of corporate finance for fourteen western states, the same title I had at Hentz, except that McDonnell *was* in the investment banking business in a big way.

I came into McDonnell with the understanding that I would be permitted to form within the house my own small, tightly-knit organization, employing my own people, and that I would function with a large degree of autonomy.

Without a whit of dissent, McDonnell agreed to this arrangement. Had the house not agreed, I would have gone elsewhere.

I hired three secretaries, two brokers to execute routine retail orders, and since I could do only so much traveling and investigating myself, I employed and trained two assistants in the deal end of my operation. They were responsible for providing me with the first wedge of information about a company in which I was interested. As I had done, they learned to ask the right questions and unearth the important details about a particular firm. My assistant deal men have performed beautifully. I value their judgment above anybody else's on Wall Street. When their basic fact-finding proves enticing, I always follow up with my own investigation, making the final decision as to whether the situation will lead to profit or pain for my clients.

From the beginning of my association with McDonnell, I operated in tandem as a broker and investment banker. My focus continued to be finding small companies destined to make a sensational impact, to catch these companies in transition from anonymity to blue chips.

I completely ignored playing the old school-tie game, which is still so much a part of the Wall Street establishment. In many houses a broker's stature often depends entirely on his contacts with hundred-year-old corporations. Such brokers wouldn't be caught dead talking to the management of a company earning a mere $200,000 a year. They wouldn't so lower themselves, even if such a company could be developed into a $200 million enterprise.

Brokers who concentrate on the old stand-by situations display not only the pride of fools—but myopia, stupidity, laziness and, worst sin of all, they do not serve their clients responsibly.

The story of Monogram Industries (no kin to the old movie production company) is a perfect illustration of spotting a comet ahead of the crowd by using my *modus operandi* before a company's sparkle and glitter is seen through the lens of every telescope on Wall Street, before it becomes "respectable."

My initial information about Monogram came (while I was

still at Hentz) from a friend who was an investment adviser. In the most casual, offhand way, he remarked: "Monogram's doing promising things. You ought to take a look."

I'd had dozens of similar "tips"—and Monogram appeared no better or worse than many other companies brought to my attention.

At the time, the stock was selling at 8 on the over-the-counter market.

Only because Martin Stone and Harvey Karp, the two driving geniuses behind Monogram, had excellent reputations did I decide to probe further. I met them at lunch. Theirs was a company already on its way. Stone and Karp had bought control of faltering Monogram when it was on the verge of bankruptcy. They had turned it around into a healthy little firm that was doing an annual sales volume of between $9 and $10 million.

Their basic product was the most utilitarian of creature comforts. Stone and Karp hadn't discovered how to make automobiles fly. They weren't groundbreakers. Their product didn't have the glamour of television, computers, a Polaroid camera or a Xerox copying machine.

Their business was producing chemical toilets.

Nothing could be less interesting. Nothing less exciting. Nothing less glamorous.

But there is nothing more interesting, exciting and glamorous to the investor than the appreciation of a stock, and the more a stock appreciates, the more interesting, exciting and glamorous it becomes, no matter what the firm manufactures.

Canny investors and brokers take this for granted. But it is a lesson still to be learned by the major segment of the investing public and most brokers.

Stone and Karp were ambitious and knowledgeable, their eyes set realistically on a boundless future for Monogram. Their product wasn't new, even within its field. Monogram did not invent the chemical toilet, but Monogram had refined and improved the convenience to the point where it was the best in the industry.

The company had contracts to supply its flushing, portable

toilets for all Boeing 707's and Douglas DC-8's. And I could foresee a vast market penetration for the portable toilet among the rising number of people who owned boats and mobile homes. An additional advantage to Monogram's product was that it didn't pollute the water or land since the same water was recirculated and purified by chemicals.

Hospitals were also a rich market. Monogram was selling its new Mobile Monomatic as a replacement for the venerable bedpan. The company's literature to hospital administrators about its product made no claim to glamour, only to practicality.

> *The offensive, archaic bedpan is quite out of place in to-day's jet age. Patients forced to assume the unnatural postures required to utilize the bedpan often suffer constipation resulting in complications that interfere with complete comfort and perhaps recovery. It is important also to consider the personal embarrassment on the patient's part when requesting this service or when, indeed, the service is performed.*
>
> *It is equally inappropriate for nurses and attendants to have their more important duties constantly interrupted because they must be engaged in the disagreeable task of handling and servicing the patient's bedpan need.*
>
> *To answer this critical need, Monogram Industries has applied the same principles used in the flushing toilets they manufacture for jet airliners.*

Perusal of that brochure copy might possibly spoil a client's dinner, but if the company prospered he would have a great deal of financial consolation.

I came away from my meeting with Stone and Karp completely convinced that I had stumbled on another luminescent situation. The three key elements were present in abundance—top-drawer management, rising earnings and my third ear telling me the situation was right.

There was, it seemed to me, gold in chemical toilets.

I put every client who would listen—and most did—into Monogram at 8.

When I joined McDonnell the stock was at 22, the company by this time having increased its sales to $26 million, its earnings to $1.1 million.

I stayed very close to management, and was kept informed as a matter of course on every development within the firm. I never stopped recommending the stock, buying continually for old as well as new clients.

In the spring of 1967 Monogram was ready for an ambitious merger. The price of the stock was now in the 60s!

Monogram offered 250,000 shares of new common at $64 per share to acquire a totally unrelated business, the Spaulding Fibre Company, which made laminated plastics, vulcanized fibre products, electrical insulation papers and transformer boards for industry, parts for television and radio sets, luggage, shoes and light switches. Spaulding also produced materials essential in computers and military and space systems.

Spaulding's sales volume was larger than Monogram's. It was doing $40 million a year, $14 million more than Monogram.

Monogram planned to acquire Spaulding through a 250,000-share underwriting. Stone and Karp needed an investment banker to handle the deal. They approached me, and I was delighted at the opportunity.

Then outside pressure built until Stone was put in a position where he couldn't possibly honor his commitment to me.

Spaulding was controlled by the trustees of a charter member of the Ivy League, Dartmouth University. The trustees insisted that the lion's share of the underwriting be assigned to Lehman Brothers, whose old school ties were of long standing. If Lehman Brothers did not get the business, it was made evident to Stone, the trustees wouldn't sell Spaulding.

Stone fought as hard as he could against what amounted to financial blackmail. Stone did demand, and it took quite a bit of demanding, that McDonnell be in the first bracket of underwriters, with me handling McDonnell's participation in the new financing.

Marty Stone felt bad. He was caught in a vise. Stone was a totally honorable man. Ethically, he had every right to choose his own underwriter. But I understood the politics perhaps better than he did.

Of the 250,000-share underwriting, which was quickly sold, my portion was a scant 500 shares.

Spaulding was acquired, and in the first six months of 1967, Monogram's net sales rose to $48 million. Earnings galloped to $2.3 million, more than double the previous profit.

Only five months later—in September, 1967—Monogram took another giant step, acquiring the National Screw and Manufacturing Company of Cleveland, Ohio, a $38 million firm, a leading producer of fasteners, chains and hoists. Monogram made a tender offer, which was accepted, of $60 for National Screw's 369,724 shares.

Building from a functional fortune generated by the production of chemical toilets, Monogram spread its wings from a $26 million company to one doing more than $100 million in yearly sales. By diversifying into Spaulding and National Screw, Monogram in 1968 showed sales of $121.4 with net earnings of $6.7 million, a six-fold profit spiral from early 1967.

Before it split 3 for 1, Monogram zoomed to 240, a fantastic 232 points from where it hovered when I first heard about it.

Monogram was more than a comet. It had traveled faster than the speed of light. Some of my clients who had bought in at 8 got out, against my advice, around 108. I was still buying at 150, so intimately did I know this situation, so complete was my faith in Stone and Karp. Only after the split did I take all my clients out, feeling that the stock had had its run.

Many clients had gone all the way, from 8 to 240.

It is only fair to point out that a situation like this was possible in 1967, a sensational year for the bulls. In the bear market of 1969–1970, Monogram—despite its solid management and profits—would perhaps have moved to 30. A leap to 240 would have been unthinkable, given the vastly different climate.

Monogram had the fundamentals going for it in 1967, and I knew that its two swift acquisitions in the prevailing atmosphere would set off a chain reaction. Almost everything was selling, and Monogram couldn't help but go up. Although it was basi-

cally sound, much of Monogram's rise was a stock play: It rode
to its incredible heights on the crest of a roaring up market.

In 1967 the psychology of the investor was such that anyone
would buy anything. Unfortunately, many buyers bought the
wrong stocks, discounting five years in advance.

My success in Monogram was due partially from being in
the right place at the right time. By itself, Monogram was an
excellent situation. The two acquisitions were a booming bonus.
When I had first decided to go with Monogram I had no inkling
—neither did Stone or Karp—that the two big acquisitions
would be made.

The achievement of Monogram is a textbook illustration of
the importance of management. Management is far more important than earnings. With proper management, earnings will
always be there. In 1969–1970, because of Stone and Karp,
Monogram would have been a successful investment, although
far less profitable.

Monogram certainly wasn't a blue chip by traditional definition, but it moved like few blue chips have in a long time.

If enough brokers push any stock or group of stocks hard
enough, anything will move—temporarily. A classic instance
took place during the first few months of 1970 when brokers
capitalized on the public's sudden awareness of the pollution
crisis.

All at once there was a craze for companies involved in fighting pollution. Any company that had "ecology" or "environ-
ment" in its name rose, although many of these firms were selling at brutally unrealistic prices of 40 and 50 times earnings.
Most had no earnings at all, or were operating at a loss! This
round of speculation into the latest, zinging glamour industry
was senseless. Investors who bought these shares in haste are
going to have a long, long time to repent in leisure.

I didn't touch a single environmental issue because none of
them met my standards.

The brokers who recommended these companies were doing
so with no realistic expectation of appreciation. They were
selling glamour, which is unbankable. No broker should climb

aboard a shaky, questionable bandwagon until the risk is measured, the situation thoroughly explored.

The art of the broker is to uncover a basically good stock, no matter what product the company makes. If the stock rises, as Monogram did in part because of a bandwagon atmosphere, that's all gravy. But it is important to repeat and underline that Monogram was a triumphant situation going in. It would have been a winner without the acquisitions and in a bear market.

Investors swayed by fast- and loose-talking brokers and their own emotions pour money down a rathole, forgetting there's always a new bandwagon, always a new winner around the corner.

But the new winner must be built on a firm foundation and guided and protected by eminently capable men at the top.

That's why gold flowed from a near-bankrupt company with an unromantic basic product.

No wave of tomorrow.

No razzle-dazzle.

No spurious blue chip.

Just chemical toilets . . . magnificent management . . . and astronomical profits for all.

SIX

LET THE GOOD TIMES ROLL

Money is always there but the pockets change.

GERTRUDE STEIN

Although 1967 was an electric year for the market, not all brokers by any means made money for all their clients. A bull market doesn't guarantee that every investor will prosper in every stock, any more than a bear market means every investor will lose money.

There are millions who cling to the fable, seldom if ever discouraged by the booster literature that flows from brokerage houses and planted stories by Wall Street's paid public relations men, that in a surging market they can't lose—no matter what offal they buy. Conversely, millions refuse to buy in a down market even though such a climate sometimes, but not always, offers marvelous opportunities to purchase underpriced shares that will come back.

Many investors who make their buy decisions on the basis of the happy headlines caused by a rising Dow Jones forget this index is an average for only thirty stocks. If you're in the wrong situations, you can watch the Dow rise all the way to the welfare rolls.

A bull market is not an automatic, free ride to prosperity, and brokers who brainwash clients into placing orders on the specious reasoning that "the market is up" are immoral.

Choosing stocks for clients—whether the atmosphere is bull or bear—is still, and always will be, a process of careful, ruthless, unsentimental selection by the conscientious broker who has done his homework before asking anyone to risk a dime.

That is the very heart of the matter.

A sunny market can and will propel a sound situation to undreamed of heights. But the right stock even in a black market will tend to appreciate somewhat, hold its own or, at worst, show a minimal loss. The right stock will generally weather the gale of plunging prices. The issue may take a battering, but once the storm is over it will be ready to ride the wave of the inevitable turnaround from bear to bull market.

Survival is not a question of when a client puts his money into the market, but where.

The good times rolled in 1967, 1968 and part of 1969 only for those who considered the where, not the when.

In the 1950s a team of four brilliant men, led by Bernard Levine, started their business in a garage with a bankroll of only $25,000. The quartet who thus founded Vernitron Corporation constituted a management team of whiz kids, very profit-conscious and acquisition-minded.

The company's rise had been impressive. The $25,000 investment by 1960 had snowballed into a firm with annual sales of $1.1 million and earnings of $48,000. In 1965 Vernitron had a $5.5 million volume year, earning $300,000. The company closed out 1966 with $9.3 million in sales, and profits of $513,-000.

When I first began scouting Vernitron, it looked like a steamroller, despite the hard reality that its Torrance, California, plant was in the highly competitive electronics-aerospace business, producing control and electrical components, circle mechanisms used in engine computers, digital encoders and solid state converters—nothing that dozens of other firms weren't shuttling out just as well.

Perhaps that was why Vernitron was largely overlooked by the market. It was selling on the American Exchange in the 12–13 area.

In discussions with management I learned of a bright potential for the company. The Vernitron executives expected to *double* their earnings by the end of 1967. I didn't doubt their word for a moment, having established to my satisfaction the top-drawer quality of the men running the company. The goal of earning at least $1 million in the next twelve months was to be accomplished by vigorously increasing present business and through mergers.

There was another prime factor in the gathering Vernitron situation that I liked very much. As with House of Fabrics and

Monogram before their big moves, Vernitron had comparatively little stock outstanding, just under 700,000 shares. That meant great leverage, and anything the company did would be reflected very heavily in the price of the stock.

I recommended Vernitron to all my clients.

The garage-spawned firm swiftly proceeded to carry out its acquisition program. Three companies tumbled into the parent corporation. Vernitron bought Trailco Manufacturing Company, putting them into the transportation business. Purchase of the Dataport Company brought them into information processing. And control of Radalab, Inc., gave them a division in the highly specialized field of manufacturing communications systems for telephone terminals.

Venitron coursed the hallelujah trail of high finance without committing a single sin—no misjudgments, mismanagement or mistakes. The amens rang out in the bible of a corporation, its financial statement. In 1967 Vernitron, with the considerable aid of its three acquisitions, chalked up $21.8 million in sales, more than *tripling* rather than doubling its profits. Earnings grew from $513,000 in 1966 to $1.7 million.

The bountiful earnings were reflected in the price of the stock. It climbed to the mid-40s, at which point I took most of my clients out. A few clients, with my concurrence, stayed with the stock longer and saw a rise of ten more points before I finally urged them to sell. Every stock inevitably reaches a level where its major play is behind it.

Not a single client in Venitron failed to at least triple his money. Many did much, much better.

An executive with growth on his mind is always an executive worth watching. A skillful, properly executed merger can achieve wonders for the parent company and for clients who buy a piece of the action at the right moment.

In 1966, through a friend of mine in New York, I met Irwin Solomon, president of the relatively small but extremely efficient and successful Colonial Life Insurance Company. Solomon was merger-minded. He was a terribly impressive executive. "Winner" could have fittingly been tattooed across his forehead. As an imaginative, cautiously daring man, he saw new vistas for his company. Obviously competent, I was certain he couldn't miss. And so when he decided to bring Colonial public and acquire Seaboard Life Insurance Company, a much larger firm, I took a position in the underwriting for my own account, buying 15,000 shares at 9.

Once the merger was sealed, the stock drifted off in price to 5, primarily because the acquisition had seemingly diluted the per share value of the combined company. But at 5 the stock was a splendid opportunity to buy, a virtual steal. To me it was only a question of time until Solomon's acumen in running his company would be reflected on the tape.

I put everybody in at a range of 5–9.

In less than a year I took everybody out at 15–16. Every client came close or went over the point of doubling his money. My own position in the stock brought me a huge profit. I was at last in a position to benefit personally from my own detective work. I have no reluctance to put my own money into any situation I urge my clients to purchase. That's another test for a good broker: Is he ready to put his own funds into the same stock he is recommending to his clients?

The rise in the price of this issue was again predicated on increased earnings engineered by an excellent executive. Today the company is much larger. Its holdings now include three mutual funds. I had taken the bulk of clients out of the situation when they had nearly a 100 percent gain on their investment, feeling once more that the stock for the time being had made its major move. If a broker can double his clients' money inside a year he need not apologize. He is performing extremely well.

I set no absolute increase on the amount any stock will rise. That would be idiotically presumptuous and arrogant. I look solely for appreciation per se, without, of course, knowing how large the appreciation will be. I don't, and can't, promise that any stock will double, triple or do even more than that.

The crest of the rise depends on prevailing circumstances. Sometimes I'll recommend that a client hold even after a stock has increased six, seven or ten times over its purchase price. On other occasions I'll take clients out with a gain of only a few points.

There were not many firms in America more woebegone than Inglewood Gasoline Company when my attention was called to it in 1967 by a friend with whom I had participated in a previous deal.

Inglewood was so woebegone that the people who owned the company couldn't wait to dump it. The controlling interest in the firm was for sale. Inglewood was a tiny outfit going absolutely nowhere, trading over-the-counter at 90¢ a share. Its aggregate annual sales in 1967 were a puny $100,000, and it had lost $70,000. The net worth of Inglewood, $271,000, was less than half the salary of the president of General Motors.

But I didn't see Inglewood as a corpse. It struck me as a perfect opportunity, for the first time in my career, to build a company for myself and my clients instead of for others, a perfect opportunity to create a firm in my own image, one that would reflect my ideals and business concepts. If it had the right elements, Inglewood could rise phoenixlike. The proper elements included innovative management ideas I wanted to put in motion, fresh financing and an aggressive acquisition program. I helped locate the new management team and put together the group that not only purchased Inglewood but jumped its value immediately by buying another company simultaneously, another company I had thoroughly investigated. Although Inglewood was still trading at 90¢, we offered $1.06. Our tender on 145,000 shares was accepted. At the same time, we borrowed $860,000 from a bank to acquire the second company, the Dr. Pepper Bottling Company, a thirty-year-old Fullerton, California, concern that owned exclusive rights to bottle and distribute that soft drink and others throughout populous Orange County.

Inglewood and Dr. Pepper emerged under a new name that I coined, Pacific American Industries, Inc.

By the end of December, 1967, nothing much had happened to the company so far as the price of its shares was concerned. At its highest, it traded at $1.50.

By the end of 1968 four more acquisitions were bolted into Pacific American: Ericson Yachts, specializing in manufacturing ocean-going fiberglass sailboats; Dual-Wide, Inc., which made custom mobile homes; Sweetheart Bakers, Ltd., supplying the boom demand in snack foods; and Michigan Bulb Company, a flower and bulb concern.

New management, a change in direction and an active merger program proved to the market that the company was in good hands and that what it was doing it was doing very well.

At the end of its first year of operation as Pacific American, the company totaled sales of $8 million, with almost $300,000 in after-tax earnings.

The stock had run from 90¢ to $20.

Throughout 1969, Pacific American acquired seven additional companies, all involved in leisure-time products. Going after the self-gratification dollar and the impulse spender, Pacific American prospered, reaching sales in 1969 of $25 million with earnings of $750,000.

The stock scored a 1969 high of 46.

In the teeth of the bear market of May, 1970, Pacific American, unlike almost all companies, big and small, continued its acquisition program, on a cash basis, acquiring San Diego's Canada Dry Bottling Company, San Diego's Hires–Dr. Pepper Company, and a major entry into the fast-growing gourmet food field, A & N Foods.

Pacific American had swelled into a brawny conglomerate. It closed out 1970 with a sales rate of $35 million in soft drinks, modular construction, entertainment and fine foods. It is a financially sound growth company, which succeeded triumphantly, even in a rough money market.

Most of my clients bought Pacific American well under 5, and a great many sold with at least a thirty-five point profit. A few became wealthy through this one investment alone. It was not a situation that had been plucked idly from the smoggy Southern California air. I'd been with Pacific American every step of the way. From the beginning it was carefully tailored for growth. Knowing the situation so intimately allowed my clients to reap rich rewards. How better can a broker serve himself and those who entrust their money to him? Pacific American's stock suffered in price in the 1969–1970 bear market, but because of its strong earnings growth it will be among the very first to bounce back in price in a bullish atmosphere.

One of the outstanding success stories in the recent history of American business has been that of National General Corporation and its driving, visionary board chairman, Eugene V. Klein, a one-time Volvo distributor and savings and loan executive. In 1961 he began running National General. The company, which owned a string of theaters and had been involved in several unsuccessful movie and television production ventures, was beset by losses when Klein took over.

He whipped the firm into shape with the kill-or-be-killed skill and intensity of a Marine D.I. He set up a $7 million loss reserve for National Telefilm, the company's losingest division. He shed National General of the Cinemiracle movie process and sold off an expensively-produced film opus called *Windjammer*.

Klein then made an extremely daring move. In the midst of an era when television held the American public in thralldom and virtually no movie theater had been built in ten years, he began constructing about twenty film houses a year, a seemingly reckless rate. Klein had judged that the surfeit of mediocre entertainment offered on television would cause a widespread public backlash. His judgment was absolutely correct. People came to his new theaters in droves.

At the end of only two years Klein and his associates had turned a losing company into a money-maker. By 1963 National General showed a profit of $1.5 million. In 1966 earnings leaped to $3.7 million, and by 1967 National General had earned $3.8 million on sales of $77 million. The company now had a chain of 260 theaters in the United States, plus a half-interest in 50 movie houses in Canada. To help supply its theaters with product, NGC financed eight to twelve films a year, the majority of which were commercially successful. National General today has close to 300 theaters, is still financing new films, and distributes all the movies produced by CBS, at least a dozen a year.

The Los Angeles financial community is relatively small; and as in all financial centers there is an ever-quivering though not always reliable grapevine. I wasn't the only broker hearing good things about Gene Klein and National General but, unwilling to trust the grapevine, I was probably one of the few brokers who checked out the situation in detail.

I called Klein for an appointment, and this led to a series of meetings with him and his two top aides: Irving H. Leven, executive vice-president, and Samuel Schulman, senior vice-president. They were the talented trio running the company. Like Klein, both Leven and Schulman had been successful businessmen in other enterprises before joining in the challenge of building National General.

And build is what they wanted to do. The trio was Bunyanesque in outlook. They had flare—and they were growth-oriented. It didn't take long to conclude that these men could stand with any management team in the nation when it came to efficiency and effective decision-making.

With such helmsmen at the wheel, National General at 15 seemed a bargain when I unconditionally recommended it to clients in mid-1967.

When the fulsome 1967 earnings were announced, the stock rocketed. By February, 1968, it had almost doubled, clients now paying 28–30, a range at which I still considered it an excellent buy.

This judgment proved out—1968 was National General's big, breathtaking year.

It acquired Grosset & Dunlap, Inc., a hardcover book publisher that also owned one of the largest paperback houses, Bantam Books. Grosset & Dunlap added $68 million in volume to National General's $77 million in sales. National General had almost doubled its size.

Hard on the heels of that merger, National General acquired another company in a move that still leaves financial observers hyperventilating. It went after and won (à la Wilder/U.S. Smelting) the Great American Insurance Company, which in 1967 ranked as the nation's twenty-fourth largest stock. It was a huge fire and casualty insurance firm.

National General's price bounded to a high of 60½. Some of

my clients got out in the 55–60 range. Everyone who sold in that delicious area doubled, tripled or quadrupled his investment.

The next big winner to surface came in the form of what I knew would be a hot underwriting, strictly a short-term situation. I traveled to Dallas to investigate the company, and I was awarded a block of Scientific Control Company, which manufactured a new line of computer hardware. Because of its fragile position in an extremely competitive industry, I felt the stock would be a gamble if held too long. Also, management did not impress me. But I hadn't the slightest doubt, once I investigated the situation, that the company, going public at 7½, would flash forward. It was the right industry in the right market climate. The underwriting sold out on December 22, 1967. Thirteen days later it was at 23. On February 5, 1968, it reached 25. At that level, I began recommending that my clients sell. Some clients, and I considered it a good risk, held on. My last client in the stock sold the shares he had purchased at 7½ on December 22, 1967, at 53½ on June 25, 1968, a 46-point increase, with the added largesse of nipping in under the wire of the lower six-month capital gains tax bite.

I had read Scientific Control as a stock that would shoot up fast, figuring everyone would make at least four or five times his investment within six months. It proved out, and I didn't let anyone linger beyond six months.

In the spring of 1966 I began looking into Occidental Petroleum. So pleased was I with its earnings projection that I began buying it for clients at 26. I was still buying it in mid-1966 at 45. By November, 1967, the stock reached 120 and split 4 for 1. At that level we took our money and ran.

Interstate Engineering was yet another fortunate situation. After a thorough investigation I began buying at 20 in May, 1966. Thirteen months later the stock was 34⅝. I sold it out of clients' accounts two weeks later in the 45–46 area.

As I've already indicated, the last impression I want to give is that I'm invincible or infallible as a broker. Although I haven't hit a winner every time, the care I've taken with my selections has prevented any of my clients from taking a bath in any stock.

Some of my clients have lost money in certain transactions. Sometimes this was the fault of the client, sometimes it was my fault.

I've had clients who lost money in Sargent, House of Fabrics and Monogram because they wouldn't wait. They bounced in and out too quickly even though I assured them they had the right stocks and the right moves were coming. Impatience can be extremely expensive.

Then there are those times that try a broker's soul. A company can look exactly right and earnings do come in at the estimated level, yet the market ignores the stock. This doesn't happen often, but inexplicably it does occur. And there is always the unpredictable event. A case in point is National General. The stock in 1969 fell to a low of 16½ after the company reported a whopping $70.3 million loss as a result of extraordinary, nonrecurring writedowns in connection with its acquisition of Great American Insurance and a 38 percent interest it acquired in Performance Systems, Inc., the franchising unit for Minnie Pearl fried chicken outlets.

Aside from these writedowns, National General had a substantial operating profit for 1969.

I miscalculated when National General hit its high of 60½. I didn't think it was overbought in that area. I thought the price would continue to rise.

I was wrong.

But my clients who bought anywhere in the 15–30 area have been hurt only in terms of losing time.

The company finished 1970 with earnings of $2.30. National General at its 1970 price range of 13–20¼ was an excellent buy since the company is fundamentally sound, its nonrecurring losses behind it.

As the good times rolled on for my clients, many became very, very wealthy. Some who were millionaires had new millions piled on their fortunes. No client who stayed with me through all my buy and sell recommendations failed to come out a big winner.

In running up profits for my clients, I had also run up enormous profits for myself. From my brokerage business, deal income and investments in the same situations I sold to clients, I was in the multimillion-dollar bracket by the end of 1968.

Meticulous investigation of my situations and assessment of management had proved out enough times to overcome the losers by a wide margin.

A seven-figure bank balance is waiting for any broker or investor who chooses to operate in the same way. But he must wait for the proper market climate.

The real achievement in masterminding the fortunes of my clients and amassing my own fortune was that it was accomplished in the eye of a hurricane whirling unceasingly through McDonnell & Co. As mentioned earlier, I had hoped that McDonnell & Co. would be my last move. But I resigned from the house, after an unbelievable series of events, on March 1, 1969.

When I handed in my resignation I was in excellent financial condition. The same could not be said for McDonnell & Co.

SEVEN

THE RISE AND FALL OF A BROKERAGE HOUSE

*It requires a great deal of boldness and a
great deal of caution to make a great fortune;
and when you have got it, it requires ten
times as much wit to keep it.*

JAMES ROTHSCHILD

I am the richest man in the world.

*WILLIAM HENRY VANDERBILT, circa
1880*

The public be damned.

WILLIAM HENRY VANDERBILT, 1883

Twenty-two years after Vanderbilt's legendary gaffe, the son of
an Irish immigrant named James F. McDonnell slipped quietly
into Wall Street and established a brokerage house bearing his
name. It is unrecorded as to whether McDonnell agreed or dis-
agreed with Vanderbilt's attitude concerning the public. But
McDonnell founded a house that efficaciously sought out and
catered to influential and powerful clients.

The Wall Street atmosphere to which McDonnell came in
1905 was volatile. It was the age of the stock market buccaneer
and the industrial pirate.

As now, the United States was in social and economic fer-
ment. Trust-busting Teddy Roosevelt was in the White House,
and the former Rough Rider was riding roughshod over the
fabled financial titans who set the moral and ethical tone of
American industry and Wall Street.

Roosevelt brought the king of kings, J. P. Morgan, to his
knees by filing a suit against Northern Securities, a holding
company that he charged Morgan had hammered together
solely to help a group of western railroads evade the provisions
of the 1890 Sherman Anti-Trust Act. The Supreme Court up-

held Roosevelt, and Morgan's outfit was dissolved. During Roosevelt's presidency forty-three federal suits were filed against major corporations. In the most significant cases, the government ended John D. Rockefeller's oil trust, James B. Duke's tobacco trust, and in *Swift v. United States* the beef trust was declared illegal and consigned to oblivion.

"The United States," said the New York *World* editorially, "was never closer to a social revolution than at the time Roosevelt became President in 1901."

Despite Roosevelt's reform efforts, there was still much reason by 1905 for the average man to consider social revolution. Typical of the era was a Supreme Court decision which struck down as unconstitutional a New York statute fixing the daily labor of bakery workers, many of them women and children, at ten hours a day. Grounds for the decision were that such a law, even in that period a not unreasonable demand, "violated the right of contract."

The bakery workers and their toil-weary counterparts in New York's sweat shops went back to fourteen- and fifteen-hour days, earning a pittance for their labor.

It was also the era of crusading muckrakers. Ray Stannard, Charles E. Russell and Thomas W. Lawson, writing in *McClure's* and *Everybody's* magazines, raged against the continued social and economic abuses of the railroads, the meat packers and the no-holds-barred practices of Wall Street which made the rich richer and churned under the small investor, a syndrome that hasn't really changed much to this day. Regulation of the stock market was nonexistent. The Securities and Exchange Commission, a body that still has a long way to go in effectively policing the industry, was not created until 1934.

From its beginning, the House of McDonnell was well-connected. It did a great deal of business with organized religion. Among its major accounts were the Catholic Church and several Protestant denominations. Also among its clients were some of the wealthiest individuals in the nation.

This tradition of relying on clients in high places with high-bracket accounts lingered until the day McDonnell closed its doors in 1970. The house was never truly comfortable with the small investor. It never wavered in its basic philosophy—cultivating the most established of establishmentarians.

Six decades of prosperity for the House of McDonnell was helped along by a fortunate marriage on the part of James F. McDonnell. The Irish immigrant's son wed the daughter of Thomas E. Murray, a celebrated inventor and president of the Murray Manufacturing Company of Brooklyn, New York.

Many of the fourteen children of James and Anna McDonnell also made fortunate, sometimes spectacular, marriages. One daughter, Anne, is the ex-wife of Henry Ford II. Son Murray, who in 1945 at the tender age of twenty-three was made titular head of the firm under the always-watchful scrutiny of his father, married the daughter of a prominent New York banker.

In 1958 the seventy-nine-year-old senior McDonnell died, leaving behind a viable, financially healthy family business. The principal owners of the house became the founder's widow, Mr. and Mrs. T. Murray McDonnell, a brother named Morgan and the former Anne Ford.

Set on a solid course by its progenitor, McDonnell & Co. had breasted good and bad markets, supplementing the business from millionaire clients with the somewhat reluctant but necessary embrace of the smaller investor. By the late 1950s the house was doing a large amount of retail trading for clients in all income brackets. It had also developed a huge, profitable business in placing warrants and participating in underwritings.

In 1967, my first year at McDonnell, the house ran up record earnings of $1.1 million on a gross of $24.7 million. McDonnell was so rich that it could afford $300 chairs for secretaries, company limousines and a private dining room for top executives. Its printing and stationery bill alone was nearly $1 million a year. Its twenty-six offices stretched from Hawaii to Paris. It had three seats on the New York Stock Exchange. Among the high and mighty of Wall Street, McDonnell was firmly entrenched.

So bullish was the overall picture that McDonnell executives said aloud they envisioned the day when they would surpass Merrill Lynch, Pierce, Fenner & Smith, the largest brokerage in the world.

That was the enormously sanguine picture at the end of 1967.

But barely more than two years later, the House of McDonnell was no more. The firm was liquidated, the collapse so catastrophic its full implications will not be known for years.

What was responsible for this incredible turnaround of a sixty-five-year-old brokerage business? How could such a venerable bastion of Wall Street be obliterated with such dramatic suddenness?

McDonnell succumbed for the same basic reason any company fails: bad management.

There is irony without end in the fact that McDonnell fell from its lofty perch because it could not find an executive team to successfully operate its own affairs, while my team within McDonnell was recommending companies to clients precisely because they were well-managed. In fairness, McDonnell wasn't and isn't the only house to suffer from poor management. The brokerage business as a whole undoubtedly has the worst management of any industry in the nation.

I spent my two years and two months at McDonnell headquartered in the *ne plus ultra* Century City office in the heart of the new business and apartment house complex built on land that once was the backlot of 20th Century-Fox Studios.

In 1968 I sold about $100 million worth of stock, producing commissions of almost $1 million for the house and about $400,000 for myself. And all my sales had been to individual clients, not institutions and mutual funds that trade in large blocks. In addition, I produced about $2 million in deal income—commissions from the underwriting of stock issues and fees for arranging mergers between companies. Some $1.2 million went to McDonnell, my share being the remaining $800,-000.

I was far and away the biggest producer in the McDonnell organization. By myself I generated 50 percent of McDonnell's *total* profits. I therefore had good reason to believe that the house considered me something of an asset to the firm.

I was soon to learn otherwise.

Since the death of his father, Murray McDonnell had done little administrative work, preferring to concentrate his energies on handling many of the firm's large accounts. The house pretty much ran itself, but any business allowed to run itself will ultimately run itself into the ground.

Day-to-day management passed in 1966 to the youngest McDonnell son, thirty-three-year-old Sean. He was a good administrator and not a bad businessman, and he brought a much needed steadying influence to the firm.

In the early part of 1968 the house was still enjoying success. Orders poured in with every jangle of the telephone. The ballooning business, however, ballooned the paperwork. McDonnell was quickly trapped in a mountainous paper jungle.

To attempt to sort it out, Sean decided to install a complex new computer system. The effectiveness of the computer in unraveling the paperwork mess was still in doubt when Sean died unexpectedly of a heart attack in June, 1968.

Murray then became administrative head of McDonnell—and things changed fast. The stability that Sean had brought to the business, his attempt at problem-solving, were virtues no longer apparent in the house.

What was already a bad dream became a nightmare.

The situation in the back office worsened, a horrible foul-up beyond description and hope. It was so bad that the only realistic course would have been to close the doors until the paper underbrush was straightened out, if it ever could be straightened out.

In the back office all was pandemonium. Dozens of employees ran around helter-skelter, totally unaware of what they were doing or supposed to be doing. Even if they had time to sit down, there were no chairs. Nobody knew where anything was. Nobody followed through on anything. Nobody took any responsibility. It was all like a Marx Brothers movie, except that it wasn't funny.

My staff was spending 40 percent of its valuable time doing nothing more than trying to rectify back-office errors. But it was an impossible job. How could you rectify an error when you couldn't trace its source? Clients, rightfully, were screaming bloody murder. They wanted errors in their accounts adjusted, they wanted their dividend checks, they wanted their stock certificates.

At one point in 1968, and these are statistics released by McDonnell itself, the situation stood as follows:

Forty thousand admitted errors in the accounts of 47,000 clients!

Uncollected dividends for clients totaling $872,000!

And, most incredible of all, McDonnell had $9 million worth of stock certificates and neither computer nor man knew to whom they belonged!

Despite this barrage of inefficiency, McDonnell miraculously ended 1968 with a profit of $414,000, but well beneath its 1967 revenue of $1.1 million. McDonnell now was in the position of earning less than half the profit of the previous year although its gross was up almost $9 million. The 1967 volume was $24.7 million; 1968 volume was $33 million.

McDonnell's inefficiency became notorious among insiders from Los Angeles to New York. Rumors of the muddle reached the *Wall Street Journal,* and the paper assigned a reporter to look into McDonnell's affairs.

Its chaotic condition became public on the *Journal's* November 6, 1969, front page in a column-one leader under a RICHES TO RAGS headline.

Staff reporter Richard E. Rustin wrote a long, trenchant, well-researched story, including the admission from one of McDonnell's former back-office employees, "I never could get any direction or instructions from the boss who was in charge of my section. He always was too busy chasing errors and running around with a batch of nasty letters from customers. There was always some kind of flap going on."

The story quoted an executive in the operations department of another Wall Street firm: "You'd call a McDonnell clerk about a dividend problem, and he'd either give you a fast shuffle, or promise to call you back and then never phone. McDonnell was a second-line, badly-managed firm that tried to make you think it was first-rate."

Observed another executive aware of the situation, "McDonnell hadn't any written standard operating procedures for any of its back-office functions."

Rustin's piece also revealed, "Confidential Big Board statistics indicated that last year [1968] McDonnell ranked 35th in efficiency among the 38 member firms doing business with the public."

I shudder to think of the efficiency level at the three firms rated below McDonnell.

The vaunted computer—we were told it would "revolutionize" Wall Street—proved to be an atrocity. Sean McDonnell's optimism that the sophisticated system could remove the bedlam from the firm's order-processing and record-keeping procedures proved to be unfounded.

The computer rig was designed and installed by a Waltham, Massachusetts, company, Data Architects, Inc., no stranger to McDonnell. The house had handled Data's underwriting, and McDonnell owned 20 percent of Data's stock.

Sean's death occurred while the computer was still undergoing tests. After his death, management copped out. No one at McDonnell would make a decisive decision on whether the full system should be installed, although it was glaringly obvious that an incomplete system was worse than none at all. "We had the front end of a Rolls Royce and the back end of a Model T," said one McDonnell official.

The incomplete McDonnell computer ranks as a white elephant beside Howard Hughes' wooden flying boat. Neither ever got off the ground.

The computer botch was very costly. Three million dollars had been tossed away, $2 million in salaries and other direct expenses. Data received $500,000 for its work and equipment. Then came the expenditure of another $500,000. This half-million bundle, of all things, was lavished on renting outside computer time.

Even so, McDonnell couldn't begin to catch up with its paperwork. Everything remained snarled and tangled.

All of us at McDonnell sighed in amazement at the computer episode, which caused so many more problems than it solved. I was almost tempted to agree with Stewart Alsop, who observed:

"Invention should have halted with the flush toilet a century ago —what sensible man has a good word to say for the ballistic missile or the bomb, or even for the automobile, and the airplane? But the worst invention of the lot was the computer."

Although machines had failed, men—the right men—might have rescued McDonnell, as thousands of troubled American companies have been rescued by first-rate management. My impression is that Murray McDonnell had the unfortunate proclivity for choosing the wrong man at the wrong time for the wrong job while firing, bludgeoning into silence or forcing his best people to resign.

One particular tragedy was the premature death of a young controller, a friendly, highly competent and dedicated man. He died of a sudden heart attack at the age of forty-one. He was under enormous pressure and in a position to know perhaps better than anyone else how bad things really were in the back office.

At home one evening I received a phone call from the McDonnell executive who had hired me. He didn't go into great detail. He said tersely and wearily. "I've had it. I'm quitting." His loss was yet another body blow to McDonnell. This was a seasoned, conscientious man who, given the chance to function properly, could have helped the house through its time of crisis.

With his resignation my own troubles really began. Without my knowledge, he had been acting as a buffer between New York and myself. I was aware that there was a good deal of jealousy within McDonnell, as within the industry, about my success. But there is jealousy in every company, and it never occurred to me that, given my performance, my own position was in jeopardy.

In September, 1968, I was called to New York for what proved to be a momentous meeting with Murray McDonnell.

"From now on we're going to do business only with the *right* kind of people, my kind of people," Murray said. He obviously meant the firm's business would be confined solely to wealthy clients.

Murray ushered into the room a man I subsequently learned

had logged thirteen years with the old-line, old school-tie First Boston Company, the nation's leading investment banking house. I went slack-jawed when the man was introduced to me as the new head of McDonnell's corporate finance department. Murray said there was no longer going to be a western head of corporate finance. This man was now in complete charge— period.

It didn't matter that I had produced 50 percent of McDonnell's overall profit. When I reminded Murray of this, he replied, incredibly, "I don't care about profit!"

A businessman who doesn't care about profit will soon enough have none to care about, as Murray would shortly discover.

It was only natural for me to wonder what my replacement had produced in thirteen years with the nation's leading investment banker. If he was all that good, if he was a hotshot, why would he want to leave his prestigious firm for a house that was in deep, deep trouble?

The fantastic confrontation reached a zenith of incredibility when Murray said to me, "You can go on salary if you want to."

Taking a salary would have meant an income of between $35,000 and $50,000, a not inconsequential cut from the $1 million-plus I was earning annually. Murray's suggestion in my mind was a calculated insult, a slap in the face. I refused to sink to that level. As calmly as I could, I told Murray, "I'll think about your offer."

It was now a foregone conclusion that I would leave McDonnell. But I needed time to regroup and make plans for the future. I wanted to leave at my own convenience.

Murray suddenly turned friendly after giving me the option of going on salary. I could barely suppress my laughter when he asked me in dead earnest, "If you leave McDonnell, what do you think you'll do for a living?"

He was completed convinced, so far removed was he from the sound and fury and the chaos of everyday operations in his own firm, that I needed his name in order to continue to function successfully.

Murray apparently believed that his firm's former prestige

and prosperity were still a reality, when everyone on Wall Street knew the House of McDonnell was ready to cave in.

Although a cataclysm was threatening the very existence of his firm, Murray McDonnell was living in a dream world. A friend of the Kennedys, a confidante of leading churchmen and Ivy League millionaires, a social lion who was a well-known commuter along the New York-Palm Beach axis amid what passes for high society these days, he was convinced that every broker who was making money at McDonnell owed his success to the McDonnell name.

But who really cared that Murray McDonnell knew the Kennedys? How much money was that going to earn for a client who came to a McDonnell office and placed his trust in a McDonnell broker?

Said Murray: "We have a great firm because it's backed by the McDonnell name." The man was fantasizing as the seconds ticked away toward the destruction of his house, as well as the name of which he was so proud.

It had been a nasty, disheartening confrontation.

When I returned to Los Angeles I told my staff and my wife that the house was no longer viable. Murray was forcing out all the men, others as well as myself, who were producing profits for him. Meantime, he had raised the salaries of his acolytes on the executive committee. I gave McDonnell & Co. up to a year and a half to live.

For a time the situation settled into an uneasy truce. I continued to operate as usual. New York ignored me. I ignored New York. No one asked me what I was doing. I told no one what I was doing. No one said boo to me. I said boo to no one.

It was preposterous.

Management at McDonnell was nonexistent.

The truce turned to battle again when that overblown "superbroker" story appeared in the Los Angeles *Times*.

I had not sought the publicity. Arelo Sederberg, a staff writer for the paper's financial section, had set out to do a story about four successful Los Angeles brokers. He heard of me through a public relations man at Pacific American.

Sederberg interviewed me at lunch, and I gave him a factual rundown of my track record and my investment philosophy.

The next thing I knew I was informed that the story was going to be on the front page of the *Times*. I assumed that meant the front page of the financial section. When the story, complete with my picture, broke on page one of the news section, I was completely surprised. And more surprising was that the long piece was confined solely to me. The idea of including three other brokers had been discarded somewhere along the line, an obvious editorial decision by Sederberg and the *Times*.

When Murray McDonnell read the story he was incensed. He was wild over the fact that I had publicly revealed that by myself I had produced half of all McDonnell's income.

Now Murray had fresh ammunition.

Now Murray McDonnell demanded my immediate dismissal.

Getting rid of me, however, wasn't that simple. To dismiss me, McDonnell was obliged to show cause. Otherwise I could sue, as Murray well knew.

Murray and his tremulous executive committee held a meeting for the express purpose of finding some grounds on which they could fire me. But they were unsuccessful since I still was outperforming everyone in the organization.

There was just no way to throw me out. I was still planning to leave, of course, but at my own convenience.

By this time Murray had brought in a formidable new man as president of McDonnell, the brilliant political tactician Lawrence Francis O'Brien, capo of the famed "Irish Mafia" that had masterminded John F. Kennedy's surge into the White House.

The day I heard of O'Brien's appointment, I predicted that he wouldn't stay long. It didn't take much common sense to realize that O'Brien had been duped. Murray McDonnell certainly had not given O'Brien anything resembling the true picture of the firm. But how could he? Murray himself didn't really know the depth of the crevasse into which McDonnell had slipped.

Gifted as O'Brien was in presidential politics—Kennedy had called him "the best election man in the business"—I knew that the former Presidential kingmaker and ex-Postmaster General was out of his element at McDonnell.

I knew of no background or qualifications that O'Brien had for presiding over a Wall Street firm, particularly one with such serious difficulties. With his acumen, O'Brien, given enough time, would unquestionably have learned the business and made an effective administrator, but O'Brien didn't have that kind of time.

I'm certain that if he had known the true state of McDonnell's affairs he would have as soon turned Republican as accept the presidency of a Wall Street ruin. Murray had evidently persuaded O'Brien to lend his prestige and contacts to McDonnell on a "trust me" basis.

Although O'Brien was instrumental in making Kennedy the thirty-fifth President of the United States, I knew he couldn't salvage McDonnell. The man who could do that—considering all the circumstances—would be a man who could also walk on water.

On February 10, a little more than two weeks after the story about me appeared, O'Brien worked out an agreement with my attorney that I would resign from McDonnell on March 15. My attorney, powerful in California's Democratic Party ranks, was a friend of O'Brien's. He and O'Brien shook hands on the March 15 date for my resignation—time enough, I had decided, for me to put my own house in order.

But March 15 wasn't soon enough for Murray McDonnell. He wanted me out as quickly as possible. Two days after the handshake deal, O'Brien called my lawyer and said that I now had to be out by February 15. That gave me only three days to clean up my considerable affairs. It wasn't fair or logical. "I won't do it," I told my attorney. "I'll stick to the March 15 date on which O'Brien shook hands."

My attorney phoned O'Brien to negotiate another month's time for me. "My hands are tied," O'Brien said. "Murray wants him out in the worst way."

A compromise between Murray McDonnell, O'Brien, my attorney and myself was finally arranged. I had bought sufficient time. I agreed to leave March 1, and I left March 1.

When I walked out of the McDonnell office for the last time, the house's obituary had been written but not yet published.

The situation at McDonnell was even worse than anybody

had suspected. The house was losing $1 million a month in the back office alone, customers' accounts were still in massive disarray, stock certificates still weren't being delivered, ten branch offices had been closed and one of McDonnell's seats on the exchange had been sold to raise money for daily expenses.

By August, 1969, only eight months after joining McDonnell, O'Brien evidently reached the conclusion that he had walked into an impossible job. There were many things that the gifted O'Brien could do. Walking on water, however, wasn't one of them. O'Brien resigned and went into the public relations business, then found his true métier again when he became national chairman of the Democratic Party.

O'Brien's formal resignation statement was a masterpiece of understatement. He was leaving because his post "did not afford me the opportunity that I had envisioned it would."

"When I came to McDonnell & Co.," he said, "it was with the understanding that the firm would be in a position to broaden its horizons in a variety of ways. It has become apparent, however, that this will not be possible, and, in fact, the company is retrenching into a smaller entity with concentration in its areas of traditional specialty.

"Considering the state of the economy and the stock market, the decision to retrench is a prudent one."

The Associated Press story that carried the news of O'Brien's resignation also carried Murray's comment concerning the loss of his president. O'Brien "has performed an outstanding service for the firm and its customers during his tenure," Murray said.

The nature of that "outstanding service" was not spelled out.

In conjunction with O'Brien's departure, Murray also announced a major reorganization of the firm and that it was divesting itself of something known as the McDonnell Mutual Fund.

"An examination of the company's business indicates that the outlook for earning improved returns will best be met by limiting the nature of the business," said Murray.

Then, talking in a code I understood only too well, Murray added that the firm was seeking to "reduce the quantity of its business and to increase the quality of its business."

Meantime, the presumed hotshot from First Boston, who was going to do great things for McDonnell with the right kind of people, reaped disaster. Part of his deal upon entering McDonnell was buying stock in the house. He was to invest $250,000, which he didn't have. He borrowed the money from a bank, Murray purportedly arranging the loan.

The gentleman from First Boston stayed with McDonnell for about five months. Then he too came to the conclusion that he was aboard a sinking ship.

Further disasters continued to ravage the McDonnell operation.

Cost-cutting and a desperate attempt to find fresh capital to keep the firm going were now the primary concerns.

Gone were the VIP limousines (Murray kept his, but paid for its operation himself). The executive dining room was closed. People were being fired at a rapid rate. The staff of the corporate finance department was halved. There was also a 50 percent personnel reduction in the research department, which is particularly significant. Research is the last department a house should cut. With half its analysts gone, how could McDonnell's stock recommendations, which were weak enough even with a full staff, be given to the public in good conscience? I had always avoided McDonnell's research recommendations, putting my clients into situations I had investigated myself, but other brokers relied on house research which was only a bare notch better than no research at all.

Also fired were brokers who weren't producing minimum commissions of $50,000 a year. Even the $50,000–$100,000 salaries of Murray's yes-men were shaved 10 percent. More branch offices were shuttered. And the contract with Data Architects was finally cancelled. The full computer system would never be installed. McDonnell continued to farm out its back-office bacchanalia to an outside computer service.

Murray was now pushing stock in his dying firm to his vice-presidents, remaining branch managers and brokers. The stock was pegged at 70! But it was worse than worthless. I read it at a price of minus $5 a share.

I warned many of the friends I had among the executives and

brokers at McDonnell's Century City and Beverly Hills offices
not to touch Murray's stock. I told the manager of the Hono-
lulu branch the same thing. Interestingly enough, these same
men who would buy any stock I recommended—no questions
asked—thought I was attacking the Church when I advised them
against investing in McDonnell. Many key men in what remained of McDonnell's operation didn't know or didn't want to
know that the firm's illness was terminal. They could not or
would not believe it. They all felt, because they were employed
by McDonnell, that they had a moral obligation to buy stock in
the house.

Needless to say, everyone who bought lost his shirt.

Brokers still at McDonnell could not take any orders for in-
expensive over-the-counter stocks. Such orders were too costly
to process, brought little profit to the house and only piled up
more unmanageable paperwork. Said the *Wall Street Journal,*
"There were plenty of cases where these orders were disobeyed,
because there were salesmen who just were interested in getting
their commissions, and to hell with the firm. Their immediate
superiors, who should have stopped this, simply didn't do it."

Chaos at the top had bred chaos through the ranks.

Murray McDonnell did not set out to intentionally wreck his
own firm. He is not a stupid man or a man bent on committing
financial suicide, despite his assertion to me that he wasn't interested in profit. Rather, I regard him as a classic example of a
bad manager. He hadn't the slightest conception of how to
administer a complex business.

Murray was a good salesman. To put it in Dr. Laurence J.
Peter's terms, he had reached his highest level of competence.
His highest level of competence was as a jet-set broker. Because
of Sean's untimely death, Murray was hurled to his highest level
of incompetence when he became chairman of the firm. Not the
least of Murray's mistakes was that he had the money to hire
experts who might have bailed him out at several places along
the line. Instead he chose to surround himself with puppets,
while driving from his temple precisely those men who could
have helped him the most by continuing to rack up profits for

the house and give him candid assessments and knowledgeable suggestions for solving his problems.

Thus Murray McDonnell and so many others in the firm were to pay because of bad management.

But what about McDonnell's clients? Who was protecting them? Who was protecting and doing anything for the 47,000 shareholders that McDonnell admitted had 40,000 errors in their accounts? Who was protecting the clients who had a heady $872,000 due them in uncollected dividends? Who was protecting those perplexed and angry investors who hadn't received $9 million worth of stock securities that were presumably flapping around somewhere in the mayhem of the McDonnell back office?

In the whole sorry saga of the McDonnell debacle, this was the sorriest aspect of all.

Who should have been protecting the public is the SEC. Who should also have been protecting clients was the New York Stock Exchange, the presumed watchdog over member firms under whose supposed Argus-eye the public may purchase stocks with total confidence.

The NYSE is fond of running opulent ads in leading magazines. The copy is full of joy and jargon. The Exchange is "promoting high standards in the public interest," said a typical ad in *Time* magazine. "Four basic concepts characterize the marketplace," continued the puffery. The first three "concepts" relate only to routine trading practices on the floor, which help keep an orderly market. But the fourth guarantee offered by the NYSE is "surveillance by the Exchange to help enforce the rules governing trading."

Where was that surveillance in the debacle at McDonnell?

The moment the news of McDonnell's ailing condition sifted onto the Street, the Exchange should have brought those self-proclaimed "high standards in the public interest" and its self-declared surveillance into force. The Exchange had the muscle to shut down McDonnell and protect the money of McDonnell clients before the situation became impossible.

On paper the policing powers of the Exchange sound extremely potent, but the policing action of the Exchange in practice is ludicrous.

A year before I was forced out of McDonnell, I knew how bad the situation was. The executive committee and many lesser managerial employees at McDonnell knew how bad the situation was. The financial underground had spread the story of McDonnell's malaise from sea to shining sea.

Why didn't the NYSE know how bad the situation was, and why didn't this august self-styled protector of the public's welfare act?

The NYSE is a private club, composed of members of the nation's principal brokerage firms. Every house that owns a seat is a member of the club. A member of a private country club who breaks enough rules gets thrown out, severely reprimanded or punished. The same thing should have happened to McDonnell once its condition became so widely known. Once the first rumors started tripping along the Street, they should have been checked out.

Virtually every brokerage house carries a line in its mass newspaper and magazine advertising that reads: Member of the New York Stock Exchange. To the man in the street this implies standards, responsibility and protection. But the NYSE doesn't provide half the protection it should. Sanctions by its board of governors are occasionally visited on smaller houses. The big houses, however, are seldom touched.

The old school tie is more important than the faceless shareholder in the crowd to the NYSE, but those faceless shareholders who in sum make up the investing public are transcendently more important than protecting fellow club members.

The NYSE had an absolute responsibility to the public to police McDonnell. But where were the men from the NYSE asking McDonnell the hundreds of questions that should have been asked? Where indeed were they?

McDonnell's problems didn't bloom overnight. There was ample time to step in to lessen or avoid the final disaster. The responsibility of the Exchange is to prevent Humpty-Dumpty's great fall, not try to put the yolk back together.

The Exchange should have a task force of hardheaded, no-

nonsense sharpshooters who, like the Inspector General of the Army, would descend unannounced on all member firms for periodic, microscopic spot checks, making certain the back offices are in shape and that minimal capital requirements of member houses are being maintained. Even the threat of a surprise inspection would trigger most houses into reforming many of their procedures. The NYSE above all should be protecting the investment public against fraud, manipulation and deceit, sins practiced on a daily basis by many member firms.

The Exchange sharpshooters, like Internal Revenue agents, would show fear or favor to no one.

The old school tie is a tattered, tainted and stained tradition. The securities business is too big, too fundamentally important to the nation's economy for a small group of men to treat the public with lordly disdain.

The public-be-damned philosophy of William Henry Vanderbilt is still alive on Wall Street today. It's been more than eighty-five years since Vanderbilt expressed his contempt for the average man, and Wall Street hasn't learned its lesson yet.

Although generally I abhor more Federal regulation, I think the time has come for the government to step in. It's not likely that the NYSE will descend on its member transgressors before the barn has burned down. Congress should formulate legislation for the hard-hitting task force, which perhaps would operate out of the Treasury Department or under the aegis of a revamped SEC. The SEC in practice is as ineffective as the NYSE as an instrumentality of public protection. The government agency should also have been in the McDonnell picture long before it finally moved to stop the financial rape of trusting clients.

The stakes are too great for the government to ignore. We are talking about the underpinnings of the American economy and much of the nation's treasure. We are talking about the protection of at least one in thirteen Americans who own stock. We are talking about the families of these stockholders. We are talking about the protection of every American whose life insurance company, pension fund or union invests in the stock market. We are talking about almost 15 billion shares of stock on the New York Stock Exchange worth $675 billion at the end of 1970.

The government regulates the airlines, the drug industry, the meat packers and scores of other industries. Why should the securities industry be an exception to tougher regulations sternly enforced?

Additional Federal regulation of brokerage houses would inspire additional investor confidence and result in a higher volume of business for the industry. With such protection, a lot of investors would sleep a lot better.

The deepest concern I have is to see the securities industry prosper and grow, but I want to see it grow on a sounder basis. With the right kind of policing, the incredible excesses at McDonnell would never have reached the point of no-return.

When the NYSE and the SEC finally came into the McDonnell mess they came as undertakers, not saviors. In November, 1969, McDonnell was prohibited from participating in underwritings, hiring new brokers, or replacing any brokers who were fired or quit. McDonnell was barred from advertising or promoting itself. McDonnell was forbidden to handle more than 12,000 trades a week, a meaningless restriction because orders had already plummeted to some 4,000 trades weekly from 17,-000 during the heyday of the firm.

Timid as the sanctions were, most of them were quickly removed by the Exchange and McDonnell, after so shamefully and shabbily serving its clients, was allowed to limp along, still permitted to do business with the public.

On the Black Friday of March 13, 1970, the House of McDonnell collapsed completely.

McDonnell was shut down, according to SEC New York Regional Administrator Kevin Thomas Duffy, after a lengthy investigation. But the SEC's investigation had been too lengthy. The risks of investing in the market itself are sufficient without clients losing money because of NYSE–SEC laxity in cracking down on a mismanaged and inefficient house.

Murray McDonnell's account of the reasons for the collapse came in a prepared statement: "It is with deep regret that we have decided to close McDonnell & Co. after 65 years of business on Wall Street. The firm, started by my father, has had a long tradition of integrity and reliability and it is in that spirit that we have made our decision.

"Circumstances, many of them beyond human control, created problems for our firm that have turned out to be insoluble. These included the sudden death of my young brother, Sean, who had played a key management role until June, 1968, the untimely death of the firm's controller and of its senior vice president for operations in 1968 and 1969, the failure of a new computer system to operate as it had been planned, compounding the back-office problems during the latter part of 1968 when stock brokerage volume was at a record level, the sharply declining stock market of 1969, and the subsequent drop in brokerage volume and other investment banking activities.

"The properly stringent requirements of the regulatory bodies concerning net capital have made it impossible to weather the storm any longer. Therefore we will terminate our business over the next few months, keeping faith with our customers, with our colleagues in Wall Street, and with our loyal and devoted employees."

But that pious explanation wouldn't wash.

The SEC lashed out at last with thunderous action and allegations that reverberated into the halls of Congress. Not only was McDonnell out of business, but the fissure was deeper than anyone had guessed.

The SEC revoked McDonnell's broker-dealer license and announced hearings on charges * that fourteen McDonnell executives and brokers had violated various Federal securities laws regarding margin, registration and antifraud sections of government regulations.

Murray made a deal with the SEC. Without admitting the allegations, Murray nevertheless consented to findings that:

• He failed to exercise the type of supervision that might have prevented the violations.

• Common stock and promissory notes of McDonnell & Co. had been sold without being registered.

* Detailed and documented in the Securities and Exchange Commission's File No. 3-2409, April 9, 1970.

• Such sales were in violation of antifraud statutes because the defendants failed to advise purchasers of the "true condition" of the firm's back-office operations, books and records.

• Had not advised those who bought stock in the house of "large operating losses" suffered by McDonnell & Co., especially from September through December, 1968.

• McDonnell & Co. had not met a number of financial requirements of the NYSE.

• That McDonnell brokers had made false and misleading statements concerning the prospects of Norsul Oil & Mining Ltd. and Waltham Industries Corporation. Norsul, a Canadian company, was suspended from trading on January 27, 1969, for what the SEC called a "false and misleading" announcement the company issued about its oil interests in Ecuador. The suspension was lifted on February 25 after the company issued a clarifying announcement. But McDonnell brokers had violated antifraud regulations of Federal securities law by recommending Norsul's stock without first making a "reasonable and diligent inquiry" about the shares and "in disregard of information about Norsul's financial condition and business operations."

Regarding Waltham, the brokers had recommended the stock without first having made the proper inquiry about it. Further, that the brokers recommended the stock to customers for whom it wasn't suitable "in light of the customers' individual investment needs and objectives," and that they made "false and misleading" statements about certain aspects of Waltham's operations and financial condition.

• McDonnell & Co. further violated antifraud regulations by inducing customers to engage in stock transactions that were "excessive in size and frequency" and to engage in certain "speculative" investment practices that weren't suitable to the customers' needs.

• Making unauthorized trades in customers' accounts.

• Establishing unauthorized credit accounts for customers.

• That McDonnell & Co. also violated credit-extension regulations by, among other things, giving credit to customers without collateral.

• That executives also failed to exercise proper supervision to prevent the alleged violations.

In a separate action,* Murray and McDonnell & Co., again without admitting or denying the allegations, consented to an injunction issued by a Federal district court in New York barring Murray and his associates from "further violations" of the registration and antifraud provisions of Federal securities law. The court order stemmed from the SEC charges.

Seldom, if ever, has there been such public condemnation of the failure of management.

As for Murray McDonnell himself, he was subjected to a penalty rarely meted out.

The immigrant's grandson who inherited a rich family business, confidante of the Kennedys, the churches, broker to bluebloods, was visited with a singular punishment.

Murray McDonnell, without SEC approval, was barred for life from assuming any managerial position with a Wall Street broker-dealer firm.

Winston Churchill said in November, 1942, "I have not become the King's first minister to preside over the liquidation of the British Empire."

Neither did Murray McDonnell become the chairman of his family's empire to preside over its liquidation.

Yet the British Empire and McDonnell & Co. are no more.

Winston Churchill, of course, could not long prevent or change the forces militating against the continuation of colonialism.

But Murray McDonnell had had his chance to recover. He threw it away, writing his own bizarre epitaph:

From now on, we're going to do business only with the right kind of people, my kind of people, and I don't care about profit.

In Washington, the McDonnell fiasco, the failure of other houses and the looming threat of even more failures stirred a tempest. A Senate banking subcommittee began hearings with

* See File No. 1473, United States District Court, Southern District of New York, Securities and Exchange Commission, Plaintiff, against McDonnell & Co., Inc. and T. Murray McDonnell, Defendants.

a view to writing legislation that would provide Federal insurance to protect investors from losses when brokerage firms go under.

Representative John E. Moss, sponsor of a similar measure in the House, declared such a bill might be the only hope "for stemming the crisis of investor confidence that would inevitably develop in the case of the failure of another brokerage house."

There was panic now in Washington as well as on Wall Street.

The NYSE, which at this point was said to be considering its own sanctions and disciplinary measures against Murray McDonnell, did not think a government insurance program was a good idea. But during the course of the hearings the NYSE changed its mind "in order to restore investor confidence."

What emerged after six months of intensive and agonizing negotiations between Congress, the SEC, and the NYSE was the creation of a new Securities Investor Protection Corporation comparable to the Federal Deposit Insurance Corporation that protects customers of banks. Signing the legislation, President Nixon called it a "vitally important advance in the consumer protection field."

It is no such thing. The SIPC is a sham and a hollow victory for beleaguered shareholders.

At best it is supposed to provide up to $50,000 worth of insurance protection against losses resulting from brokerage house insolvencies. But it is possible that the rate of brokerage failures will be so high that no investor can be assured he is really protected.

And why isn't the man who has more than $50,000 in the market covered? President Nixon acknowledged that the new law "is for the protection of the small investor, not the large investor."

I'm all for the small investor getting all the protection possible, but it is manifestly unfair to arbitrarily set protection at $50,000. Every investor, no matter the size of his commitment in the market, should be covered equally. Imbedded in this section of the law is the reared head of politics. There are more small investors than large investors, which translates into more votes. Under a fair program, the man with $5,000 or $5 million in the market deserves equal protection.

The SIPC is funded by an assessment of less than 1 percent from brokerage houses. Additionally, the SIPC has authority to borrow up to $1 billion from the U.S. Treasury if its own failure fund is depleted. Thus Wall Street, the nerve-center of capitalism, free enterprise supposedly in its purest form, can now go to the taxpayers' well and ask all Americans—whether they own stock or not—to come up with money to remedy its own incapacity to manage itself.

I deplore a development where more than 200 million Americans can be taxed for the losses of 31.9 million Americans who owned stock market shares at the beginning of 1971, where the entire nation might have to pay for the ineptitude and greed of Wall Street. Even more frightening is that the $1 billion will not be enough to cover all the future losses I anticipate.

What happens then?

Wall Street has become so inept that it has now reached the historic crossroads where an industry trumpeting and selling free enterprise must ask the government to underwrite the security of its customers. Unfortunately, Wall Street inefficiency is so staggering that government underwriting *is* necessary. However, it should be done much more effectively.

The SIPC legislation puts the emphasis in the wrong place. It is nonsense to provide a fund only for houses that have already gone under or are certain to go under. That's buying water to put out the fire after the barn has burned.

What should be created to put the entire Wall Street structure on a healthier course is a new regulatory agency of the Federal government that would function in much the same manner as the Federal Reserve System, which provides inspection and borrowing facilities for banks. Under such a set-up, the brokerage houses could go to the public window to borrow funds to maintain their solvency *before* they fail, thereby keeping them liquid and under close scrutiny, the government making certain that they are not violating securities laws and trampling the rights of any investor. The present Federal Reserve System was put into effect as an outgrowth of the wave of bank failures that occurred in the 1930's, and it has worked very well. Why not initiate the same kind of machinery to ward off future failures of brokerage houses?

How things have changed on the Street of the mighty! The mighty have become maggots, feeding off the public's body. As matters now stand, investors are not offered nearly enough protection. The securities business has become too big, too important, too much a force in the American economy, to leave investor protection to the doubtful efficacy of the SIPC, a weak SEC and the NYSE, which still remains a private club.

The NYSE in February, 1971, chose to accept Murray McDonnell's offer to suspend himself as a broker for 12 months, of which 10 months were remitted for reasons of "extenuation." Murray also agreed not to apply again for exchange membership or a supervisory position in a member firm.

When Murray was barred for life from the Street less than a year before, the story rated headlines. The announcement of his settlement with the NYSE was quietly buried. Even the *Wall Street Journal* carried the details on page 16.

It was clear that everyone on the Street wanted to forget the story of the rise and fall of McDonnell & Co.

"If you have to keep reminding yourself of a thing," wrote Christopher Morley, "perhaps it isn't so."

EIGHT

A BLUE CHIP IS A STOCK THAT GOES UP

It requires ages to destroy a popular opinion.

VOLTAIRE

Bloody but unbowed after being whipsawed out of McDonnell, I was in temporary professional trauma.

The vexing question was what my next move should be.

I remained *hors de combat*—removing myself entirely from the market from March 1–December 1, 1969. It was time for soul-searching.

I had thought McDonnell would be my last house, and now I was unemployed, a broker in exile suffering mental but not monetary anguish. The securities industry, through travail and triumph, had been magnificently generous to me. During the nine-month period in which I hunted for fresh commitment and involvement, I could enjoy the luxurious amenities of a fulsome bank balance, a comfortable red-brick home in fashionable Brentwood, a Rolls Royce with telephone, a capacious boat. Never would I have serious financial problems again, but at the age of forty-one I felt that I hadn't begun to hit my stride.

There were many options open to me. Yet, ironically, upon detailed examination there weren't all that many possibilities.

I considered starting my own brokerage firm. However, that would unavoidably tie me up in administrative detail, the day-by-day trivia of running a business, and I had no particular desire to so dissipate my energies.

I also considered initiating my own mutual fund—a comparatively small, no-load fund, capitalized at $50 million, a financial boundary in which I thought I could perform most effectively. The titanic funds with $500 million to play with, or much more, have become the albatross of the market. I decided against my own fund in the end because this move would also involve administrative trivia and, more importantly, there weren't that many lush stocks around that would meet my in-

83

vestment standards. In any case, I could perform more profitably for clients by clinging closely to a relatively small number of individual situations, pinpointing winners through my own detective work.

I could have made a career acting as a financial adviser and sitting on the boards of directors of several companies. I had been asked repeatedly to join the boards of firms who knew me by reputation and firms that I had helped build and in which I held large amounts of stock. But sitting on a board is generally a waste of time, an essentially stagnant, nonimaginative task that can quickly become routine and dull. For the most part it is noncreative participation. Besides, I wanted more action than would be offered by making the rounds of board meetings.

Joining another brokerage presented still another problem. I immediately had to exclude all but a very small number of the reigning Wall Street houses. I knew how they thought—more to the point, how they *didn't* think. I had no desire to become mired down again in another house where, as at McDonnell, management stupidity gushed like water over a broken dam.

To say this is not to say or imply that I considered myself made of special they-threw-the-mold-away clay. It is only to say that the way in which I had built the assets of my clients and myself was a way that worked. I couldn't possibly function within the confines of a house where yesterday's outmoded methods still held sway, where in spirit and philosophy and outlook nothing was significantly different from Wall Street's buttonwood tree days.

Surveying the scene, it was all quite discouraging. I turned down offers to join one brokerage after another. These houses might not suffer the fate of McDonnell, but they, too, were involved in what at bottom was a blind, senseless policy of eventually butchering clients. They were houses of financial prostitution where management acted like madams, brokers operated like whores. The focus was solely on making a commission by selling whatever stock could be sold—good, bad, indifferent or horrendous.

Not until I met the men who ran Newburger, Loeb & Co. did I find a management team whose thinking coincided with mine. The firm was well established. It had seven offices in New York, two in Los Angeles. It was almost as old as McDonnell had been, founded in 1899. In capital, prestige and strength it was richer than McDonnell had been, although it had nine offices compared to the twenty-six owned by McDonnell at its peak. But number of offices is not the way a brokerage firm should be gauged. McDonnell's twenty-six had been more hindrance than help; in fact, its widespread expansion was one of the important reasons for its failure. The operative principle of a brokerage firm for me is the thinking of the men who run the house.

And the thinking at Newburger, Loeb was perfectly attuned to mine. It was a member of all the exchanges, research-oriented, depth-investigating its situations. It was profit-minded, deeply committed to investment banking, amenable to change in areas where change seemed necessary and beneficial.

I was offered a partnership, which I accepted. I was made western head of the corporate finance department—the usual euphemism for running the deal end of the business, which is where the real action and opportunities exist.

I was given more autonomy than I had had in any previous association, allowed to point my laser beam in any direction I cared to take, at any company I cared to investigate. I had carte blanche to stitch together any deal I wanted, and I had an atmosphere of tranquility and serenity, free from the yapping, howling and baying hounds of indecision, in-fighting and exotic, hothouse personalities.

I reconstituted my team from McDonnell and brought them into Newburger, Loeb. I had slipped into gear again.

Now the search was on again for blue chips, my kind of blue chips.

I joined Newburger, Loeb at a time when the market was in its longest bear period since 1962. For the most part, I went into hibernation as far as recommending stocks was concerned. A clever broker once said, "Sometimes the best way you can double a client's money is to advise him to fold it over once and put. it in his pocket or his bank."

I bought stocks for some clients, stocks I thought were underpriced, particularly Pacific American, House of Fabrics, National General, and a growing firm called Wells Industries, which subsequently changed its corporate name to Continental Transportation Systems, Inc. Headquartered in Santa Fe Springs, California, it was a company I had been close to for several years. Continental had changed its thrust from dependence on uncertain, low-profit, big-headache government contracts for the manufacture of aerospace parts to a private-sector, fully diversified transportation company, the only company in its field with a complete range of nationwide services—leasing, carting, storing, repairing and manufacturing container chassis. It was expanding under a keen-minded, fourth-generation transportation executive, Stephen C. Wyn, the firm's new president. It had also acquired a number of distributorships for Timpte trailers, and would prosper further through acquisitions. A $3,317,961 loss resulting from some earlier government contracts had been turned around. Once the Federal business was cancelled and a couple of deadweight divisions sold off, Continental showed a small net profit of $16,000 in the first quarter of 1969. Given all its elements, in my opinion the only way the company could go was up.

With these exceptions, I did virtually nothing for clients. All I lost was commissions, infinitely preferable to losing a client or having a client lose money in a market atmosphere I considered temporarily unsuitable for investment. I found out early in my career that the wisest course of action in the throes of a bear market is no course of action. Sit, hold tight and wait. The opportunity to find a real blue chip will always be there.

Of all the myths in the stock market, the myth of blue chips is the hardest to kill and the most difficult to explain to clients.

The first thing to be recognized is that there isn't a blue chip that conforms to conventional definition. Blue chips are supposed to be the very best stocks in that they are the most stable, the most widely held, responsible, dependable, safest, with profits and dividends rising year after year.

But there are no such stocks.

Not one.

In a poker game, blue chips are of highest value (hence the

origin of the term). But the market to me isn't a poker game. And what Wall Street calls blue chips are by no means always of the highest value.

The term is a misnomer, as millions of investors have discovered. For the public as well as investors and brokers there should be only one realistic, acceptable definition of a blue chip:

A stock that goes up.

Anything else is a bad investment.

"Stick with quality," advised a 1969 research report from one influential house with coast-to-coast offices. But what constitutes quality is as subject to interpretation as the philosophical conundrum, "What is truth?"

"Many people," the report said, "feel they have to find something that nobody else has ever heard of, or discover a so-called hidden value."

This is the sort of "research" that perpetuates the myth of blue chips. Hidden value, if it can be discerned in a particular corporation, is exactly how the investor profits most. There was hidden value in House of Fabrics, Monogram and a whole string of other issues into which I put my clients. Their hidden value wasn't "so-called." It was real.

The report went on to sing the praises of the cliché giants— AT&T, General Motors and DuPont, the triumvirate that supposedly is the holy trinity of the market.

But these stocks in my view were not blue chips in 1969. They were companies beset with the kinds of problems that virtually prohibit the investor from making money. They also were companies that long ago had had their major play. At best it can be said they are blue chips only in a good year. In a bad auto year, for example, General Motors is not a blue chip. It is a highly questionable investment for a profit-minded client.

The fact that companies are widely held only proves that most people can be impressed by size. Of the twenty-four companies with the largest number of stockholders in 1969, only three performed the way blue chips are supposed to, although these two dozen giants are among the most illustrious, powerful dreadnoughts in the American corporate fleet, the flagships of our industrial might. In the bear market that dominated 1969, most

proved to be leaky vessels, as vulnerable—some more vulnerable—than many of the worst speculations in the over-the-
counter market.

The following table is instructive:

Company	Number of Stock-holders	Closing Market Price 1968	1969	Net Change
AT&T	3,142,000	53	48⅝	−4⅜
General Motors	1,349,000	79⅛	69⅛	−10
Standard Oil of New Jersey	774,000	78⅝	61¾	−16⅞
General Telephone & Electronics	544,000	39⅞	30	−9⅞
General Electric	541,000	93⅞	77½	−16⅜
IBM	501,000	315	364½	+49½
Ford Motor	384,000	53	41⅛	−11⅞
U.S. Steel	349,000	42⅞	33¾	−9⅛
RCA	321,000	46¼	34	−12½
Sears, Roebuck	252,000	62¼	68	+5¾
Standard Oil of California	248,000	72⅛	51⅛	−21
Bethlehem Steel	237,000	31⅜	27⅛	−4¼
DuPont	235,000	165	105	−60
Consolidated Edison	228,000	33¼	25½	−7¾
Mobil Oil	219,000	58¾	46	−12¾
Tenneco	217,000	31⅝	23⅛	−8½
Texaco	212,000	83¼	30⅝	−22*
Union Carbide	210,000	45¼	37	−8¼
Eastman Kodak	199,000	73¼	82⅜	+9⅛
Columbia Gas System	186,000	30¼	26	−4¼
Pacific Gas & Electric	175,000	38⅛	32¾	−5⅜
Standard Oil of Indiana	173,000	61⅜	48	−13⅜
Gulf Oil	172,000	43⅛	31	−12⅛
Commonwealth Edison	171,000	48⅝	37½	−11⅛

* adjusted for 2 for 1 split

Even more to the point, try telling those who bought AT&T
at its 1965 high of 70½ and watched it sink to a 44½–53⅞
trading range in January–May, 1970, that they owned a blue chip

stock. Some buyers saw as much as one-third of AT&T's value trickle away. And Ma Bell is showing her age. Chairman H. I. Romnes freely admitted in 1970 that the company's growth rate would be about 8½ percent compared to 10½ percent in 1969. Despite that warning signal, the company continues to be the ninth most popular stock in portfolios of the seventy-one leading college endowment funds. It was the fourth-ranking favorite of individual buyers in 1969. In the last quarter of 1969, some 736,000 shares of AT&T were bought by fifteen mutual funds, about $36 million worth. No one is going to go completely broke buying AT&T or any other vaunted blue chip. But no one is going to make any real money either. And what of the thousands who have sold Ma Bell in disgust, losing money? Tell them that Ma Bell is a blue chip.

General Motors, the nation's largest industrial firm, has undergone important management shifts, and although it ranked number one on the list of *Fortune* magazine's 500 largest industrial corporations in 1969, its net income dropped $21 million despite worldwide dollar sales of $24.3 billion. GM earned $5.95 per share in 1969, compared to $6.02 per share in 1968. Try telling the man who paid 113¾ for the stock in 1965 that it was a blue chip at its trading range of 67½–80 in 1970.

DuPont in its 167th year of existence has seen its growth stunted. The company "has been on a plateau for the past few years. It is at a high plateau, but it is still a plateau." This is the judgment of Charles Brelsford McCoy, the man who is the president of the world's largest chemical company. Net income as a percentage of sales slipped from 20 percent in 1956 to 11 percent in 1968. The company has proved extremely vulnerable to competition from chemical firms in Europe and Japan. Its condition is no secret. The January 5, 1970, issue of *Time* concluded: "DuPont managers are plainly worried. Many stockholders share their concern. Though Wall Street still considers the company to be among the bluest of blue chips, DuPont shares have dropped from 261 in 1965 to last week's 106." A client can get awfully blue holding that kind of blue chip.

Fortunes of companies, even the biggest, rise and fall. They are subject to yearly variation and considerable long-term variation. I'm certainly not the only observer who thinks so. Nationally-syndicated financial columnist Sylvia Porter observed: "Of all the sobering lessons we can learn from 1969, among the most valuable can be: fashions in stocks shift in a relatively short period; you can't put even the high quality favorites 'away and forget'; few of yesteryear's blue chips are today's and few of this year's blue chips will be tomorrow's."

The 1946 blue chip list—the stocks most favored by brokerage houses, mutual funds and individual investors—had shifted dramatically by 1969.

Top Fifty, 1946	Top Fifty, 1969
1. Montgomery Ward	IBM
2. Standard Oil of New Jersey	Xerox
3. Kennecott Copper	Atlantic Richfield
4. North American Co.	American Telephone
5. Union Carbide	Standard Oil of New Jersey
6. Chrysler	Polaroid
7. Johns-Manville	Texaco
8. Paramount Pictures	Royal Dutch Petroleum
9. DuPont	Burroughs
10. Gulf Oil	Eastman Kodak
11. International Paper	General Motors
12. Electric Power & Light	Sperry Rand
13. General Electric	Control Data
14. General Motors	General Electric
15. Sears, Roebuck	Avon Products
16. American Gas & Electric	Gulf Oil
17. American Viscose	Mobil Oil
18. B. F. Goodrich	Standard Oil of California
19. Hercules Powder	Continental Oil
20. Continental Oil	Sears, Roebuck
21. American Radiator	International Telephone
22. Armstrong Cork	Minnesota Mining
23. Electric Auto-Lite	Goodyear Tire
24. Firestone Tire	Ford Motor
25. Goodyear Tire	Honeywell
26. International Nickel	International Paper
27. U.S. Rubber	Philip Morris
28. Westinghouse Electric	S. S. Kresge
29. Texas Co.	Caterpillar Tractor
30. Allied Stores	Aetna Life & Casualty
31. American Tobacco "B"	Westinghouse Electric

Top Fifty, 1946	Top Fifty, 1969
32. Celanese Corp.	International Nickel, Canada
33. Deere	Cities Service
34. Great Northern Railway pfd.	Merck
35. Phillips Petroleum	Chrysler
36. Standard Oil of California	Northwest Airlines
37. American Cyanamid	Continental Can
38. CIT Financial	Crown Zellerbach
39. Eastman Kodak	Household Finance
40. Greyhound	Standard Oil of Indiana
41. International Harvester	Dupont
42. Sherwin-Williams	Mohawk Data Sciences
43. Standard Brands	Union Carbide
44. United Light & Railways	American Home Products
45. Youngstown Sheet & Tube	Procter & Gamble
46. American Power & Light pfd.	Weyerhaeuser
47. Middle West Corporation	Delta Air Lines
48. Monsanto Chemical	Phillips Petroleum
49. Commonwealth & Southern pfd.	Columbia Broadcasting
50. Phelps Dodge	Aluminum Company of America

Even the hallowed Dow Jones industrials are anything but invincible protection in a bear market, nor are many of them all that good in a bull market.

The Dow averages, zinged into the public conscience as a blue chip barometer, are nothing of the sort. The big thirty are not necessarily true blue chips in a good or bad market. The Dow averages closed in 1965 at 969.26, in 1966 at 785.59, in 1967 at 905.11, in 1968 at 943.75 and in 1969 at 800.36. Anyone naive enough to hold a portfolio of the Dow stocks through that five-year period—and millions did—saw his blue chips drop in overall value by 168.90, hardly a blue chip investment in any sense of the word.

Stock by stock the princely Dow thirty performed dismally, for the most part, in 1969:

Stock	Closing Market Price 1968	1969	Net Change
Allied Chemical	36	24⅜	−11⅝
Aluminum Company of America	73	71¼	−1¾
American Brands	37¾	35¾	−2

Stock	Closing Market Price 1968	1969	Net Change
American Can	57¼	40⅞	−16⅜
AT&T	53	48⅝	−4⅜
Anaconda	64½	30⅛	−34⅜
Bethlehem Steel	31⅝	27⅛	−4½
Chrysler	56	34⅜	−21⅝
DuPont	165	105	−60
Eastman Kodak	73¼	82⅜	+9⅛
General Electric	93⅞	77½	−16⅜
General Foods	81½	83⅛	+1⅝
General Motors	79⅛	69⅛	−10
Goodyear	56	30¾	−25¼
International Harvester	37¼	24¾	−12½
International Nickel	39	43½	+4½
International Paper	37⅝	37⅛	−½
Johns-Manville	87¼	30	−57¼
Owens-Illinois	71½	62	−9½
Procter & Gamble	86½	109½	+23
Sears, Roebuck	62¼	68	+5¾
Standard Oil of California	72⅛	51⅛	−21
Standard Oil of New Jersey	78⅝	61¾	−16⅞
Swift	29¾	31¼	+1½
Texaco	83¼	30⅝	−52⅝
Union Carbide	45¼	37	−8¼
United Aircraft	65⅞	39¼	−26⅝
U.S. Steel	42⅞	33¾	−9⅛
Westinghouse Electric	68¼	58⅛	−10⅛
Woolworth	32⅞	37¾	+4⅞

Only seven of the thirty finished on the upside. Most of the others were bombs.

Buying the Dow Jones stocks for safety is like doing business with a brokerage firm because it says it's a member of the New York Stock Exchange. It's unjustified blind faith, sheer ignorance.

Capital gains appreciation is what the market is all about. Making a profit, as large a profit as possible, is the only reason anyone should risk a dollar in any stock.

Anyone who expects to become a millionaire in the market or add sizably to his wealth isn't going to accomplish that goal by buying AT&T and the other bruited bulwarks on the NYSE.

There are many investors who have become millionaires or extremely wealthy in the market without ever owning a single share of the supposed big-shouldered blue chips on the Dow list.

Among the blue chips, blue chips because they were winners even in the tough 1969 market, were the following twenty stocks, not one of them in the Dow club.

Stock	Closing Market Price 1968	1969	Net Change
Allied Maintenance	24½a	36	+11½
American Air Filter Co.	37	54⅞	+17⅞
American Research & Development	44⅛a	83¼	+39⅛
AMP Inc.	34¼	56½	+22¼
Avery Products	26½a	40¼	+13¾
Baxter Laboratories	19⅞a	29⅝	+9¾
Computer Sciences Corp.	21¾a	33⅞	+12⅛
Copper Range Co.	46½a	67⅝	+21⅛
Disney Productions	83⅜a	134	+50⅝
Eckerd Corp.	22⅛a	34½	+12⅜
Japan Fund	21⅜	45⅛	+23¾
Johnson & Johnson	106½	180	+73½
Kendall Co.	31⅞a	46	+14⅛
McIntyre Porcupine Mines	88	144	+56
Memorex Corp.	82¼	148¼	+66
Natomas Co.	35¼	63⅜	+28⅛
Northwestern Steel & Wire	50⅝	74¼	+23⅝
Ryder System, Inc.	32a	46¼	+14¼
Schlitz Brewing Co.	51¾	75	+23¼
Unishops, Inc.	27⅝a	43⅛	+15½

a = adjusted for stock dividends, splits, etc.

Investors should avoid being impressed by the term *blue chip* as it is commonly used by brokers. In any given year, a blue chip is a blue chip only if it shows a net gain, that and that only. As with any other stock, the issues on the Dow prove out as good or bad investments depending on performance.

An October 28, 1969, research department report by one major house titled UNDERVALUED BLUE CHIPS declared, "We think that many blue chip stocks offer outstanding value in today's market." Advantages cited were "a unique combination of capital appreciation potential and limited downside risk."

Ten alleged blue chips were recommended. Assuming a buyer purchased this package at the time of recommendation, this was his position six months later (before the worst of the bear market):

Stock	Price October 28, 1969	Price April 30, 1970	Net Change
American Can	48¼	40½	−7¾
American Electric Power	32¼	28⅛	−4⅛
AT&T	52	47⅞	−4⅛
Bethlehem Steel	29¾	26⅜	−3⅜
General Electric	84	72¼	−11¾
International Paper	33½	34	+½
Monsanto	41½	35	−6½
National Lead	30¾	22⅞	−7⅞
Reynolds Metals	36¾	31	−5¾
Standard Oil of New Jersey	67	53⅝	−13⅜

If the investor had to sell his "undervalued blue chips" in six months, he took a beating in nine of the ten issues, scoring a gain of only half a point in one stock, International Paper. And even this miniscule increase would have translated into a loss after he paid commissions.

Unfortunately, the investor has been educated to believe that the companies listed on the Dow Jones along with other giant firms, are the safest investments.

I recall urging one client to sell GE and buy House of Fabrics. For him to sell GE was like desecrating the flag. But when I finally convinced him to make the switch in holdings, he watched GE drift down and House of Fabrics zoom up. The man who is seriously interested in making money in the market follows the advice of a broker who knows his situations.

Some bank trust officers deal primarily or solely in Dow Jones stocks. They sock the money into the "best" blue chips, and when the blue chips fail to react as blue chips are supposed to, they have a cop-out. The investor is told he was put into stocks of the highest caliber, no risks were taken, quality was bought, there wasn't any speculation.

But part of the blue chip myth is that one stock can be labeled conservative, another speculative. The reality is that every stock involves some speculation, and to claim otherwise to a client is criminally misleading.

It would be ridiculous for me not to point out that traditional blue chips can be good investments. But everything depends on timing, and I am not adverse to buying such stocks at a propitious moment. There are some excellent companies among America's 500 leading firms that can be bought at various times. Although I do not do much buying in such stocks, I will purchase them for my clients' accounts when I believe they will truly perform as blue chips should, i.e., rise in price. In 1964 and 1965 I was interested in the oils, particularly Standard Oil of New Jersey, Standard Oil of California, Standard Oil of Indiana and Phillips Petroleum. At the time I felt that earnings of these companies would be up and that they were extremely good investments for widows and orphans, in and out traders and those going for capital gains. I earned money for clients in those issues as I did in 1965–1966 in Johns-Manville and American Cement.

There *is* money to be made in the corporate giants—*if*.

It all comes down, finally, to analysis of a particular company, knowing the situation, knowing what the earnings are going to be, knowing what the conditions are that affect each stock.

But to think of making a killing in old-fashioned blue chips goes beyond fantasizing and wishful thinking. It goes beyond foolishness. To dream of becoming wealthy in anything but carefully considered specific situations is mental masturbation.

That the best of all possible worlds for the investor is the world of old-line blue chips stands up under no criterion.

Another myth about these blue chips is that at least the dividend is safe through good times and bad. This is generally true among large companies, but it is not always true. In 1968, before the 1969–1970 bear market, 107 important companies decreased their dividends and 130 omitted dividends entirely. In

1969 some 101 major firms lowered payouts and 124 omitted them altogether.

Buying a stock for the dividend as against buying a stock for appreciation means the investor is going to be badly outperformed.

An investor who sits nursing his dividends is losing money, because no matter what the dividend is, it comes nowhere near matching the rise in the cost of living. He is fighting a losing battle against inflation, which by 1970 was eroding the dollar at the rate of 6–7 percent a year, with no sign the trend would be meaningfully lessened.

From 1964–1969, food, clothing and shelter and all the other essentials that go into the tally of the U.S. Labor Department's cost-of-living index went up 21 percent. The cost of services of all types had risen 28 percent in the five-year period.

Item	Percentage Rise Between 1964 and 1969
Electric bill	4.6
Gas bill	5.3
Shoes	6.2
Bank service charge	9.1
Airplane fare (coach)	11.6
Household rent	11.8
Bowling fee	14.6
Funeral services	17.1
Eye examination and glasses	20.9
Parking fees	21.9
Dry-cleaning bill	21.9
Woman's haircut	23.4
Auto repairs	23.5
X-ray fee	23.6
Taxi fare	25.1
Piano lessons	25.2
Bus fare (intercity)	25.5
Tailor's bill	27.6
Property taxes	29.7
Meal at a restaurant	29.7
Dentist's fee, filling tooth	30.4
Local transit fare	32.7
Man's haircut	32.9

Item	Percentage Rise Between 1964 and 1969
Lawyer's fee, drawing will	33.4
Babysitter's fee	36.5
Physician's fee, office visit	37.8
Auto insurance	38.1
Mortgage interest	39.2
Replacing a sink	40.2
Reshingling a roof	40.3
Laundry bill	42.3
Repairing a furnace	44.3
Pay of household worker	44.7
Repainting a room	50.4
Hospital operating room	67.4
Hospital room, semiprivate	86.0

In April, 1970, one advisory service published a list of "Ten Stocks Everyone Should Own." The reasons everyone should own these stocks, said the advisory service, were because of attractive long-term appreciation possibilities, dividends and percentage yields. Those who bought these stocks were not only touted into shaky, purported blue chips, but the percentage yield on their money in eight out of the ten stocks was virtually nonexistent. At the time of the April, 1970, recommendation, the percentages and promise for the investor were dreadful.

Company	Price	Annual Dividend	Percentage Yield
American Electric Power	29	$1.64	5.7
American Home Products	60	$1.50	2.5
Coca-Cola	76	$1.44	1.9
DuPont	112	$5.25	4.7
Eastman Kodak	72	$1.28	1.8
First National City Bank	67	$2.40	3.6
General Foods	78	$2.60	3.3
Georgia Pacific	50	$0.80	1.6
IBM	310	$4.80	1.5
Minnesota Mining & Mfg.	95	$1.75	1.8

Buying stocks strictly for dividends is absurd. Dividend-minded investors would do better to place their money in a routine commercial bank passbook paying interest of 4½ percent.

Through 1969–1970, a commercial bank certificate of $100,-000 and up held for one year paid 7½ percent. Ninety-one–day U.S. Treasury bills, with a minimum $10,000 investment, were earning 7.2 percent. Three-year Treasury notes were yielding 7.08 percent, and some high-grade utility bonds were paying up to 8.55 percent.

If $2,500 is placed in a savings and loan association account each year for a period of twenty-five years at 5 percent with interest compounded quarterly, untouched and reinvested, there will be $126,957.27 in the account at the end of the twenty-five year period.

This money is also subject to erosion through inflation, but the "I'm-interested-in-dividends-only" investor would be better served by putting his funds almost anywhere other than in the market. Why should he risk a loss of his capital?

Actually, anyone not in the market for appreciation is committing slow financial suicide. A dividend is only attractive as a bagatelle bonus in a stock that is appreciating in price.

Those seventy-one leading college endowment funds playing with a total of $7.6 billion have stashed 60.3 percent of their money in stocks. The order of popularity is IBM, Eastman Kodak, Xerox, Standard Oil of New Jersey, General Motors, Gulf Oil, Texaco, Coca-Cola, AT&T and Ford. The funds are anything but quick traders, and dividend yield is extremely important to them.

But the highest profit of any endowment as of the end of 1970 was less than 6 percent, putting aside the punishment in the prices of their stocks. The lowest yield was barely above 2 percent. Neither in dividends nor appreciation have these endowments prospered. If the trustees were having nightmares, it was perfectly understandable.

The Kennecott Copper Company in 1969 paid for a survey of 3,000 of its shareholders to find out what they thought of the firm and what the shareholders' general objectives were.

The composite shareholder was found to be over fifty-five years old, he had attended college, held a responsible managerial or professional position and had an annual income of more than $20,000.

And:
He was more interested in dividends than capital gains.
In 1954 Kennecott traded in the 22–32 range. The dividend
was $2 a year.
In 1959 Kennecott's low was 30 ½, its high was 40. The dividend five years later was still $2.
In 1969 Kennecott had a low of 37, a high of 55 ½. Its dividend was up to $2.60, a percentage yield of 5.1, a yield that
was running behind rampaging inflation.
Alex N. Campbell, business columnist of the Los Angeles
Herald-Examiner, sagely commented, "Historically then, stockholders have really done better in Kennecott because of the increased price of the stock than because of any increase in dividends. So, it is strange that shareholders would consider this
stock a dividend stock as opposed to a capital-gains stock."
So pitifully passionate do people become about dividends—
completely ignoring appreciation—that many actually buy
stocks so that a dividend check arrives each month. I quiver at
the number of portfolios put together on no other grounds than
a monthly dividend check.
To those interested only in opening an envelope each month
with a dividend check, one broker in a mid-1969 newspaper
column gave this list of companies:
"January, April, July and October dividend payers include
Baltimore Gas & Electric, CPC International, AT&T, Union
Pacific, Mountain States Telephone and Southern California
Edison.
"Among the February, May, August and November payers
are American Can, Boston Edison, Cincinnati Gas & Electric,
New York State Electric & Gas and Columbia Gas.
"Those who pay in March, June, September and December
are Borden, R. J. Reynolds, Shell Oil, Union Carbide, Chesa-
peake & Ohio, Niagara Mohawk Power, Public Service Electric
& Gas, International Nickel and New England Telephone."
Every one of these stocks took a drubbing or a severe beating in price from the close of business in 1968 to the close of
business in 1969. And their yearly dividends were anything but
outstanding. The best of them barely kept pace with inflation.

Stock	Closing Price 1968	Closing Price 1969	Net Change	Dividend	Yield
Baltimore Gas & Electric	34½	31¼	−3¼	$1.82	6.0%
CPC International	42⅜	31½	−10⅞	$1.70	5.0%
AT&T	53	48⅝	−4⅜	$2.60	4.9%
Union Pacific	52½	39½	−13	$2.00	5.3%
Mountain States Telephone	23⅛	21⅝	−1½	$1.36	6.1%
Southern California Edison	36⅛	30⅛	−6	$1.50	4.6%
American Can	57¼	48⅝	−8⅝	$2.20	5.5%
Boston Edison	46½	33¾	−12¾	$2.08	6.2%
Cincinnati Gas & Electric	31	24	−7	$1.40	5.9%
New York State Electric & Gas	41	29⅞	−11⅛	$2.08	6.7%
Columbia Gas	30¼	26	−4¼	$1.60	5.6%
Borden	34⅜	23	−11⅜	$1.20	4.8%
R. J. Reynolds	46⅜	45½	−⅞	$2.25	6.1%
Shell Oil	70⅝	44¼	−26⅜	$2.40	5.8%
Union Carbide	45¼	37	−8¼	$2.00	5.4%
Chesapeake & Ohio	73	51½	−21½	$4.00	7.3%
Niagara Mohawk Power	22⅜	16⅛	−6¼	$1.10	6.6%
Public Service Electric & Gas	35⅛	26⅝	−8½	$1.64	6.2%
International Nickel	39	43½	+4½	$1.20	2.6%
New England Telephone	42	32⅛	−9⅞	$1.77	6.8%

Brokers (and there are many such) who arrange portfolios
solely on the basis of a monthly dividend check could be replaced by adding machines. They are accountants, not brokers.
The best service they could do for their clients is to advise them
to forget about the market. People who cleave to dividends for
income are generally on fixed incomes. There is always the
danger that the dividends of many of these companies, none of
them a bargain to begin with, might be reduced as well as increased. Too, they might be omitted. And then where is the re-
tiree who has based his investment "philosophy" on monthly
stock dividends to supplement his pension and Social Security

checks? Even if he takes such a portfolio to his grave, his paper loss in capital and his inflation-flecked dividend dollar month by month has only dwindled his standard of living. Month by month he becomes poorer and must continually adjust to his constantly decreasing living standard.

Another misconception foisted on investors is that bigness alone somehow guarantees profit and safety.

Based on sales, that greatest of hollow victories, America's 500 leading companies in 1969, according to *Fortune* magazine, had only a combined net profit increase of 2 percent on total net income of $24.7 billion. There were 152 companies that reported declines in profits, and the eleven biggest losers lost an incredible amount of money, which was reflected in their market price and dividends.

Stock	Loss	Closing Price 1968	Closing Price 1969	Net Change	Dividend
Ling-Temco-Vought	$38,294,000	95	25⅜	−69⅝	$1.33⅓
Lockheed Aircraft	$32,642,000	47⅝	17¼	−30⅜	$1.70
International Minerals & Chemicals	$20,604,000	22⅞	11¾	−11⅛	$0.25
Libby, McNeill & Libby	$15,124,000	16¾	7⅝	−9⅛	none
Bangor Punta	$8,567,000	44⅝	15	−29⅝	$0.60
Hygrade Food Products*	$6,422,000	64¾	30¼	−34½	$0.25
American Bakeries	$3,177,000	27¼	13½	−13¾	$0.75
Warwick Electronics*	$2,847,000	18¾	14	−4¾	none
Sanders Associates	$1,951,000	59	27	−32	$0.30
Cowles Communications*	$1,883,000	17	10⅛	−6⅞	$0.35
Ward Foods	$1,797,000	51⅞	27¼	−24⅝	Stock

* Also lost money in 1968

About the only way anyone has come out ahead on dividends is if he was fortunate enough to own Washington Gas & Light that was purchased in 1852, AT&T bought in 1881, Baltimore Gas & Electric acquired in 1910, Dow Chemical in 1911, Bank of America in 1933. These five companies are among those that have never reduced their dividends. They are what

brokers and bank trust officers call the "perfect list," paying
never-fail dividends. But even at 1852, 1881, 1910, 1911 and
1933 prices, the punch and clout in those stocks has been in the
appreciation, not the dividends.

In summation:

1. The size of a company is no guarantee of quality or safety.

2. Stay out of the market if you're interested only in dividends.

3. Invest in the market only for appreciation.

4. A blue chip has always been, is now, and always will be
a stock that goes up.

NINE

OF LOVE AND HATE, FEAR AND FANTASY, RUMOR AND REASON

The taste for emotion may become a dangerous taste; we should be very cautious how we attempt to squeeze out of human life more ecstasy and paroxysm than it can well afford.

SYDNEY SMITH

"Fluctuating mass psychology always is difficult to interpret; and theories about it are subject to a high margin of error," opined a market letter from W. E. Hutton & Company.

Amen.

Psychological insight and interpretation of human behavior vis-à-vis the market is not my long suit. Yet I would have to be blind, deaf and dumb not to wonder at the bewildering variety of emotional hangups that afflict brokers, the individual investor and the investor en masse.

The greedy broker, consciously or unconsciously, will take advantage of the greedy investor. But at least the investor's greed is marbled by ignorance and/or trust in the broker's pitch that buying into a particular stock will make money for him, a completely normal and laudable goal.

Two unfortunate examples from situations very close to me illustrate how commission-hungry brokers have sliced their way through the bank accounts of investors who allowed emotion to overcome their reason.

Continental Transportation, before its resurrection, discussed briefly in the previous chapter, was in its early years little more than a glorified machine shop. Yet the stock had been run up to 12 by brokers who had absolutely no evidence on which to base their heady projections to clients. At that time Continental had no projected earnings. Management left much to be desired. The company was involved in costly, long-running litigation. One private placement had raised enough money to keep it going, but these funds were quickly dissipated and Continental

103

was in danger of going under completely. The firm was moribund. It had been nowhere, and was going nowhere. The people who invested in Continental didn't have the foggiest notion of what they were buying. Their investment decisions in this situation were irrational.

And greed and irrationality inevitably lead to disaster.

After touching its high of 12, the stock eventually sank on the over-the-counter market to a bid of 1¾ and an asking price of 2.

In this case the investors who bought Continental at its high will undoubtedly profit eventually, although they will have lost a good deal of time in which their money was doing nothing for them. And they will come out of it as winners only by chance.

Once I decided to guide the fortunes of Continental, I managed a second private placement at 1½, which brought more critically needed financing. Those who came in on this placement will be the greatest beneficiaries of Continental's bright future. Those who bought a piece of the second private placement in the problem-plagued company did so only because I was involved with the firm's refinancing, change of direction, finding and approving new management and directing the decision-making conferences that changed the entire philosophy of the company from reliance on Federal contracts to a nongovernment-focused business. It is not immodesty, but factual to state that if I had not become interested in Continental, the company would long since have disappeared from the corporate map. In the interim period before the second private placement was completed, I personally kept the company alive by meeting its Friday payroll out of my own funds.

Those who bought at 10, 11 and 12 were sandbagged by brokers playing on their emotions, strumming the sensitive chords of their psyches. Only lazy, irresponsible brokers would push a stock without earnings, a company mired in mismanagement, a company gasping its last breath. Continental at that time had been a rank promotion. All any broker or investor had to do to realize this was to make one trip to the company's plant and observe the lackadaisical operation and management.

And how could any but emotionally distressed investors buy such a stock when there were so many other issues available with so much more potential? These clients acted with illogical hope and a covetousness that clouded their judgment.

An even more frightening example was a dormant firm called Imperial Packing Company, which was a corporate shell that owned nothing, had nothing, participated in no business whatsoever. It didn't even have an office.

Yet a gaggle of gluttonous houses had made a market in the stock, sending the trading range up to 8½–9 in 1969. The company's 1 million shares were capitalized in the market between 8 and 9 at a moment when the firm wasn't worth a dime.

I personally owned 325,000 shares, acquired at 35¢, which gave me control. I bought control because I considered the company a potentially useful corporate shell.

But it was up to me to act. I might inject new life into Imperial, or on the other hand I might never lift a finger in its behalf. As it happens, I began to work hard at resuscitating Imperial. The name was changed to Alison International, Inc., and my plan is to turn it into a muscle and blood company.

But the brokers who sold the stock at 9 and the investors who bought it in such an overblown range were buying fantasy. At that price the buyer was in a dangerous, suicidal speculation. More than 1,000 shareholders of Imperial were led into a wild trip to tomorrow-land, a tomorrow-land that might never have come.

A great many investors do not profit in the market because they so frequently take leave of their senses, permitting emotion to substitute for rationality.

Left to their own devices, those investors who have contempt for all brokers will end up going on their own imperfect research, tips, dreams, whims, hunches, ESP, tea leaves, crystal balls and "advice" from fortune tellers and horoscope magazines. And there are still actually those who buy or sell on the old notion that the market will rise or fall in conjunction with the rise or fall of skirt hemlines.

Such investors are much worse than horse players. At least most who play the ponies chart a course.

Few investors know or care to learn how to seek out a broker who has their genuine interest at heart. They often come in with their minds made up, having arrived at their investment decisions by one, several or a combination of the aforementioned processes.

A large proportion of investors don't even bother to consult the *Wall Street Journal, Barron's, Standard & Poor's,* the business section of their local newspaper or other financial sources through which they could gain at least a modicum of fundamental knowledge. Of course, consulting such sources with their cascade of invariably contradictory information is no guarantee that the investor will prosper. But it's better than tea leaves or crystal balls.

As long as there is a stock market, people will continue to react to it emotionally instead of hedging their bets with reasoned judgment.

Consider the businessman, a genius at his own thing, who will haggle all day over $\frac{1}{10}$ of a cent before he signs a purchase order. Yet how tragically often I have seen this same stripe of businessman commit $25,000 and more, going on nothing else but a hunch or a "you ought to buy this" siren song from a broker he hasn't even met. That broker, for all the investor knows, could be calling from a men's room or a bucket shop.

I'm acquainted with a tycoon who owns an investment business. He's tough as a three-day beard and rules his considerable empire like Napoleon. He fights for every dollar and scratches for every penny of profit. But on one occasion a broker called him and said, "This stock is running and it's going to go twenty points." He went into a paroxysm of joy and flash-bought a thousand shares, "investing" some $40,000 on the say-so of a broker he knew only vaguely. The result: a hefty sum committed in a stock about which he was totally ignorant. The investment proved a wipe-out.

Although the name of the game is always profit, there are those who are not interested in coming out a winner. They are the compulsive market gamblers, motivated in part by a need to lose because they feel in their own mind that they don't deserve to win. These types are common in brokerage board rooms. The worst thing such a person can do is give in to his weakness. If he can't control his compulsion, he's better off visiting a psychiatrist or giving his money to charity instead of playing the market like a crap table. Investors in this classification always lose, and it is simple to predict that they will lose because they literally "play" the market like a game of dice or roulette. It is impossible to reach them with advice or sound investment principles. They aren't interested.

Most of my clients do exactly as I suggest. They buy when I advise them to buy, they sell when I think the time is right to unload. But there are those who cry and breastbeat in a bad market and forget about all the big money they have previously made and the ground-floor deals they were put into so profitably. They wriggle as impatiently as a five-year-old in kindergarten, unwilling to stay the course until the market turns or while a company is gestating. The majority of my clients never utter a word in a bad market because they know I have placed them in the best possible position and that I don't make prices go up or down by myself. They are smart enough to realize that they simply must ride out a bad market and that they are in sound situations that will show a profit in time.

But among my clients was one who would continually sell, and always at the wrong time. He wouldn't listen when I pointed out to him that I knew his stocks intimately and that it wasn't time to sell. But sell he did, inevitably at the bottom. Then he would watch with wretched resignation as the stock went up.

The man was a pathological trader. He couldn't stand to be in a stock for more than a few days. If he didn't get rich overnight (and very, very seldom does any investor in any situation acquire overnight riches) he would unload, invariably with large losses. But almost everything eventually increased sizably in price.

He never learned his lesson, he never changed. The commissions were fine for me as the selling broker. Yet, I repeatedly told him, there was no point in what he was doing. Many of the stocks he was in were unquestionably going to rise because earnings would be so powerful nothing could keep them from appreciating. But that didn't mean they were going to leap ahead in twenty-four or forty-eight hours. I lectured him that his quick trading was no way to make money in the market.

Time after time he sold, only to see each stock rise fifteen to twenty points. But there was one instance in which he sold and came out with a slight gain. He then was gleeful when the stock went down and stayed down for a long period. That lucky sell-off is the exception he pointed to with pride, forgetting the dozens of precipitous, knee-jerk moves he had made that were wrong, the dozens of issues he sold that would have brought him a fortune if he'd had patience.

My father is also afflicted with impatience. His emotional makeup is such that he too has frequently failed to go the last mile. When I have counseled patience, he's reacted with haste —and he's suffered financially for his inability to wait.

A look at his moves in two stocks is illuminating. In the latter part of 1965 he bought 950 shares of House of Fabrics at 3¾. He was on the inside of what I knew was a tremendous situation. But he wouldn't wait. On February 2, 1966, he sold 300 shares at 5, on April 1 he unloaded 500 at 4⅜, November 18 he cashed in 100 at 3¼, and his last 50 shares went at 3⅛ on November 28. He came out of it all with a loss of $702.63 in a stock I repeatedly assured him would be a huge winner (which is what happened when House of Fabrics reached a high of 36 in 1969 after two splits). During the time my father was selling there was a credit squeeze and House of Fabrics was doing what most stocks were doing, drifting up or down a few points or not fluctuating at all. But that didn't change the promise of the company one whit. The market price of a stock does not necessarily reflect what is happening inside the company. When you are going for a big percentage gain, a year, two years, is a very short time to wait. After he sold House of Fabrics, my father never bought it back despite my urgings. He thus missed the oceanic move.

He also missed the surge in Monogram. He bought 300 shares at 39½ on January 19, 1967. Only eleven days later he sold at 44½, netting $1,320.09, a peanut profit in a stock that rose to 240. It was again a situation I knew to the core, one I knew was due for a big ride.

As a result of all his transactions in House of Fabrics and Monogram, my father made only $617.46, a lesson in how costly impatience can be.

I had another client, extremely well-to-do, with a slightly different psychological bent. I continually recommended to him that he invest only in first-class situations. He seldom heeded me, insisting on buying stuff that I told him, in my opinion (to put it as politely as possible), was of extremely dubious merit. He passed up situations I thought sure he would buy, stocks perfect for his account. Instead he substituted issues that had no intrinsic value. He never confided to me on what basis he made his decisions. In 1963 I felt that all the airline stocks were going to cruise into the stratosphere. I especially liked Delta at that particular time because its price was lagging behind its competitors in the industry. My research showed it was going to have impressive earnings and growth, and that the market would sooner or later recognize its rosy future. I wasn't the only broker then recommending Delta. Any broker worth his telephone knew it was a comer. I made a big presentation about Delta to this client. He absolutely refused to buy a single share, thereby missing a situation that went from 18 to the middle 60s. Sometimes, however, he went along with my selections. I put him into International Rectifier, another situation I had personally taken a long look at. At the time, the stock was the smallest company on the American Exchange. But the client went in at 12 and sold in the 30s.

The baffling thing to me about this man was that I never knew which way he was going to jump, or why he jumped the way he did.

If a client can find a knowledgeable, first-class broker, he simply should come in with X amount of dollars and let the broker make all his buy and sell decisions. The client would do much better placing himself in the hands of such a broker rather than making his own decisions. I prefer clients with this point of view.

I have enough confidence in my decisions to take on the responsibilities of investing the funds of any client, whether the account is large or small. This confidence stems not from arrogance but because I've trained myself to be hardheaded and nonemotional about the market, and that's one of the prime reasons I've been able to perform successfully.

Once emotion takes over investment judgment, there is no investment judgment. If every broker and investor could be totally objective, there would be fantastic changes in the market. Gone would be the wild speculations, the stocks artificially inflated with silicone instead of hard tissue. Gone would be the high-flyers zooming up and down, situations which occasionally have made a man rich but more often left most investors holding a lot of costly, depressed paper.

But the day of total broker and client objectivity will not be with us soon, if ever. And so the uncertain yardstick of emotional judgment continues apace, handicapping investors who, even bereft of emotion, would have to cope with the already unpredictable uncertainties of the market.

The range of investor eccentricity never ceases to amaze me.

I have a number of wealthy clients who can well afford to be locked into private placements that have enormous profit potential. But they won't touch unregistered shares because they are psychologically incapable of adjusting to a situation in which even a relatively small portion of their capital is temporarily nonliquid.

One client worth between $2 and $3 million wouldn't put $10,000 into a private placement that proved extremely lucrative. Yet he owned a $20,000 automobile that began depreciating the moment he signed the sales slip.

The author of a recent best-selling book on the market spent a great deal of time poking fun at investors with emotional hangups. But there's nothing amusing about such people. Their emotional weaknesses have deprived them of earning a great deal of money and driven them into losing money needlessly.

Ponder those shareholders who in defiance of all logic refuse absolutely to take a profit. They offer all kinds of excuses for not selling a winning stock, but the truth appears to be they are afraid that if they sell, the price will increase the moment they get out. Many of these clients often show more than 1,000 percent paper profit. But if the stock should go another 200–300 percent or even another 5–10 percent and they are not with it, they'll be shattered.

Canny Bernard Baruch counted himself lucky if he sold 10 percent below the peak price of a stock, and counted himself equally fortunate if he managed to buy an issue 10 percent above the bottom. That investment philosphy was one of the reasons Baruch became a multimillionaire.

Any investor who waits for the last oink from the pig on a stock in which he has a profit is playing roulette. More often than not, the investor holding out for the last oink goes to the slaughterhouse.

Such unreasoning greed often results in the disappearance of profit. Market conditions may change overnight. The stock for any number of reasons can quickly tumble, and the client finds himself in a loss position when he could so easily have shown a gorgeous profit.

Some clients tell me they can't afford to take their profits because of taxes. This is possibly the most neurotic reason for not selling stocks in which clients are on the upside. They are going to have to sell someday and pay the capital gains bite. I point out to such clients, with varying degrees of success, that when a stock has become overpriced it should be sold, no matter what their tax problems are. Since they will have to pay the tax anyway, what difference does it make when they pay? It is far better to pay taxes on a profit—even when a client has an unusually high income year—than wind up taking a loss on a stock that moves down because its moment has passed.

I have one client who doesn't want to be on account basis. This is a man with $500,000 constantly floating through the market, a man who also trades dozens of times a year. He comes to the office with a check and insists on paying in full immediately after each buy; he visits the office after each sell, insisting on immediate payment in full via check. He won't use the mails or a messenger. Every transaction means two personal visits to the office. I haven't a clue as to why he so conducts his affairs.

But since the offbeat procedure makes him happy, I oblige.

In a good market, or when a downswing is being bucked and investors are earning money when most of their friends are taking a beating, the client-broker relationship is Romeo and Juliet. Love, the most desirable and strongest of all emotions, manifests itself, sometimes in cloying abundance. But I always remember that Romeo and Juliet ended tragically. When the market turns bad or a loss is sustained, broker-client involvement ends, if not in pure tragedy, then with barely concealed fury or verbal hatred very freely expressed.

At times when clients are making money hand over fist there are some who, if I let them, would entertain me lavishly every night of the week. In a bear market like 1969–1970 when I had few if any recommendations and I didn't want clients to buy anything and I hadn't made money for them, my phone stopped ringing. I didn't get invited to a cafeteria for a cup of coffee.

Hate and love also get wrapped up in the market in another unfathomable way. I have seen people sell excellent stocks because they've developed a hatred for a company, a hatred that's totally irrational. They suddenly decide they don't want to own a particular stock. They don't want it because the stock is a living thing to them. They wouldn't keep it even if I could guarantee that it was going to rise fifty points in a week. "Get me out of that stock—get me out now. I don't care how good it is. I don't care what you say. I don't want that stock. I don't want to own it under any circumstances."

At the other extreme, I've had clients tell me they will never sell a particular stock, no matter what. The stock may be the major holding in their portfolios or it may be a lesser piece. "I'll buy and sell anything else, but I'll never sell that stock. I love that stock."

Such haters and lovers are dead serious. The hater will scuttle a particular issue even though it could make him rich. The lover will not unburden himself of a particular issue even though it could make him poor. A broker, understanding how neurotic people can be about their money, soon learns to adjust to the alternating love and hate syndromes exhibited by his clients.

Come bull or bear market, there are those clients who absolutely need action, and against my protests and advice they'll commit large sums in cats and dogs. When I won't put them into such stocks, they'll go around the corner to another broker who will gladly accommodate them.

These clients can't stand to have idle funds in their accounts. They have to put the money somewhere. Instead of conserving cash, they'll plunge into the wildest, most unbelievable speculations. They might as well put a match to their money. They ignore my counsel that it's critically important to stay liquid against the day of a new, exciting and promising opportunity. When the day of the new opportunity inevitably arrives, I call and discover their money has been plowed into garbage and they are shorn of ready cash that could bring them more ready cash.

The usual explanations:

"I don't know why I did it."

"I just couldn't resist."

"I thought I'd take a flyer."

One client—a card-carrying, charter member of the I Want Action Now Club—actually told me, "I don't care if the climate of the market is good or bad. I don't care if the stock goes up or down! Get me into something."

Many of these clients are sometimes playing with the better part of $1 million. It's fine for the broker commission-wise, but predictably disastrous for clients who toy so inexplicably with their money. Such plungers apparently must have the feeling of being big traders, in contradiction of all reason. Perhaps they enjoy bragging to friends at lunch that they went against my advice. If so, it's expensive table talk. These types also fit into the category of those who have the self-punishing need to lose.

Many investors lose money in the market because they are their own worst enemies. They not only buy on cockeyed reasoning, but if a client finds a broker who's made money for him, his ego often comes into play. He soon begins making his own decisions, second-guessing the broker. An intelligent man wouldn't second-guess his doctor's diagnosis or his attorney's assessment of an action at law. But even the best of brokers in the minds of these clients enjoy no status and respect as professionals.

I've had clients sneak to other brokers and trade in stuff they didn't want me to know about. Picking a stock on their own gives them a sense of self-satisfaction. It's balm to their egos. Some of the clients that I've made huge sums for have sneaked a buy or several buys with other brokers. They're like closet drinkers or secret smokers, fooling no one but themselves. When these stocks turn sour, they come to me with sad stories, admit their unreasoning purchases sheepishly, apologetically and with a long sigh.

Such clients forget that they were smart enough to make money in their own businesses or professions, and they came to me as an expert in my field to make their money appreciate by capitalizing on my knowledge. But they don't see it that way at all. They are tortured by the realization that they had to come to another man to make money for them. Some couldn't make any money in the market until they started dealing with me. Deep in their hearts they believe they're at least as smart if not smarter than I am, and they're going to prove it to me. And off they go to throw a random dart into some random stock. Thus they lose money they needn't have lost.

The most intriguing solution I've heard to deal with the emotion-riddled market is the brainchild of Dr. R. Bruce Ricks, professor of investments at UCLA and a former E. F. Hutton broker and analyst.

The doctor joins me in deploring some of the reasons clients buy a particular issue, including a desire to outwit the broker, perhaps to gain the broker's approval, or for other emotional reasons.

"If I were to predict the major shift in brokerage firms during the next ten years, maybe five, it's that they'll staff themselves with resident psychologists to advise the customer's men," Dr. Ricks says. He stresses brokers wouldn't be taught to "psych people out" but instead to discover what really turns the investor on.

Until that utopian day, one of the most important realizations that investors should be constantly aware of is that every time they sell, somebody is buying their stock. Every time they buy, someone is selling. Surprisingly few comprehend that on any given day, at any given moment, each buyer and seller has a different opinion, a different emotional fix on each stock.

It's incredible how many people do not understand this basic fact about the market, incredible how many clients believe that buy and sell transactions are consummated automatically by a machine. They have no conception that the stock exchanges are only auction markets, clearing houses where men of polarized opinions buy and sell; no idea that the gigantic New York Stock Exchange merely provides floor space where buyers and sellers can be matched.

If clients absorbed this simple fact they often would not be in such a hurry to trade. It would take much of the emotion out of their buy and sell decisions. The seller in Los Angeles should take cognizance of the stark reality that a buyer in Butte, Montana, disagrees profoundly with his opinion. The buyer in Hartford, Connecticut, should realize he has an 180-degree turn of mind from the seller in Omaha, Nebraska.

Why am I selling this stock? Why am I buying this stock? Most investors never approach these questions logically. They will trade on rumor, supposition, Second Coming headlines.

Momentous national or world events routinely activate a massive sell-off or a buying spree. Grief and fear, hope and optimism are the operative psychological forces, although it should be cliché-clear to investors that passing events have nothing to do with the basic values of sound stocks.

President Eisenhower's heart attack and the assassination of John F. Kennedy induced a broad-based gloom psychology with resultant down markets. Such news, however tragic, had nothing to do with the fundamental strength of stocks inevitably slated for upside performance.

A man should pray for the recovery of a stricken President and a man should cry at the murder of a young President shot down in the prime of life by a psychotic. But it is psychosis of another sort when such events affect a man's investment judgment.

Any temporary piece of bad news that has an adverse effect on the market should be considered a buying opportunity. The smart money, cynical money if you prefer, always buys. The scared money always sells because of crisis headlines that in the long run are irrelevant to good situations. And there is always more scared money than smart-cynical money. In any event, the market soon resettles into whatever pattern it had been following prior to whatever has appeared on the front pages.

The death of North Vietnamese leader Ho Chi Minh was one of the principal reasons cited for the Dow Jones nosedive of 10.37 on September 9, 1969. Of 1,552 issues traded that day, 931 declined and 343 advanced. Even superficial thought would have reminded those who were so easily panicked that Ho's death was not unexpected. Reports of his illness had been appearing in the press for some time. Ho's demise, without a clear indication that his death would materially alter the course of the war, only proved what everyone knows—that every man is mortal. His passing certainly had no primary effect on the value or lack of value in any one stock, much less anything to do with why stocks basically increase or decrease in worth.

The market is the greatest rumor mill in the world. But rumor by definition is a story or statement without confirmation or certainty as to facts.

On December 18, 1969, Arthur F. Burns, then chairman-designate of the Federal Reserve Board, said he *hoped* that the Board would reconsider its tight money policy *when* it received more information on the pending tax-reform bill and the new budget of the Nixon Administration.

Nothing more than a hope and a when. Yet the Dow averages soared 13.86, although the value of a single share of a single stock was not inherently changed by Burns' less than precise semantics.

On December 24, 1969, Paul W. McCracken, chairman of President Nixon's Council of Economic Advisers, said no more than that current monetary restrictions could not be continued indefinitely without damaging the economy. Because of McCracken's pithy declaration, the Dow again rocked upwards—10.36 points. The market was not reacting to hard news.

McCracken had said nothing factual. But again millions of shares and millions of dollars changed hands solely on the basis of a gossamer statement, a few words that churned up a lot of sound and fury signifying nothing.

On February 4, 1970, Treasury Secretary David Kennedy brought the speciousness of semantics to pathfinding vagueness. "Once the inflationary psychology is broken and the business community and the public in general begin to look forward to greater stability, interest rates will drop to a more reasonable level and other salutary effects will be felt throughout the economy," Kennedy jawboned.

He gave no date, no timetable for lower rates or the easing of credit. The key word in Kennedy's statement was "once." But once could mean tomorrow, six months, two years or never. At the precise moment Kennedy was talking, trading on the NYSE was drifting along listlessly. The Dow at 743.07 was off more than three points for the day. When Kennedy's remarks reached the floor there was an immediate blast of buying. The averages jumped seventeen points in two hours before settling back to close at 757.46, up 11.02 for the day.

"Wall Street has been waiting for a remark such as Kennedy's," chortled one analyst.

But Kennedy's word-mongering again did nothing to change fundamentals. Reality settled in the next day and the Dow fell nearly three points.

A week later even more tenuous whispers triggered another temporary upswing. "The stock market grabbed at vague rumors of imminent interest rate cuts and took off with an explosive rally in late trading," the Associated Press reported. "Brokers said rumors circulated on Wall Street that a major bank would cut its prime interest rate and that the Federal Reserve Board might act to ease credit restraints."

The rally chalked up a 10.7 rise in the Dow. "It's very difficult to say whether the rumors spawned the rally or the rally spawned the rumors," observed Bache & Co. analyst Monte Gordon.

It turned out that the prime rate wasn't lowered or credit loosened.

Such wispy emanations from government officials can do immense damage to thousands of investors who rush in lemminglike with trading orders on the basis of vague statements like the above.

If I bought and sold for my clients on the basis of such amorphous noninformation, I should more fittingly be selling shoes. A pox on brokers maneuvering their clients into trades because of such filigree.

Burns, McCracken and Kennedy—acting, one must presume, with White House approval—ill-served the investor with their comments. Their words, and they knew it, had the power to artificially stimulate the market. It smacks of government manipulation of Wall Street by rumor, by raising false hope, with Pollyana prose instead of hard facts, which the market could realistically and intelligently react to and assess.

The only ones who benefited from all the frenetic trading induced by the careless verbiage of government spokesmen were the professional traders who owned a seat on the exchange or acted for a brokerage house that had one or more seats. These pros do not pay a commission on a trade. They can and do sometimes buy and sell a stock twenty times a day and come out with a profit on each transaction. The average man in the market not only has to pay a broker's commission, but he can't move fast enough, he isn't in a position to keep pace with the lightning trades on the floor. The traders made quick killings; the small investors, per usual, were shafted. Professional traders can come out beautifully on a stock that moves only a point, but ordinary investors need a full point rise just to break even.

When the fast shuffle was all over, the traders were long gone, profits snugly pocketed. The small investor had been had once more.

Consciously or otherwise, the professional traders are usually master psychologists. The cleverest of them can anticipate the emotional reaction of the general public to a particular piece of news. And the more emotion average investors exhibit, the more they will be hurt.

Another truism of the market: If the investor acts in emotional haste, he will repent in rational leisure.

"Every imaginable kind of bullish rumor hit the floor of the NYSE," said the lead paragraph of a story by Los Angeles

Times financial writer Ernest A. Schonberger on May 6, 1970.

The buying splurge was touched off by the announcement the previous day of lower margin requirements, dropped from 80 percent to 65 percent.

"But many professionals said the buying was intensified by purely emotional considerations," Schonberger added.

The Dow rose sixteen points on heavy trading, moved by the margin drop. But fifteen points of the rise evaporated shortly after midsession.

Then came the wildfire rumors that the discount rate (the interest rate banks charge on loans to member banks) would be shaved one-half percent; the war in Vietnam was about to end.

None of these rumors proved out.

"You name it, there was a rumor on it," said one trader. Another noted, "The public gets excited by the slightest bit of hope." And another asserted, "If enough people are sucked in today the rally won't last."

He was right.

The Dow closed on May 6, at 718.39, up 8.65.

On May 7 the closing was 723.07, plus 4.68.

Then all turned to gall and wormwood, the rumor epidemic having spent itself like a whirling top. On May 8 the Dow posted a final average of 717.073, a loss of 5.34. The Dow was now below its price before the rumors started on May 6. It had been a three-day exercise in futility, loon-crazy mass childishness.

The penalties of emotion are paid not only by small investors and outsiders but by some of the nation's most brilliant businessmen, who should know better. Lust for power and the weakness of greed have made fools of many of America's smartest tycoons.

An excellent example is the madness that occurred in the late 1960s on the part of affluent men and corporations who began tripping over one another in a frenzy to buy obsolescent Hollywood movie studios, although they knew nothing about the complex industry.

Financier Kirk Kerkorian had a number of good things going for him in Las Vegas and elsewhere. Then he barged into the MGM picture, overpaying tremendously in his zeal to control the company. Thus, at the moment he did acquire control, he had a $280 million paper loss. And of course he didn't really own MGM. The banks did. Kerkorian didn't need the company. Why did he want MGM? Perhaps he wanted to be bigger than Howard Hughes. But all he got was a giant migraine. In 1969 MGM lost $25 million. The man Kerkorian installed as president of MGM, James T. Aubrey, Jr., promptly consigned to limbo three ambitious productions on which millions had already been spent. "We had to do it," Aubrey said candidly. "Either we cancelled them or we went out of business; it was that simple."

In an attempt to raise cash, 180 acres of MGM's storied Culver City lot were put up for sale. No revenue source was overlooked, so dire was MGM's need for money. What was described by ex-MGM luminary Betty Furness as a "depressing" auction was held on the "rundown lot." MGM was reduced to running a second-hand store, soliciting a little petty cash against its huge deficit.

Among the items placed on sale were eight slave whips, eight rickshas and 167 spears. Also a genuine Sherman tank.

Judy Garland's $14 red slippers worn in *The Wizard of Oz* brought $15,000. Clark Gable's raincoat went for $1,250, and Elizabeth Taylor's *Father of the Bride* wedding gown sold for $625.

In all, Metro raised about $1.5 million from the auction. It didn't help Kerkorian much. He had to sell almost half his Vegas hotel-casino holdings to the Hilton chain to raise money to meet his obligations to the banks.

Kerkorian wasn't the only one who risked so much for so little. Corporations are nothing but people, and the people in corporations, even those at the highest level, can have a lapse of reason.

Kinney National Service also overpaid tremendously to acquire Warner Brothers. Paramount cost Gulf & Western far too much. Half the Paramount lot was subsequently sold to an Italian real estate company, the previous highest bidder, fittingly, had been a cemetery.

Only the Disney operation in the current Hollywood scene has the know-how in a swiftly changing industry to earn a profit with a big studio operation. In 1970 Disney reported a record net income of $22.4 million.

Two attempts to sell Universal have failed, and the studio to some degree has kept its head above water not by making movies and television shows, but by turning the lot into a highly successful tourist attraction. About five million visitors have spent a fortune touring the place.

The corporate executives who acquired MGM, Warner Brothers and Paramount more than likely were dreaming of becoming movie moguls. They saw themselves as reincarnations of Louis B. Mayer, David Selznick, Harry Cohn and Darryl Zanuck. Of that quartet, only Zanuck is alive, and he, after a lifetime in the business, is still having his troubles.

Emotions ran rampant at the May, 1970, stockholders meeting of Twentieth Century-Fox Film Corporation in Los Angeles. It began with unpleasant news. Zanuck said that Fox showed a profit during the first three months of 1970 of $967,000, or 11 cents a share. That was a drop from the $2.5 million or 31 cents a share earned in the comparable quarter the year before. Zanuck declared he was optimistic that the net loss of $25.2 million for 1969 would be turned around in the ensuing nine months because of the release of six or seven major features.

Zanuck was followed to the podium by his son Richard, president of Fox. "I'm no happier than you," young Zanuck told the shareholders. "Too often by following yesterday's formula for success, we have produced today's failures."

But Fox had saved considerable money, Richard Zanuck added, by slashing employment 40 percent; cutting advertising $5 million; and eliminating six branch offices, which reduced domestic distribution costs by $1.5 million.

"I believe we have an excellent chance to continue the upward trend," young Zanuck concluded.

Darryl Zanuck then resumed the podium and called for questions.

One shareholder wanted to know why Richard Zanuck's salary had thrusted from $125,000 in 1969 to $350,000 in 1970, and why Darryl Zanuck himself had been raised from $110,000 to $200,000.

Zanuck's answer was that his son deserved the $135,000 increase because he was acting both as head of the studio and as an executive at the company's New York headquarters.

As to his own salary nearly doubling, Zanuck declared—his voice filled with enough drama to match any of his screen productions—that when he took control of Fox seven years previously, "I wanted to come back like I wanted a hole in the head. I came back when the company had touched bottom and I realized that my family depended on the [Fox] shares" it owned.

"I went to Spain," he continued passionately. "I went to work on *Cleopatra,* and I'm proud to say that the highest-costing motion picture in history now shows a profit."

A stocky figure rose, left hand arched to a hip, the other cradling a menacing microphone.

The shareholder was Broadway's most famous producer.

"My name is David Merrick," David Merrick said. "I own in excess of 200,000 shares, alas and to my regret."

Darryl Zanuck did not smile, and must at that moment have longed for the beautiful days before television.

Merrick thundered that figures provided him by "some of your disloyal employees in high places" had in reality produced a net loss for the company during Zanuck's seven-year reign.

It was David Merrick's belief that the $60 million in profit reported by Darryl Zanuck in that period represented money earned from the sale, lease or rental to television of films that were made prior to Zanuck's assuming control. If that sum and nonrecurring profits from sale of real estate and other assets were subtracted from the reported profits, the net loss would be $60 million.

Zanuck, eyes darting, flashed back his answer. He said he had worked for Fox for years as a producer before taking command of the company and that he deserved the credit for much of the television revenue. "The pictures you are talking about are pictures that I made," he added in a voice that could have been clearly heard without a microphone.

Undeterred, David Merrick asked Darryl Zanuck to anticipate how much money was going to be lost on several of the
new Fox films.

"You're a good one to talk about failures," roared Zanuck.
"You've had your fill of them."

Merrick roared back, "Sixty percent of my product has got-
ten into the black." Merrick accused Zanuck of employing "the
old Senator Joe McCarthy technique."

Boos and hisses and cries of "sit down, unfair" were hurled
at Merrick. Others shouted that Merrick's remarks were "hurt-
ing the price of the stock."

"You've got your clique here to give you support," said David
Merrick to Darryl Zanuck.

Merrick, who released the full text of his attack to the press
and other shareholders before the meeting began, suggested that
the meeting had been held in Los Angeles rather than New
York to assure attendance of a majority of employees loyal to
the Zanucks.

In an interview after the conclusion of the stormy meeting,
Merrick told reporters that Zanuck "has a chance to turn the
company around." However, he was planning to "watch very
carefully" in the following months. If overhead wasn't reduced
to an acceptable level he said he would try to take control of
Fox or at least file a mismanagement suit.

Less than a year after this meeting, the situation was very,
very different. The heady optimism of both Zanucks concerning
future profits failed to materialize and young Zanuck was dis-
missed under fire and with the apparent consent of his father.
Then the elder Zanuck himself became a figurehead when he
was eased out as chief executive officer of the board.

Fox, too, had held an auction, selling off about 2,000 props,
raising a ridiculous $364,480, especially ridiculous when mea-
sured against a 1970 second-quarter loss of $17,072,000 and a
$5.2 million loss in the third quarter. Fox ended the fiscal year
with a Brobdingnagian $55 million loss and possible insolvency.

Darryl Zanuck had lived to see the parade pass by. The
parade had long passed by when the aspiring moguls bought
the other film factories. The day of the vast studio complex was

over and the complexion of the movie-going audience had changed. Young people under twenty-five were buying most of the tickets. "This is not a phase," according to MGM's James Aubrey. "It'll never get back to what it was. Anybody looking for the good old days won't find them again. The audience, I think, is ahead of the business and we've got to get ahead of them. The revolution has been rapid and we all got caught. We're fortunate to have the audience we've got."

The writing was already on the wall when the studios were acquired, but nobody bothered to read it.

If reason instead of tangled emotions had been the measuring rod, these expensive, high-risk acquisitions would not have been made. Why buy trouble going in?

The same verity applies to the individual investor. If he can't keep his emotions out of the market, he should keep himself out of the market.

In Los Angeles there are three restaurateurs who own millions of shares of stocks, shares once the coveted possessions of buyers who acted with emotion instead of reason and detailed knowledge. Among the holdings of the restaurateurs are 2,000 shares of Sunset Pacific Oil, 6,000 of Lightning Spark Plug, 2,000 of Mineral Mountain Mining and some 65,000 additional shares in twenty-one other companies.

The restaurant men utilize the stock certificates of these firms in the only way they can be utilized:

They have papered them to the walls of their establishments.

TEN

CANYON OF CHAOS

Institutions which handle other people's money have a special obligation to conduct their affairs in such a way that public confidence is maintained.

Wall Street forgot that lesson in the 1920's, much to its own ultimate regret and that of the country as a whole.

From a Los Angeles Times *editorial*

On staid, stodgy old Wall Street, banker and stockbroker to the world, October 4, 1968, was as usual a day of bulls and bears. More unusual, it was also a day of an awesome bust, albeit not of a financial nature.

Derriere swinging with more momentum than the tape, a black-booted California brunette, flown in especially for the purpose, paraded down the powerhouse canyons in a flaming, fuchsia mini-dress, 47-inch breasts marching in front of her.

A special detail of twenty policemen struggled to maintain order as more than 10,000 not-so-staid-and-stodgy Wall Streeters cheered their lusty admiration at the young woman exhibiting more than her share of common stock.

All in all, it was a good day on the Street. Aside from the spectacle of a walking treasure chest, an impressive display of blue chips, the Dow closed at 952.95, up 3.38. There were 106 new highs on the NYSE, only 4 new lows.

In October, 1968, there was still time for fun and games on Wall Street, but the brunette's eye-popping appearance was one of the last happy, frivolous diversions in lower Manhattan's financial center.

The market was already mired in quicksand.

Less than fifteen months later, the quicksand was neck high, and the canyons of Wall Street were in chaos. Nothing like it had been seen since the 1929 crash.

Anarchy hovered.

Like the figure of a pregnant woman, the chaos and anarchy

125

had swollen imperceptibly but inevitably. However, it had taken a gestation period in excess of nine months for retarded Wall Street to give birth to its retarded, deeply troubled child.

The financial fortresses, once thought impregnable, were sowing a crop of calamity, reaping a bitter not undeserved harvest, the payoff for years of neglect and mismanagement. And the trouble inside the brokerage houses was monumental.

Brokers, brokerage houses and clients were all caught in a recession, and everyone was unhappy.

Clients had more reason than anybody else to be unhappy. Their disenchantment was justified and crucial. Wall Street had been reaming the client for years, and who would blame any investor for crying foul? The client, big and small, had been crucified by the securities business. Wall Street had shown monumental contempt for the stock purchaser, arrogantly believing it was doing the client a favor in allowing him to put his money in the market. Of course, the reverse was true.

Clients had been conned into purchasing billions upon billions of dollars of the wrong stocks at the wrong times in the unholy drive for commissions. But the greed of the brokerage houses had been so piglike when volume was huge in the 1960s that they ignored their responsibility to provide fundamental services to clients, services that in a properly organized, well-administered industry would have been routine.

The unmanageable paperwork had piled to Himalayan heights, one of the most stupendous failures of management in the history of American business.

"Bookkeeping is snarled and orders cannot be matched with customers," said one observer with considerable understatement.

Magazine writer Max Gunther, an objective and conscientious journalist, painted this picture of Wall Street on an evening in 1968. Time: 9 P.M.

"Every building still had lights burning in many windows. Coffee shops were busy, filled with weary men and women trying to stay awake. The sidewalks were full of people carrying paper: messengers lugging sacks of securities, executive types clutching envelopes and folders. The wind blew paper along the gutters and across the roadway and up building walls.

Corded stacks of paper lay on steps and inside doorways, awaiting transfer. The street was awash with paper."

By December 31, 1968, member firms of the NYSE had inexcusably failed to deliver an incredible $4.1 billion worth of securities because of back-office inefficiency.

Right then the situation could have been brought under control or enormously improved if the NYSE, the ASE and/or the SEC had declared an emergency—which is what the situation was—and urged a moratorium on business. The NYSE could have made such a moratorium stick if violation brought severe penalties and sanctions. The houses should have been all but shut down, brokers forbidden to solicit new business; brokers should have been allowed to service only clients already on the books, clients that in the first place had been ill-served. Well-trained, decently paid back-office employees should have been put on round-the-clock shifts to straighten out the muddle before the houses were allowed to reopen. This would have meant a short-term decline in brokers' commissions and profits to the partners, but in the end it would have saved millions for every house that was in a paperwork predicament. In the end, too, it would have allowed many houses to turn the corner. Instead, the paperwork jumble activated the downfall of many firms.

The March 18, 1969, Los Angeles *Times* editorial quoted at the beginning of this chapter also said:

> *A few years ago a campaign was launched to persuade ordinary Americans to participate in "people's capitalism" by buying stocks.*
>
> *The campaign was an outstanding success. Today more than 26 million people own stocks, and a volume of 12 million or more transactions a day has become common.*
>
> *The exchanges and the brokerage houses have been slow to invest in automated equipment to handle the increased volume. In the view of many experts, they have also been niggardly in salaries to their "backshop" employees who do the paperwork.*
>
> *Under the horse-and-buggy system still in use, each transaction goes through about 50 steps culminating in the*

delivery of certificates of ownership to stock purchasers or their agents.

This system is proving pitifully inadequate. Failures to deliver certificates on time have become chronic. So have errors in the monthly statements issued by brokers.

This is irritating; it is also potentially dangerous.

There is concern that, should trading volume increase dramatically for some reason, delivery failures would shoot up—triggering a crisis of confidence that might leave some brokerage houses unable to meet their obligations to customers.

By the end of 1969, fails-to-deliver fell to $1.84 billion, a welcome 55 percent drop. But even that fail rate was a staggering, unnecessary, inexcusable hardship on clients.

By March, 1970, the fail rate moved down to a still-inexcusable $1.46 billion.

The houses were so confused that clients' certificates were, as one Wall Streeter put it, "vanishing like lightning" in the back offices. How long would GM (or any other corporation) remain in business if it failed to deliver the product on which its business was based?

There was no mystery as to why the back offices were uproariously inefficient. Wall Street had been caught flat-footed. Its guiding lights had no contingency plans to handle the zoom in trading volume, which had been growing at breakneck speed from the beginning of the 1960s, reaching a zenith of frenzy in 1967–1968.

When the shower of new shareholders descended, Wall Street ad-libbed, improvising very badly. Many houses simply pulled any live bodies they could find from the sidewalks and put them to work without even token training.

At the end of July, 1969, Stanley A. Rasch, vice-president in charge of personnel and training of giant Bache & Co., said: "The need was so great until very recently we all hired a great many mediocre people. Now we are taking a more critical view to eliminate the fat while retaining the muscle in anticipation

of the higher volume expected later this year." He added un-
easily: "But it's altogether possible we'll have to return to a
mass hiring situation to meet our needs then."

Declared Adrian L. Banky, director of membership services of
the Association of Stock Exchange Firms: During the crunch
"it got so bad that anyone who could do virtually anything was
hired."

The Association, representing 80 percent of the more than
600 NYSE firms, instituted a long overdue innovation, but it
was a grain-of-sand effort. A school for back-office employees
was begun. However, the training lasted only one to three weeks,
and even this brief amount of familiarization with some very
complicated back-office procedures was received by a mere 400
people. The purported number of employees shunted through
the school in 1970 was a scant 1,500. And some firms began
their own training programs. Bache, for example, conducted a
one-week "orientation" course for all new employees.

This puny effort did not come close to solving Wall Street's
manpower shortage in terms of either quantity or quality.

And undoubtedly the major reason is those "niggardly" salaries. At the height of the people shortage in the late 1960s,
body stealing of back-office employees grew to epidemic proportions, with firms pirating each other's workers—often during
lunch hours. In many cases it took a lure of as little as $5 a
week for an employee to switch firms.

And why not? There wasn't much economic inducement for
a back-office worker to remain loyal. While the houses were
showing astronomical profits in 1967, the typical Wall Street
clerk earned a base pay of $103.47. It rose a mite to $115.92 in
1968. Overtime added between $15 and $25.

But Wall Street would shell out when it had to. Many firms
hired and paid for limousines to transport teen-age girl employees who worked late, because the young women were fear-
ful of riding the subways at night.

The pay scales are little higher today and it is necessary, if
obvious, to state that management gets exactly what it pays
for.

Because of such parsimony, Wall Street, which needs efficient people like the Pope needs churches, is not likely to gather a force of dedicated, reasonably happy employees.

An upgrading of wages as well as better and more extensive training would go far to guarantee every house a back-office team that could contend with future logjams. (By 1980, according to one NYSE prediction, volume could hit a fantastic 60 million shares a day, compared to the current 8–20 million daily trading range of shares.)

Better-paid and better-trained people are only part of the answer to all the ailments that afflict Wall Street. But it is an important element. I have made it a practice to pay members of my own team—from secretaries to my assistant deal men—generously. In the end, it's good business, a minimum investment for a maximum return.

One test of good management—and good management on Wall Street is as rare as moon rocks—is to cope with problems before they get out of hand.

Of the woes besetting the Street, most of the "problems should have been foreseen with more clarity," said Associated Press business analyst John Cunniff.

The truism was also pointed out to 450 representatives of brokerage firms in a September, 1969, speech by SEC chairman Hamer Budge. With far more optimism than was warranted at the time, Budge said: "Today everyone is in far better condition not only to recognize the problems but to deal with them. The very fact that we skated so near the brink in that experience [the paperwork pileup] reaffirms my conviction that perhaps our number-one problem . . . is to anticipate crises rather than merely react to them."

In another speech only three months later to the Investment Bankers Association of America in Boca Raton, Florida, Budge found Wall Street still at the brink.

He cited "alarming signs" that the brokerage industry had not yet solved its paperwork difficulties, and warned that some member firms might be in violation of antifraud provisions of securities laws because of their operational problems. He said fails still represented 52 percent of the capital of member firms.

The volume of negative mail received by his office had increased sharply, Budge continued. Of 2,600 complaints in 1967, some 67 percent were related to back-office problems. In 1968 the number of complaints shot up to almost 4,000. And in 1969 the outraged letters were running at the rate of 14,000, not to mention the uncounted number of phone calls from irate investors.

"The number of complaints," Budge added, "is more than an interesting statistic. It is another barometer of the operational capacity of the securities industry, and we shall be monitoring the current complaints with a view to determining whether some commission action is required."

Commission action *is* required, particularly the aforementioned indefinite closing of houses until the foul-ups certain to occur in the future are dealt with. The early Wednesday market closings to allow back offices to catch up on their paperwork wasn't at all effective. Under a rigorously enforced system of compulsive closing whenever a firm falls behind in its paperwork, the partners of the pregnable houses would soon enough spend the money for more employees and more computer time to clean up their nests.

The SEC, a publicly-funded agency, owes such action to the public it was created to protect.

One SEC investigator confided to journalist Gunther that he was terribly worried about the increasing public distrust of Wall Street. "Suppose," he said, "this distrust spreads, grows more intense. There could be a kind of 'run' on Wall Street, like a run on a bank. Can you imagine what it would be like? Millions of investors clamoring for their securities all at once."

A run is unlikely despite all the gargantuan gaffes of Wall Street. But clients needn't be put into the humiliating position of "clamoring for their securities."

By 1969 all the big exchanges and large brokerage houses had long since acknowledged that the cherished, engraved, fancy-bordered stock certificate was outmoded. Yet the securities industry moved turtle-fast in an age of supertechnology in finding a substitute during a period when many firms were still chalking up yearly $300,000–400,000 losses in their back offices, a big chunk of this total due to the manual handling of certificates.

The traditional stock certificate is antediluvian, primitive, old-fashioned. It is no longer needed or necessary.

The conventional 8 × 12-inch piece of paper has been maintained primarily because of custom. Big Board companies are still required to portray a human figure somewhere on the certificate.

Why?

For no important reason except that it's always been done this way. Tradition dies hard on Wall Street, even if many though not all the Street's traditions are costly, irrelevant and not worth preserving. The before-the-flood thinking persists in the heart of hearts of most members of the securities industry that the certificate must *look* impressive, solid, prestigious. It ought to *feel* good in a man's hand. But the certificate itself (even in the past its principal advantage was that it was difficult to forge) has no value except to compound the paperwork in back offices.

"How we'd love it if all the engraved stock certificates in the world could be burned and computer punch cards adopted in their place," said an executive of Paine, Webber, Jackson & Curtis. And a Merrill Lynch manager added, "If we were fully automated, we could do in a few minutes what now takes weeks."

Unfortunately, the art of the computer has not yet reached a level of efficiency where punch cards instead of certificates can be churned out fast or reliably enough, at least for the big firms.

It is an interesting paradox that the securities business was among the last—if not the last—to utilize the technology of the very computer companies they were banking, not only in the matter of processing certificates, but in taking care of payments, commissions and other back-office work. The brokerage houses sold a Niagara of shares in computer companies using the technology of tomorrow and the day after tomorrow, yet remained hopelessly antiquated in their own operations.

Expensive though computers are, no brokerage firm can remain in business now without such equipment, efficiently designed. If Wall Street had had any management worthy of the name, the necessity for computerization would have been anticipated and dealt with no later than 1967 when the paperwork bottleneck was already glaringly obvious.

By 1970 all that the exchanges and brokerage houses had done to meet the stock certificate problem was to authorize two long-range, costly studies by a pair of "think tanks." These supposed brain factories, after due and expensive consideration, will no doubt emerge with a recommendation everyone acknowledges: to replace the certificate with a punch card.

Wall Street might better call on the computer manufacturers to design, as fast as possible, hardware that would do the job. Dozens of other industries have been efficiently computerized for years. (Computerization in the world's largest bank, the Bank of America, began in the 1950s!)

Effective automation is coming. But at the current pace it may take ten years.

Some small companies, unyoked to NYSE regulations, have not waited to automate. They have been issuing IBM cards instead of the formal certificates to shareholders. And for these small firms at least, the system has been working. The cards they issue are one-third the size of the conventional certificate and far less costly. "We would pay $2,000 and up for 10,000 blank certificates of the normal type," said Donald Miller, vice-president of Ingenuics, Inc., a Maryland firm. "But for the cards it costs us only $700 for the first batch, and mere pennies for later ones." Ingenuics uses five separate printing plates and three different colors for its card certificates. "We have just as many safety features as the fancy engraved certificates required for companies listed on the New York Stock Exchange," he added.

Automated Services, Inc., of Fairview, Oregon, is another company using IBM cards in place of certificates. President Louis J. Nelson says the chief benefits of the cards are simplification and monetary savings. He estimated handling costs at about half what they were with the standard 8 × 12-inch certificate.

Until the day that the big houses have full computerization, a suggestion by John D. McClure, a senior vice-president of Bateman Eichler, Hill Richards, Inc., would be an extremely helpful interim procedure: "Although the securities industry is using the most sophisticated computers to process a great deal of their work, most of the processing in the securities cage is accomplished by the same methods that have been used for years," said McClure.

Condemning the present stock certificate as a "cumbersome document," McClure urged eliminating it altogether, adding that each brokerage firm or transfer agent should "maintain a record of the holders of its stock and send a statement either quarterly or annually showing the holdings."

If such a system was instituted now—critical because when volume is high the average fail time between order and delivery of securities exceeds by far the fail time during the pit of the 1929 crash—it would do much to avert the "crisis of confidence" that is very real among clients, particularly among Wall Street's favorite patsy: the small investor.

The small man and the odd-lot trader are, ironically and unfairly, paying the freight for Wall Street mismanagement while also being frozen out of the opportunity in most cases to earn a dime in the market.

Member firms were screaming bloody murder during the 1969–1970 bear market that lower volume was killing their profits. So the NYSE in its infinite wisdom placed what was termed a temporary $15 surcharge on all transactions. The SEC in its infinite wisdom approved the hike.

In an attempt to justify the surcharge, NYSE president Robert W. Haack in a two-page ad in mass circulation magazines and newspapers ticked off "eleven facts to help you understand the changes in stock fees."

What Haack's position amounted to was that the little guy was getting it in the groin again. The man who could buy only $1,000 worth of stock was being charged the same $15 as the institution that could purchase a 10,000-share block of GM.

The "eleven facts" stated by Haack:

1. Commission rates have not been increased in twelve years.

2. As for the broker, he has been hit hard by rising costs.

3. The commission you pay when you buy and sell stock is among the lowest anybody pays for the transfer of any kind of property.

4. If the securities industry, like many others, had increased its rates in each of these twelve years, in step with the increases in costs, the increase needed now would be barely noticeable.

5. For most firms, the cost of handling the small order has become a losing proposition.

6. In the light of the fact that many firms have lost money handling small transactions, it is certainly understandable that some firms have either discouraged the small investor or even turned him away.

7. The new interim service charge will mean greater service to the small investor.

8. It is the right of investors to service that prompted the . . . proposal to increase commissions to a fair and realistic 1970 level.

9. Brokerage firms, in common with every other business, must place themselves on a sound economic footing—not only for today, but for the future.

10. It is not realistic to say, as some people insist, that profit on the big trades should cover the losses on the small.

11. Finally, it is a fact, in every sense of the word, that the securities industry wants and needs the individual investor.

Careful scrutiny of "facts" 6 and 11 show a contradiction. Haack admitted in his sixth point that the small investor had been turned away, and in the elaboration under his eleventh point he said the securities industry wants and needs the individual investor and a "steady flow of small orders as well as big."

All of Haack's assertions are open to challenge and argument, none more so than his number 7 claim that the surcharge would mean greater service to the small investor.

The small investor did not get greater service for his $15. Had Mr. Haack disguised himself as a man with less than

$1,000 and tried in the wake of the surcharge to open an account at any but a handful of houses, he would have been treated like dirt.

The great majority of houses would sooner do business with a prosperous bank robber than a small man.

Merrill Lynch and a minority of other firms have grown wealthy by serving the small investor. Capable management procedures would have brought similar wealth to all the other houses that once—but no longer—begged the average man to "Invest in America." Wall Street used to call it "shirt-sleeve capitalism."

It is not inherently fair to the small investor that his options to choose a house are automatically restricted to the few firms that will not treat him with contempt or arrogance when he walks through the door. In my own operation, as a matter of dignity and equity, I service both large and small clients with equal diligence. To do less would disqualify me in my own mind as a conscientious broker. Every client, whatever the size of his account, deserves a fair shake and the same opportunity to profit in the market in proportion to his investment. Running up a small investor's $1,000 is as important to me as adding another million to the net worth of my wealthiest clients.

The surcharge was ineffective from all points of view, even for the brokerage firms it was designed to help. The houses figured the added fee would bring in some $450 million, but nothing like that amount accrued because the bear market had dwindled volume even below the expected level, from an average of 13 million shares a day in 1968 to a daily 10 million or fewer shares in 1969–1970.

Raising the charge "drives the individual investor out of the brokerage house and into mutual funds," according to A. V. Dowling, Los Angeles *Herald-Examiner* Financial Editor.

"If you are a small investor, you have good reason to be confused about brokerage commissions. Ever since Wall Street got bogged down in paperwork, brokers have been trying to discourage the little guy, either by refusing his business or raising the commission he pays," noted *Changing Times* magazine.

The surcharge, let it be remembered, was an extra fee piled

onto the commissions houses already charged the small investor. "Many brokers happily loaded the new surcharge on top of their own $15, $20 or $25 minimums," added *Changing Times*.

Commenting on the $15 fee, Alton Cedar of Bache & Co., the nation's second largest house, said: "Brokers are going to get killed. They don't get any of the surcharge money. It's probably going to lead to a unionization of brokers."

Under the surcharge plan, all proceeds were supposedly earmarked to improve the operation and financial position of brokerage firms (this alleged improvement, however, was as invisible as air). The practical effects of the surcharge were to hike the tabs of small investors and force many houses to increase the commissions they paid their brokers, an all-but-empty gesture at that moment since brokers were doing very little business.

The surcharge was designed as a stopgap. When the NYSE finally settles on a new commission rate, the shirt-sleeve capitalist will still be paying more proportionately than institutions to invest in the market, despite Mr. Haack's assertion that "the securities industry wants and needs the individual investor."

So shabbily has the small man been treated that there may come a day of mass revolt when the individual investor will no longer want or need the securities industry. "Many brokers fear that small investors now forced to sell everything to cover margin calls will never return to the market," *Life* magazine said in June, 1970. A large-scale boycott of stocks in this age of aware, militant consumerism is by no means out of the question. That boycott could well extend eventually to the mutual fund industry, which by and large has also turned in a poor performance for the modest investor while shafting him with huge load fees.

As the bear market persisted and the surcharge failed to generate the expected income (or that promised "greater service to the small investor"), Wall Street thrashed wildly about looking for new ways to scoop up additional money.

One prominent firm, Burnham & Co., imposed a "custody fee" on dormant accounts. The firm said it would make a $50

charge at the end of six months in clients' accounts which did
not produce at least that amount in commission or other management income.

Such a practice, which did not catch on among other firms, is
psychological and financial pressure, a mailed-fist inducement to
force clients into trades, whether there are good stocks around
or not. A client might be wisely waiting for a bear market to
bottom out before risking his funds. He thus is paying a premium for using better judgment than his broker.

A spokesman for Burnham said, "One of the problems here
is that we've been doing a lot for no compensation." He was
referring to the long-standing practice of houses to service clients by storing their securities without charge, collecting dividends and issuing regular statements as well as a few other
courtesies that should continue to be provided to the client for
goodwill, if for no other reason.

But to raise capital in a really big way, Wall Street came up
with a new, precedent-shattering wrinkle.

The new passion: issuing stock to the public. Investors would
be given the dubious privilege of buying into diseased Wall
Street firms with no assurance that most of the infected patients
would recover. The public was going to be asked to place its
money in a volatile, non-blue-chip business run for the most
part by a clutch of the least talented executives of any industry
in the nation.

For close to 200 years the NYSE had been the most private
of private clubs, the most privileged of privileged sanctuaries.
From the days of its formation, the Exchange had insisted that
ownership of its member firms be guarded like vestal virgins.
The profitable business was drumtight-closed to any but a
handful of partners, their families, a few chosen executives and
a smattering of other key employees.

Now suddenly Wall Street wanted the public to participate in
ownership of the houses. There was no thought of public participation when it was all wine and roses, only when the wine
had turned sour and the roses had wilted.

Like any other industry, Wall Street, under the right circum-

stances, could be a good investment for clients. But buying into
a brokerage firm in 1970 was akin to buying into any movie
studio but Disney. Investors were merely buying high risk and
doubtful future performance at a time when a client, if he felt
compelled to risk his money any place in the market, could have
done so in situations that had far, far more promise.

The NYSE came reluctantly to the decision to allow public
ownership of brokerages.

An upstart, a relative newcomer to the private club, forced
the acceptance of the principal of public ownership after a long
crusade. Only eleven years old, the firm of Donaldson, Lufkin
& Jenerette, Inc., compelled the NYSE to forego monopoly
ownership of the securities business.

DLJ was the first brokerage firm to go public, and the Street
held its breath, waiting for public reaction.

DLJ's underwriting was 800,000 shares at 15. The firm had
originally pegged its public price at 30, but in the market atmosphere of April, 1970, half that amount seemed more realistic. Even at 15, the first brokerage to go public did not prove
an immediately promising or successful investment for those
who bought in. By May 21, 1970, the price was down to 6⅝
bid, 7⅛ asked.

An editorial in *The Christian Science Monitor* called the DLJ
move "an historic moment for the New York Stock Exchange."
The paper gushed that "the Exchange rightly figured DLJ was
on the side of history. One feels the public can only benefit from
a more strongly funded stock brokerage industry."

Until Wall Street is cured of its many ailments, and until the
point in time when quality people who know what they're doing are at the helm of the houses, I would as soon put my clients into a firm manufacturing Herbert-Hoover-for-President
buttons than any of the other brokerages planning to go public
at a more auspicious moment.

Finance magazine's 1969 ranking of the nation's largest
brokerage houses on the basis of assets does not give any investor or observer great cause for confidence in the Wall Street
establishment's handling of its own financial affairs. The top
twenty firms and their assets were:

	1968	1969
1. Merrill Lynch	$254,368,000	$271,330,000
2. Allen & Co.	91,032,000	100,024,000
3. Bache & Co.	96,423,000	94,100,000
4. Loeb, Rhoades	76,541,000	78,580,000
5. Salomon Bros.	58,700,000	64,700,000
6. Lehman Bros.	69,572,000	60,648,000
7. Francis I. duPont	66,330,000	60,120,000
8. Goodbody & Co.	49,600,000	60,000,000
9. Walston & Co.	58,391,000	56,665,000
10. Eastman Dillon	53,000,000	50,000,000
11. White Weld & Co.	40,749,000	49,405,000
12. E. F. Hutton & Co.	48,095,000	46,134,000
13. Goldman Sachs	41,038,000	46,000,000
14. Dean Witter & Co.	51,023,000	44,620,000
15. Smith Barney	30,000,000	40,000,000
16. Burnham & Co.	44,300,000	39,078,000
17. Hayden, Stone	49,478,000	38,964,000
18. Reynolds & Co.	36,224,000	38,300,000
19. Dempsey-Tegeler	18,851,000	36,119,000
20. Stephens, Inc.	36,983,000	34,696,000

In asset value, ten of the brokerages were on the upside, ten on the downside. But assets do not reveal the true picture. The value of assets can change for better or worse with dramatic suddenness. The test must be profit.

Despite its nearly $17 million increase in assets in one year, Merrill Lynch had a 41 percent plunge in profits by the end of 1969, down to $32 million from $54 million. Even the world's largest brokerage firm could not buck the Wall Street malaise, which was not due solely—as many contend—to the onslaught of a bear market.

Bache & Co. incurred in 1969 what is probably the largest deficit of a brokerage firm in recent times, a walloping $8.7 million. The house blamed huge increases in costs, wages, prices, automation and rent, as well as shortened stock exchange trading hours and reduced trading volume for its monumental loss. Six hundred of its 6,000 people in 130 offices were fired.

Yet Merrill Lynch, operating under the same conditons, chimed in with a profit—a lesser profit than the year before, but a substantial profit nonetheless.

Why should one giant house show a profit, another a record loss?

As always, the answer is the same: management.

Francis I. duPont, the seventh-ranking house, tallied a loss not too far removed from that of Bache. It ended 1969 with a deficit of $7,701,000, although in 1968 it had an after-tax profit of $4,526,000, an incredible negative turnaround. To help keep it afloat, the firm merged with two other houses. But even this amalgamation could not prevent a 1970 loss of some $16 million. The firm was rescued in early 1971 by a $30 million loan from Ross Perot's computer fortune. "As long as there is a Wall Street, we will owe a tremendous debt of gratitude to Ross Perot," said New York Stock Exchange Chairman Bernard J. Lasker. He added he would be "eternally grateful" to Perot because the Texan's loan saved not only duPont's 180,000 customers and the firm's partners and backers, but the integrity of the financial community itself!

Right behind duPont in the rankings was goliath Goodbody & Co., which had a 1969 pretax operating loss of $832,000, shorn through partners' tax recoveries to $433,000. In the first two months of 1970, however, the estimated loss for the house approximated $1.5 million, almost twice the pretax operating deficit for the entire year of 1969. In 1968, by way of startling contrast, Goodbody earned a hefty $8.7 million before taxes and a still hefty $4.1 million after taxes.

Senior partner Harold P. Goodbody blamed the loss on continuing high costs and sagging trading volume. Some 200 of its 2,100 employees were dropped, 4 of its 105 branch offices consolidated, bonuses for partners temporarily suspended and a 10 percent pay cut planned for executives earning more than $20,-800.

All that wasn't enough. In December, 1970, it took the creation of a special $15 million NYSE trust fund and $15 million more from Merrill Lynch to keep the crumbling house afloat. Goodbody with 200,000 client accounts was merged with the affluent Merrill Lynch.

Hayden, Stone, seventeenth-ranked colossus, was bailed out only by a massive heart-transplant loan of $17.5 million from a group of Oklahoma investors. Unable to process a mammoth amount of paperwork, Hayden, Stone had closed ten offices throughout the country. The fresh infusion of capital was to aid the house in covering other operational difficulties. The loan, said Chairman Alfred J. Coyle, would increase Hayden, Stone's equity and capital base to more than $50 million. But by early 1971, Hayden, Stone was also earmarked for a merger.

A massive injection of new financing was needed, too, for the rescue of nineteenth-ranked Dempsey-Tegeler, yet another house in deep distress, although interestingly, its 1969 assets were listed at nearly twice their 1968 value. The firm had been through parlous times, so parlous that President Jerome F. Tegeler had been suspended as an allied member of the NYSE by its board of governors. A loan of $8 million to keep the firm alive came from Colorado financier John M. King, members of his family, and the King Foundation, a charitable organization. Thus Dempsey-Tegeler remained vexatiously viable. The strictures leveled against the house by the NYSE included a forced cutback in the number of offices it operated. Dempsey-Tegeler was ordered to reduce its total of sixty branches, a move calculated to enable the house to comply with the capital requirements demanded by the NYSE. The Exchange decided that Tegeler, as chief executive officer, was responsible for all the firm's operations and the difficulties brought on by unmanageable financial problems arising from accounting and other paperwork enigmas. Tegeler was replaced as president by Lewis J. Whitney, formerly executive vice-president of the house. After the King loan was in the kitty, the NYSE promptly gave Dempsey-Tegeler a clean slate, lifting all restrictions. By late 1970, however, Dempsey-Tegeler was in liquidation after a loss of $18 million and former clients had filed an estimated 150 lawsuits against the house. Two of the suits alone asked $50 million in damages, alleging that eight Dempsey-Tegeler officials misappropriated company funds, wasted corporate assets, were engaged in a conspiracy to defraud, breach of contract and breach of fiduciary duty.

Taken together, brokerage houses that reported publicly had

a combined 1969 loss of $58 million. Thirteen firms lost $1 million or more.

The extremely nettlesome, disturbing question arises as to how Wall Street, unable to keep order in its own house, with many of its plutocratic firms incapable of turning a profit, can morally, ethically or pragmatically tell clients how to earn money.

It is a situation as ludicrous—and dangerous—as a man who cannot swim advising and supposedly teaching others how to survive in deep water.

In a desperate attempt to find solvency, dozens of houses have merged. Many others are planning to merge. But shotgun marriages do not have a reputation for longevity.

In union there is strength, the Wall Street reasoning goes, but in union there is likely to be only more shared misery.

My own forecast is that most of the mergers will not ultimately work. Bringing two or more flawed entities together increases problems rather than solving them. It's still true that a chain is only as strong as its weakest link. And virtually all the links in the chain of Wall Street houses are weak.

Fourteenth-ranked Dean Witter & Co. (sixty-nine offices and 1969 commissions of $100 million) announced plans to merge with a smaller, California-based house, J. Barth & Co., which did about $15 million in commissions during 1969. Dean Witter's capital was listed at some $50 million against Barth's $12 million. But even joining forces would not provide enough financing. Said Dean Witter executive vice-president G. Willard Miller, "Obviously we are going public sometime in the future, whether it's three years or five years away. We will go the public ownership route because sooner or later we, like everyone else, will need the added capital."

Two other important NYSE firms, Sade & Co. and Charles A. Taggert & Co., announced an agreement in principle to consolidate. Auchincloss, Parker & Redpath, generaled by no less an establishment fixture than Hugh D. Auchincloss, senior partner of the firm and stepfather of Jacqueline Kennedy Onassis, announced a wedding with Thomson & McKinnon, Inc., the resulting firm to have fifty-eight offices and assets of some $160 million.

Said Auchincloss and William E. Ferguson, president of Thomson & McKinnon, in a joint statement, "From the standpoint of range and quality of investment services offered, each organization will benefit from the other as they weld into one firm."

Blyth & Co., one of the nation's ten leading investment banking firms, took an oblique path to consolidation. It merged not with another banking house or brokerage firm but with INA Corporation, a wealthy insurance holding company. "This is going to give us a lot of permanent capital," said Blyth chairman Paul Devlin, while declaring that his firm did not merge because of any financial difficulties.

In March, 1970, two-gun Kleiner, Bell & Co., which functioned both as a retailer and investment banker, announced it was giving up its retail operation but remaining foursquare in the deal end of the business. "The firm thinks it can make more money in pure investment banking than by continuing in the public brokerage business," said Seymour Goldfeld, general counsel for Kleiner, Bell. "Over the past few months it has become apparent . . . that the public brokerage business has become less profitable for the securities industry and for our firm." The announcement was followed shortly by the firm's withdrawal from business altogether.

In all, during 1969–70 more than 150 Big Board members of the precious NYSE had closed their doors or merged with larger firms! Every one of these failures was an expensive monument to inefficiency and incompetency. No one toted up how many millions were lost by partners and clients in these wipeouts.

That's only the beginning. It's hardly a secret along Wall Street that dozens of other houses are in a nip-and-tuck battle to avoid going under.

The mortally wounded firms were the first casualties among brokerages since 1963.

There will be more.

In fact, there will be so many more bankruptcies and mergers

that I envision within the next decade an almost certain cata-
clysmic shakeout among brokerage houses, the reverberations
of which will stun Wall Street as never before in its history.

NYSE rules require on paper that its member firms maintain
a ratio of $1 of capital for every $20 of debt. But the NYSE
doesn't know what ratio is being maintained between audits.
Supervision is so lax that a house can get itself in shape for an
audit and a day later be on the brink of disaster.

What I believe is going to ultimately emerge after the big
shakeout is a handful of giant firms, each with 300–400
branches, and they will have an absolute stranglehold on the
entire retail end of the business.

Everybody else is going to be deep-sixed, so manifold are
the problems and so bearish is the market in competent management on Wall Street.

The Street simply does not have the motivation or enough intelligent manpower in positions of authority to save itself.

The brokerage business as it presently exists will be no more.

The irony is that the crash of the Wall Street houses will
eclipse any crash in the market itself, which, however painful, is
always temporary.

There *are* superbly knowledgeable, highly qualified, for-
ward-thinking men who could rescue every house on the Street,
if the hidebound current crop of establishmentarians would step
aside. The men who currently run the majority of the houses
simply do not have the necessary resources as managers to keep
their firms profitably alive.

The gigantic survivors, probably less than half a dozen,
will monopolize the securities business like GM and Ford
monopolize automobile production.

These swollen houses will operate in the black almost exclusively on retail business. By then computer cards will have surely
replaced stock certificates, and other back-office problems will
have been dealt with and brought under control.

But the inevitable rise of these massive chain-store houses
does not bode well for the individual investor. Every client will
be buying virtually the same stocks. The dinosaur houses will
have the power and will institute rules to tell the client he can

only buy what is on their recommended lists. Some houses already have such rules. The client is already in a struggle against brokerage-house dictatorship. Needless to add, brokers who work in such firms serve only as robots.

Thus the client, if he wants to be in the market—and it is intriguing to consider how many will want to be in the market under such circumstances—will be compelled to buy anything that emerges from research.

The chance of clients finding the right brokers who will get them into the right situations will be practically nil.

Already the balance of power in the market has shifted from the individual client to the institutional buyer. In the aggregate, millions of small clients dominated the market until the recent growth of mutual funds and other money-rich institutions, which now account for some 60 percent of trading volume and three-fifths of the dollar value of all trading.

The market now is no longer liquid in its traditional sense. Stocks are bottled up by institutions. They have assumed a heft in the market that is nothing short of scandalous.

But since the institutions have the money, the brokerage firms compete savagely for their business, and to hell with the individual client.

As of the first half of 1970, there wasn't a single house operating profitably on retail business alone, never mind what the financial statements of most houses claim. Those financial statements are doctored. House after house makes short-term loans to show the NYSE it has the necessary capital requirements. Some firms arrange for a wealthy client to make a deposit of securities or cash, which puts them well over their capital requirements—but only for twenty-four hours. After the house makes its report to the Exchange, the rich benefactor yanks his securities or cash. So the house was undercapitalized and vulnerable for all but one day, yet the report goes in as of that one day. And that's what counts in the eyes of the board of governors of the NYSE, which knows perfectly well that such machinations are common practice.

Not only will the brokerage business as currently constituted undergo earthquake realignment, but the NYSE—in its present form—will be drastically changed, its influence reduced to practically nothing. It will become an emasculated version of what it once was and could have remained had it truly acted in the interest of the public and been tougher on its own members.

The NYSE will decline into an organization of loosely knit firms with a puny number of members.

For the surviving houses, it really won't make a damn bit of difference whether or not they belong to the NYSE.

The coming downfall of the Exchange is well-deserved. It will lose its influence not merely through an attrition of member firms but because it has failed to use its existing policing powers or create new ones to handle new abuses.

The NYSE is more interested in its image than in serving the public.

The Exchange was afraid to bring McDonnell & Co. to heel while there was still time. The Exchange hid ostrichlike, hoping it would all go away. The McDonnell bust and all the other brokerage failures needn't have happened if the NYSE had been doing its job.

The Exchange acts only when absolutely necessary. A somewhat comparable situation would be for a major city to enforce all its laws only *in extremis*. The police, as the NYSE, would descend in dire emergencies or at preannounced times to see if everyone was obeying the rules. On the days of inspections, the laws are enforced. But the rest of the time it's a jungle.

What the hell kind of situation is that?

But this is essentially how the NYSE operates.

In nine years in the business, I have been looked at by the Exchange only once. While I was at Sutro in 1964, a NYSE staff man wandered into my office. He wasn't even there to question me, only to take a glance at the firm.

He was interested in me only because he was told I was the largest producer in the house. He quickly leafed through my stock and client record books, and asked me what I thought of the manager of the house and if the manager ever looks at what the firm is buying for clients. As far as I knew, I said, the manager reviewed the trading blotter every night.

That was the extent of the Exchange's policing job in my personal experience.

The elapsed time of the interview: not longer than three minutes. I could have been the biggest crook in the business, and that Exchange representative wouldn't have had a clue.

If the NYSE really wanted to do an effective policing job now, the methodology exists. There are computer firms that offer brokerages a service that puts on the manager's desk a daily statement of every client's account, his buying power, his margin and cash position. This service will also supply a print-out of all the daily trades. With this kind of available technology, on Friday of every week a brokerage house could easily supply the NYSE with a thorough picture of its capital and liabilities, its overall financial condition.

That's only one demand the NYSE should make of its members.

The Exchange should, additionally, institute a monthly check of member firms' fail rates and inspect their error accounts.

The computer can also give the Exchange a breakdown of the heaviest purchases of particular stocks. If a firm, for example, was involved in an overabundance of margin buying for clients in a questionable, risky or too speculative stock, the Exchange could step in and put a stop to it. This practice alone is a potential disaster area. If that one stock collapsed, the house could lose a tremendous amount of money and it could affect its capital structure to the point where the firm would be ruined.

Unannounced checks should be made of branch offices and brokers at least once every quarter. Brokers usually get into trouble only because of lack of proper supervision. There isn't anyone really looking over their shoulders, at least no one who can tell if brokers are playing it fast and loose with clients or operating ethically. Such NYSE supervision would keep a lot of brokers out of trouble.

That even these minimal suggested steps will be taken by the Exchange requires an unreasonable amount of hope and faith. I don't see it on the horizon.

The granddaddy of all fallacies regarding the NYSE is the general assumption on the part of the public that having "Member of the New York Stock Exchange" on a brokerage firm's stationery means unquestioned stability, resources, honesty, integrity, knowledge, trained capable personnel, qualified money managers and consultants.

That sign is supposed to rank with chicken soup as a cure-all. But that sign in and of itself meant nothing at McDonnell, and it means nothing in the operations of most houses.

The prestige of the NYSE has already declined to the point where few member firms want to remain members.

During the period I was contemplating starting my own brokerage I visited New York and talked with a senior officer at one of the most prestigious Wall Street houses.

"Are you sure you want to be a member of the Exchange?" he wondered.

"Why do you ask?"

"It's not worth it. We are seriously considering getting out ourselves."

"Why?"

"Because they hamper you terribly in what you can and can't do. And they don't really operate efficiently and in the best interests of members."

Of course, the major reason for not tying up a large amount of capital in an Exchange seat is that the retail end of the business, for most traders and houses, will continue to be a losing proposition.

Since 1953 the number of seats on the Exchange has been frozen at 1,366. A house holding an Exchange membership must own at least one seat in order to have a representative on the floor. Merrill Lynch, as the world's largest retail firm, owns seventeen.

The highest price ever paid for a seat was $725,000 in February, 1929, a bad investment since the legendary crash followed a few months later. The lowest price in this century for a seat was $17,000 in the World War II year of 1942.

In January and May of 1969, seats sold for $515,000. By December 15 the going price was severely depressed at $270,-000. The price went lower in 1970 when a seat could be purchased for $225,000.

Many of the old-time brokers and traders who were ready to retire kicked themselves all over the canyons of Wall Street for not selling their seats early in 1969. Most of these men have spent lifetimes in the business, ignorant of what the market is all about, and their ignorance extended to their own bailiwick.

They couldn't see, were totally blind to the fact that their once-but-no-longer cherished seats were going to drop in value by 50 percent.

When Blyth merged with INA it cried no tears in giving up its seat. Not having a seat doesn't hamper the firm a bit since retail trades can easily be consummated through member brokers. Blyth, incidentally, had also resigned from the NYSE in 1930, not resuming membership until 1965.

The NYSE and the National Association of Securities Dealers have also burdened members by passing a series of villainous restrictions, which I call jealous laws. A broker who has uncovered an excellent company and invested a great deal of his own money or his firm's money in the situation, has helped to nurture the company and helped it grow, and then wants to act as an investment banker when the time comes for it to go public, is forbidden to do so. The soggy-minded, lazy men who didn't have the talent or ambition to find and finance these companies themselves have punished competing brokers who can put this type of package together by saying they can't be rewarded for their efforts. That is outright jealousy. The NYSE as well as the National Association of Securities Dealers do not want such brokers to have that kind of payday.

One of the major reasons these jealous statutes were written was because of the success of Allen & Co., the richest, most successful investment banking house on Wall Street.

Charley Allen has never been a member of the NYSE, nor would he ever join. He remains affluent without the Exchange.

If I should at some time in the future open my own firm, I would not become a member of the Exchange either. My focus would be on investment banking. As for retail, I could best serve clients as a consultant, telling them which stocks to buy, which to sell. They can easily have their trades processed elsewhere.

In its August 15, 1969, issue, *Time* magazine said, "Prosperity reached almost embarrassing proportions for Wall Street during the bull markets of the past couple of years. As stock prices climbed and trading volume rose to unprecedented heights, brokerage commissions swelled to $5 billion a year, and six-figure incomes became commonplace among customers'

men. Now the securities business is mired in painful recession
. . . [fighting] a flood of red ink."

There is no better way to show the lack of management capability on Wall Street than by inspecting the way the brokerage houses conduct their own businesses.

In a good year the big houses expand. They start buying offices all over the place. In a bad year they close offices. In a good
year they hire people in droves. In a bad year they fire them in
droves.

The houses treat their people like harvest workers, hiring
them when the crop needs picking, getting rid of them as soon
as the crop runs out.

The houses could avoid this boom and bust if they exhibited
less greed. In good markets they grab for the last piece of business, every last commission from every investor. That's when
they bring in more people. But if they grew in a planned,
businesslike way, hiring people gradually, employees of brokerage houses could honestly consider themselves career men instead of harvest workers or day laborers.

The most sophisticated of the chain-store houses, Merrill
Lynch, opens offices on a planned basis. They have a program for
expansion. They may slow it down or speed it up a bit according
to general market conditions. But Merrill Lynch seldom if ever
closes offices and lops heads en masse. It is a model of efficiency,
the best run firm of its type on Wall Street, serving both small
and large investors with consideration and dignity. Other houses
have tried to emulate its operation but have failed. Merrill Lynch
thus is a textbook lesson on how a well-managed Wall Street
house can continue to prosper, no matter whether the market
atmosphere is good or bad.

The development of a brokerage house is an interesting process, as I discovered during the time I was researching the feasi-
bility of starting my own firm. A house starts as a relatively
simple operation, essentially because a new brokerage can't afford
many frills. The firm begins by buying and selling stocks for
clients on a retail basis, and if it has the right people it develops
the capability to enter the deal business, although relatively few
houses ever reach this capability.

As the new firm becomes more successful, expenses soar. A trading room is needed, as are various departments—research, back office and a group of brokers who do nothing but handle institutional business. The personnel swells and it can be a happy, bustling, successful house. Then, if poorly managed and overextended, the whole firm can be wiped out in a bad year because it takes so much money to back up the retail end of the business, particularly the expensive and indispensable computer hardware and other automation.

If growth is not planned, if expansion is not realistic, if personnel are not added according to real long-term lasting needs, the whole enchilada goes when the market turns bearish.

Wall Street has yet to learn any of these basic lessons. It has yet to learn the ABC's of management in its zeal to gouge every dollar in sight.

Only five months after he became chairman of the SEC, Hamer Budge felt frustrated and overburdened by the multifarious problems of the Frankenstein his office was trying to administer.

Only five months after assuming the SEC chairmanship, Budge indicated he wanted out.

Who could blame him?

Who indeed could blame him for trying to bring order, stability, responsibility and honesty into chaos canyon?

The Nixon Administration prevailed on the soft-spoken Budge, a former Idaho congressman and Federal judge now in his sixties, to remain at his post.

Budge did what he could. He ordered a long-term study of the market, though it didn't take a long-term study to identify and isolate Wall Street's problems. "The study," said the SEC chairman, "will serve to look in depth into some of the things that may be wrong. Most of the activities I'm sure have been legal. Now whether Congress will want them to continue to be legal is another question."

There is a good deal of lip-service congressional support to give the SEC increased powers. The more real power the SEC has the better it will be for the securities industry, since self-regulation has been a miserable failure.

To police brokerage houses, mutual funds, bank trust departments and other institutional investors more efficiently, Budge was given thirty more people to staff his regional offices. The SEC's efforts at surveillance, therefore, were doomed to failure.

To oversee the huge Wall Street establishment, Budge had a grand total of 1,379 people.

It wasn't nearly enough. By no stretch of the imagination was it nearly enough to head off Wall Street's coming Armageddon.

Perhaps Budge realized this and perhaps that's why he did resign in January, 1971, and became president of Investors Diversified Services, Inc., the huge mutual fund outfit.

Millionaire tax lawyer William J. Casey, a personal friend of President Nixon, was chosen to replace him. Casey was quickly cleared by the Senate Banking Committee. But the hearing on his nomination was re-opened when several embarrassing matters were brought to the attention of the Committee.

However, the Senate Banking Committee voted 9–3 to approve Casey. The majority report said, "After careful scrutiny of the qualifications and credentials of the nominee and after careful consideration of all civil litigation and administrative actions brought to the attention of the committee directly or indirectly involving the nominee, a majority of the committee recommends that the Senate confirm Mr. Casey."

The minority report, written by Wisconsin Senator William Proxmire, said, ". . . He [Mr. Casey] has no direct experience with the securities industry and no publicly articulated views on the important issues which will face the Commission over the next few years."

On the Senate floor, Casey was confirmed by voice vote. Only Proxmire shouted "no."

At the moment of choosing the crucial man who would head the crucial SEC, reported the Associated Press, "a mere handful of members was on the floor."

ELEVEN

THE TROUBLE WITH BROKERS

Beware of false prophets, which come to you in sheep's clothing, but inwardly they are ravening wolves. Ye shall know them by their fruits.

MATTHEW 7:15–16

Two thirds of the people who can make money are mediocre; and at least one half of them are morally at a low level.

ALFRED NORTH WHITEHEAD

When we see what people we like will do for money, it is best to be sad and say nothing.

LLOYD PEARSALL SMITH

The reflections of these three men have not been chosen lightly to precede this chapter. They were carefully selected because of their insight into human nature, particularly human nature vis-à-vis money. Also, I happen to believe wholeheartedly in the correctness of the three statements.

Matthew before he became an apostle of Christ knew a thing or two about money. He was a professional tax collector for the Romans. Christ also knew a thing or two about money. He drove the money changers out of the temple, calling it "a den of thieves" because of the priests' machinations in making a double profit from the exchange of currency. Matthew also wisely observed, "Every good tree bringeth forth good fruit; but a corrupt tree bringeth forth evil fruit."

Matthew 7:15-17, although written in a vastly different context circa 50 A.D., is vitally applicable to the contemporary stock market.

Philosopher-mathematician Whitehead spent a lifetime pursuing the evanescent discipline of logical thought. His comment about the morality and competency of those capable of earning money can therefore be considered the wisdom of a burnished, orderly mind.

I wish I could follow the advice of Lloyd Pearsall Smith, an early nineteenth-century editor-librarian, to say nothing about what people (in this case, brokers) will do for money. It is not enough, as Smith suggests, to be sad. I feel it would dishonor my own closely held convictions not to speak out, to tell it like it is, to discuss what at bottom is perhaps the most acute problem in the securities industry—the credibility gap between broker and client.

Not to speak out would also compromise my belief that the profession of broker can be, must be, vastly upgraded. And unless there is considerable metamorphosis, the broker-client credibility gap will grow ever wider and there will never be a coming together.

Most of my colleagues are sorely beset men, and they people a profession no more or less subject to malpractice than medicine and the law.

The surgeon's scalpel fails and his mistake is often buried.

The attorney's brief is shabbily prepared and his client goes to prison.

The broker who fails in a very real sense both buries and imprisons his clients, buries and imprisons their hopes and dreams, ushers them along to earlier graves because of their financial losses. As mentioned previously, I have all too often met clients who would rather lose their lives than their money. How many clients have had their lives shortened by how many years due to emotional-physical illnesses acquired as a result of needless financial beatings they have taken because of the malfeasance, gluttony and stupidity of brokers?

Wall Street ought to underwrite a study to answer that question.

Literally and figuratively, the stock market is a deadly serious business. And the broker thus bears a responsibility to a client as important, in some ways more important, than his doctor and attorney.

Few brokers I know think of their clients' welfare in such a context.

My purpose is not to perform a hatchet job on brokers. My interest is only to prevent their performing hatchet jobs on clients. And the miserable truth is that that is what happens every day the market opens, from the moment the tape begins to roll.

Unfortunately, there is no Hippocratic oath for brokers, backed by effective supervision.

Given the lack of effective supervision, the wonder is that more brokers don't get into more difficulties than they do. The double wonder is that even more clients don't go to the showers more often than they do.

That the state of the broker's art is so depressingly low is not entirely the fault of brokers themselves. They are lashed to an inherited system, a world they never made, a system that has built-in obstacles that prevent them from performing as they should.

In Matthew's terms, the majority of brokers are false prophets, but they got that way because of false inculcation.

Some brokers are plain slothful, sluggish, indolent, inert and torpid. They do not belong in the business, and eventually most of this genre are replaced, not because of their employers' morality but simply because they can't make a living even in a bull market.

A small proportion of brokers are outright thieves, although they are seldom treated as thieves. In most states, if a man steals up to $200 his misdemeanor is punishable by a year in jail and a $1,000 fine. If he steals more than $200 he has committed a felony and can spend from one to fourteen years in state prison. But a broker or a group of men running a brokerage house can cause the loss of millions through fraud and misrepresentation to thousands of investors and get off with a NYSE–SEC wristslap.

It would take considerable research to find the last broker or Wall Street partner who went to jail.

The one quality most brokers have in common is Peter Principle incompetency. Given the natural limitation of human talent, this is not surprising. Not all doctors are Christiaan Barnards or all lawyers Percy Foremans. But there is a level of relatively high competence at which most doctors and lawyers perform. This isn't true of brokers, who as a group perform at a competency level which is painfully under par.

There is also a group of brokers who *are* doing a high-level, high-achievement job, and the client lucky enough to have such a man handling his affairs is fortunate.

The standard is there, the high level of competency exists. It remains to bring most members of the profession up to that standard and that level.

The trouble with the average broker begins with the reality that he is primarily a salesman. He could as easily be selling encyclopedias as stocks, and many would be selling encyclopedias if selling encyclopedias was as lucrative in good market years as selling stocks.

Brokers, the bulk of them, are pitchmen who don't know a damn thing about their stock-in-trade, which, of course, is the stocks in which they trade.

Most brokers are nothing more than telephone switchboard operators. They could be replaced by secretaries, who just as easily could call *their* friends, urge them to buy one stock or other and take the orders.

In matters of ethics, ignorance and opportunism, I am quick to readmit that at the beginning of my career I was as bad as the worst broker in the business now. But I was alive to the shortcomings in the system, shortcomings which so distressed me that to remain a broker I had to drastically change my method of operation. Either that or go back to my shylock contact for a fresh grubstake until I could find a new way of making a living, perhaps selling encyclopedias, which is a perfectly decent way to earn a livelihood. No home should be without a set of the *Britannica, World Book* or one of their competitors. Come to think of it, the country might be far better off with more encyclopedias instead of more stocks. If one entertains the thought seriously, it is a shame that encyclopedia salesmen do not usually earn as much as brokers or have a shot at becoming millionaires.

In an attempt to upgrade the very name of broker, a gaggle of other terms have come into usage. "Broker" always seemed good enough for me, but then these days there are places where janitors are called maintenance engineers. So in various houses the pitchmen are called customers' men, account executives or registered representatives. Not infrequently they are also called, among the more printable epithets clients use, "that son-of-a-bitch broker of mine."

Whatever he is called, the broker's lot is not enviable. He is all-hero or all-SOB, seldom anything in between.

This can and does make many brokers perpetual worriers and neurotics. They must, after all, live with the blue-sky promises they have made to their clients. And that isn't easy, especially when the very stocks they have just socked clients into drop dramatically for no reason they can understand.

The broker has the added burden of living on commissions in a boom-bust industry.

He is also a man caught in a vise—pressured on the one hand by the house to sell, on the other by his clients to perform. It's a miracle that most brokers are not in mental wards.

The broker's profession is perhaps the most democratic of white-collar endeavors. No six years of med or law school are required. And virtually anyone can qualify, as proved by my own case.

Brokers come from every walk of life. And many of them previously were, like myself, less than successful at everything else they tried.

Brokers become brokers for the same major reason anybody becomes anything. The overriding consideration is to earn as much money as possible.

The virgin broker realizes soon enough that the real reason the house has given him a desk is to accomplish the goal of earning money. And the broker usually does earn money. He earns it for the house and for himself. Maybe he also earns money for the client, the client who is Wall Street's forgotten man, the last one anybody in chaos canyon thinks seriously about, no matter what that freshet of pap says in the expensively printed propaganda barrage of brochures and pamphlets that pour from the NYSE and the brokerage houses. These self-serving handouts are about as objective and honest as *Pravda*.

Some who come to the broker's profession are celebrities by

virtue of achievement in another field. Some carry a well-publicized name, which helps them cash in handsomely on their contacts. Some are mini-celebrities with a wide range of acquaintanceship in their respective fields.

Despite what other qualifications the houses claim they are seeking in a broker, above all else they look for a man with contacts.

The son of a rich man, perforce well-connected, is still assured a desk in most houses. His pipeline to old money is prized. If his pipeline happens to be to *nouveau riche* money, it is equally prized.

For those with the proper name, no other qualification is necessary. It doesn't matter whether the proper name-carrier performs brilliantly or otherwise *for the client* once he becomes a broker. He is valuable for the commissions he generates on the sale of stocks—which, too, may perform brilliantly or otherwise.

There are a few houses that do not operate this way, Merrill Lynch again the bellwether. There are firms that won't ordinarily take on a trainee broker unless he is between certain ages and holds a college degree.

But all the standards in virtually all the houses vanish like smoke when the market is good. In a bull period most firms will hire almost anybody as a broker. They figure almost anybody can sell stocks in, say, a market like 1967. And to a large extent this is true. If the market is hot and volume is up, broker employment booms. When the market turns bearish, the throat-cutting of brokers begins because the Wall Street houses, as previously indicated, do not run a stable business through good and bad times. They expand and contract like a bellows.

Since brokers are hired essentially because of their contacts, those who have a following in whatever political, economic or social circle can find a home on Wall Street. America's first astronaut, Alan Shepard, Jr., joined a brokerage firm. Barry Goldwater, Jr., before he won a Southern California Congressional seat, was a broker. Harris, Upham's Madison Avenue office in Manhattan had an ex-fashion model holding down a desk. Another New York house employed a former *Playboy* bunny as a broker. At the age of fifty-nine, after a thirty-three-year career in medicine, a retired surgeon joined one of Good-body's California branches. And Shearson, Hammill brought in an ex-brokerage house shoeshine boy to manage a planned new office in Harlem.

From astronaut to shoeshine boy—the broker's profession is very democratic. And this is as it should be. There should be opportunity for everyone. But once given the opportunity, the broker's success should be measured not by how much money he has made for the house or himself, but by how much money he has made for his clients. The way it works out, the more money he makes for clients, the more he makes for the house and himself.

This is a yardstick applied in Wall Street houses as frequently as an atheist attends church.

Wall Street manpower needs cannot be completely filled from the available pool of celebrities, mini-celebrities and rich men's sons. Thus the profession has been dangled before everyone in enticing newspaper and magazine ads.

"Could you be a stockbroker in Shearson, Hammill's new Palm Beach Springs office? Take our free aptitude test and learn whether you qualify. If your present job is no longer challenging. . . . If you see limited chance of advancement or high income and if you are interested in the stock market, consider this opportunity."

"Could you be a stockbroker with Dean Witter & Co.? Your earning potential is limited only by your ability. (Within five years, the average Dean Witter Account Executive is earning at a level which places him in the top 2 percent income bracket for all incomes.)"

"Bache wants successful men who don't believe in ceilings. WHY—did a high school graduate earning over $25,000 become a Bache Representative? WHY—did a lawyer with four degrees (B.A., M.A., LL.B., LL.M.) change careers and join Bache? WHY—did a business executive sell his own profitable business to become a Bache Representative? WHY—should *you* consider leaving your successful career to join Bache? We'll tell you WHY—Bache is a growth company, in a growth industry."

This ad ran in the Los Angeles *Times* on May 25, 1969. As catalogued in the previous chapter, Bache, a self-styled "growth

THE TROUBLE WITH BROKERS

company, in a growth industry," lost a virtually unprecedented $8.7 million in 1969 and rid itself of six hundred employees, among them possibly some of the "successful men who don't believe in ceilings" who applied and were accepted as broker trainees.

Again I must praise Merrill Lynch. As in so many other areas, in the area of training it is the best in the business. But its full-page solicitation ad for brokers in the January 31, 1969, issue of *Time* was more fascinating to me for what it omitted rather than what it included.

"Could you make the grade at Merrill Lynch?" asked the world's largest, most prosperous house. It urged would-be brokers to "ask yourself these 18 questions. If you can truthfully answer 'yes' to 15 of them, you may have what it takes to become a Merrill Lynch account executive."

The eighteen questions:

1. Is the stock market in your bloodstream? Do you read the financial pages of this newspaper the way most men devour the sports section?

2. Can you stand up under pressure that would have most ordinary mortals climbing the walls?

3. Can you help other people handle their money as carefully and conscientiously as you handle your own? If you cannot say yes to this question, you can forget the rest.

4. Are you discreet? Our clients trust us with a lot of personal information. This is no business for blabbermouths.

5. Do you do your homework? To keep on top of the market, you've got to keep on top of your reading. Our own Research Department publishes about 60,000 words every working day.

6. Do you have a well-stocked vocabulary? Fuzzy talkers make wretched brokers.

7. Do you follow up? "Loose ends" in *any* business can drive you crazy. In *our* business, they can paralyze you.

8. Do you have the guts to say, "I don't know, I'll just have to call you back when I've got the facts." We don't deal in calculated guesses. And we don't tolerate hip-shooters.

9. Do you go out of your way to help people?

10. Could you survive a tough seven-month training program? One part of it: 12 rigorous weeks in New York City,

where you'll study and be tested on everything from corporation finance to the Federal Reserve System.

11. Are you willing to make less while you're training to be a Merrill Lynch Account Executive than you are probably making right now?

12. Do you have a compelling interest in world events? The stock market reacts to the force of the news, and you must know what's happening.

13. Do you know how to get to the point? Our account executives spend about 90% of their time on the phone—and there's no room for windbagging.

14. Do you have good energy reserves? As a Merrill Lynch Account Executive, you'll be going full blast all day. When that board starts to move, your phone will start to ring. There's no time for back-slapping at the water cooler.

15. Do you have a proven record of success in a variety of activities? Quite frankly, we look for people who have a habit of winning!

16. Do you have a good, strong backbone? Our firm has a superb reputation, but occasionally the slings and arrows of outrageous fortune come our way. We don't admire jellyfish.

17. Are you looking for a job with exceptional advancement possibilities? 160 of the 174 men who run our offices were account executives. So were 224 of our officers. So was our president—Donald T. Regan.

18. Do you like the idea of working pretty much on your own? You'll have all the facilities of Merrill Lynch behind you —research, private newswire, instant quote machine—but, when you pick up that phone, you are Merrill Lynch.

All fair questions, as far as they go.

But where is Question 19, a question unasked by Merrill Lynch or any other house, although it is far and away *the* most important question by which a contemporary broker should be judged.

In ancient and medieval philosophy the term "quintessence" related to the essential constitutent matter of heavenly bodies— air, fire, water and earth.

The quintessential constituent matter for determining a

broker's potential—the air, fire, water and earth of the calling —is embodied in the fundamental question which *should* be asked of a man who wants to sell securities:

Do you have the energy, the capacity, the ambition, the grit, the drive to investigate and evaluate your own situations so you know what the hell you're talking about when you put a client into a stock?

Each time I see one of those alluring ads, questions of my own come to mind:

Why, in the first place, is it necessary for the giant houses as well as the small ones to propagandize for brokers, virtually begging rather than offering dignified opportunity for aspirants to join the profession?

Must potential brokers be forcefed into achieving success?

Why the constant need for more brokers when the industry claims they are in the top 2 percent income level?

Why are all those desks empty?

Why is there so much turnover among brokers?

Why do so many leave the Promised Land of Wall Street?

In view of the promised payoff of summit income, why must the houses seek out brokers when the seekers should be battering down the doors for the chance to be a broker, clawing and begging the houses for the opportunity to enter the kingdom of riches?

Those are fair questions, too.

And the answers lie embedded within the bowels of ailing Wall Street, whose promises of riches to clients are no more fulfilled in most cases than its promises of riches to brokers are in most cases fulfilled.

Once the interviewing and testing jazz are over and the applicant becomes a trainee, his trouble really begins. From the outset he is frozen into a system that does not really function, that is incapable of functioning under present circumstances. The trainee goes into battle without proper equipment, and when he becomes a broker and does not make it, he wonders why. Many honest, capable men who could have made it wonder what happened.

What happened was that since a workman is only as good as

his tools, the tools he was provided in training automatically barred him from performing effectively for his clients and thus for himself. Almost the only brokers who make it and make it big year after year are those who have smartened up and ignored their training. They have come to the conclusion on their own that what they were taught bears no significant relationship to what it's all about. Or they were wise enough to emulate the one or two really good brokers, the iconoclasts, who can be found in practically every house.

The houses that do a responsible job of training brokers can be counted on the fingers of Willie Mays' two strong hands, and Mays would have fingers left over. The others do a job that is as crooked as a dog's hind leg; not usually crooked by design, but by ignorance, incompetence, doing nothing more than staying within the law while violating the spirit of the law that implies a broker should be trained so that he at least is knowledgeable if not an expert once he is licensed. Unwillingness to pay for adequate training is another factor. E. F. Hutton estimates its investment on behalf of each trainee is some $15,000. Not many houses are willing to put that kind of money into the making of a broker.

E. F. Hutton is a sixty-office house that gives the trainee twenty-six weeks of education, sixteen weeks of it in New York. "The course is rigorous and extensive," says a pamphlet entitled *A Career as an Account Executive,* issued by the firm. "Lecture courses include accounting, *securities analysis* [my italics], corporate finance, margin regulations, securities business law, municipal bonds, over-the-counter market operations, public speaking, underwriting and institutional sales. A second phase of training is concentrated on client-contact techniques."

With that sort of background—especially familiarization with how to analyze a stock—a broker has a solid base from which to build.

E. F. Hutton, Merrill Lynch and a handful of others are the exceptions.

Actual formal training in most firms consists of as little as two weeks! Some houses extend this to two or three months. As was true of my "training," the rest of the six-month period is spent listlessly checking off the days until the license comes through.

In the majority of houses the training amounts to attendance at a university extension course, a correspondence course with the New York Institute of Finance and a little boning up on the mechanics of the office and how an order is processed through the exchanges.

Even the best houses do not adequately prepare the fledgling for his responsibility to the client, or convey a deep sense of the enormous trust he is carrying on his shoulders when he begins dealing with investors.

Most trainees go through their indoctrination in something of a haze. They are thoroughly bewildered. They get a vague, general, undisciplined and amorphous idea of what the market is about.

The trainees soon begin chafing at the inaction. They want to make money (the average trainee's salary is only $500–600 a month), and the way to make money is to get on that phone and sell.

But not one of them is really qualified to sell stocks to the public *after* his training is over, much less before it is over.

The violation of trust begins in many houses even before the training period is completed. Not yet a broker, the trainee is allowed to illegally sell stocks before he is formally licensed. The practice generally starts around the fourth month of training.

Broker-trainees, as much as nature, abhor a vacuum. They are thoroughly bored, feeling they are wasting time (as most assuredly are) by the whole training charade.

So the eager beavers among them, to score points with the partners, begin calling relatives, friends, old schoolmates and any other suckers they can find, and they sell them stocks.

Thus before the trainee knows anything worth knowing about the market, he is selling.

Everyone is aware that this goes on in most houses. How could the houses help but know since a record is kept of every trade by every salesman? But nobody does anything about it.

The penalty for a trainee so operating would presumably be expulsion. But I have never heard of a trainee losing his job for bringing illegal commissions into a house.

The house looks the other way because it picks up all the gravy. The trainee-broker cannot legally earn a commission on his prelicense sales, a regulation the houses ignore because it serves their interest. The houses simply, happily, take every cent of the commissions pumped in from this sort of fraudulent peddling of securities. In toto, it amounts to a big chunk of illegal income every year.

Beside impressing management as an eager beaver, the only other conceivable advantage to the trainee making such sales is that some of the stocks he sells might accidentally rise. So when he does get his license he has client fallout. But as a practical matter these sales usually end by murdering his investors, and when as a broker he is legally entitled to sell, his client list has already been severely compromised. And those points he has scored with management will prove temporary, very temporary. If he doesn't rack up enough commissions once he is a broker, out he goes.

After the training is over there are incredibly few brokers who can read and assess a company's financial statement, nor can many brokers who have spent a lifetime in the business. Yet skill in reading a financial statement is an important part of a broker's job. Without this ability how can he critically and objectively analyze a company? But that's not his function, the typical house is quick to argue. The broker is a salesman, and the always vaunted analysts in the house research department have the task of reading the financial statements and coming up with those prized recommendations that the broker then passes on to clients. The supposed brilliance of house research is another misconception, a deceit that is explored in Chapter 13.

When I hire a broker I look for, ideally, a man between twenty-eight and thirty-five. I much prefer a man coming in as a trainee who has failed at other endeavors. Failures season and mature a man. At the very least I prefer a man who has had some experience in other fields. He is generally a more rounded individual. What does not impress me at all is a man fresh from college with a bachelor's, master's or doctorate degree. Formal academic training as such means nothing in the making of a good broker. The kid out of college wants to move too fast. I'm not downgrading ambition, but the new graduate isn't ready to move very fast in terms of previous experience, know-how, practical knowledge of people or understanding of how I approach the market.

College kids are much sought after by most leading Wall Street houses. They shove them through training and give them the commandment to sell. But what are their credentials for selling? The fact that a new broker has had a few theoretical courses, learned some of the mechanics of the business and is associated with a NYSE member house is meaningless.

The training program for all brokers should, as a minimum reform, be standardized. Here's an area the NYSE could effectively step into and clean up. And the training program should, of course, be modeled after those of the best houses in the industry.

But reform must go much further. The current system that permits a trainee to sell stocks immediately after his six-month orientation is over should be completely discarded. The commission system should also be changed.

Instead of going on commission immediately, the broker should be paid a decent salary while he grows and learns. Of the some 600 important brokerages that dominate Wall Street, to my knowledge only Merrill Lynch puts its brokers on salary in the early stages of their careers.

The commission system of the houses is responsible for much of what is wrong with Wall Street, responsible for so much of its venality, responsible for so many clients taking a clouting. To get a commission, the bulk of young brokers will sell shares to their grandmothers in companies manufacturing widgets or chamber pots and companies manufacturing nothing at all.

So long perpetuated by the houses, the commission setup triggers and plays upon the necessity of newly minted brokers to earn a living. The house, by putting on this sort of pressure, loses nothing except desk space and the price of a telephone bill, which is tax-deductible anyway. The commission system feeds a new broker's inherent inclination to make as much money as possible while he is yet in a stage where he knows as much about the market as my nine-year-old daughter.

In addition to becoming a salaried man, the beginning broker should be compelled to work as an assistant to a qualified broker for at least one year, preferably two.

With proper tutelage the inexperienced broker would come to the realization that he isn't selling chopped liver, that pushing a client into some arbitrary stock is criminal. Under the supervision of a broker with a good track record for eight or ten years and earning a realistic salary, the new broker would have that maturing, growing, learning time.

These reforms in salary and apprenticeship could be made mandatory by the NYSE. It would result in a tremendous upgrading of brokers. It would raise the standards at least 100 percent in many houses. In most houses it would result in a reign of reason that would vault standards 1,000 percent.

It is part of the lore of the American Dream that a man should be allowed to get rich quick. But no broker should be allowed to get rich quick or profit at all at the expense of clients who trust him because he works for an old-line NYSE member firm. McDonnell had an old-line name and a NYSE escutcheon, but what good did that do most of its clients?

The whole system as now constituted—commission-hungry young brokers, commission-hungry brokers who've been around for years and were themselves never adequately trained or subsequently adequately self-retrained, the pressure and the need to sell, the back-office zoo, the low standards required to work in most houses, the barely-above-welfare salaries paid the majority of employees—has contributed to yet another Wall Street problem, an unprecedented crime wave, which also is a result of poor management.

Crime is no stranger to Wall Street. The Street's outrageous history of illegalities led to the creation of the SEC and paper-tough ethics of the NYSE.

The most costly, heinous but seldom-if-ever punished crimes on Wall Street are those of lack of conscience and responsibility by the houses and brokers.

Add to this the recent rise in out-and-out law-breaking, growing alarmingly year by year—thefts of securities, churning stocks, allowing clients to violate margin requirements, violation of the rules governing the sale of unregistered stock and the old shell game, still very much in vogue, in which brokers inflate the value of nearly worthless or completely worthless stocks in final-gasp or defunct corporations. Of this last practice, SEC Commissioner Hugh F. Owens declared, "In several of these cases we have found that millions of dollars have been invested by the public in corporations that have no managements, no offices, no assets and no income."

I have heard broker after broker lie or tout to clients without shame or apparent feelings of guilt and shrug it off with a wink that I was supposed to understand meant: That's how it is, this stock market racket. Everybody's got to make a living.

But Wall Street isn't a tenderloin. The stock market isn't a racket. It hardly seems necessary to point out that as one of the principal forces in our economy, an ethical, orderly, as crime-free-as-possible market atmosphere is absolutely essential to the future of this country.

Wall Street should offer stability, confidence and reasonable hope of prosperity for clients.

It does none of these things.

Too many people and institutions have invested too much treasure for any broker with or without the connivance of the house to play fast and loose with clients on grounds that a living must be earned by exaggeration or cheating.

The stock market is not for con men.

The industry isn't selling used cars or $5,000 funerals.

In one of the most vicious cases of its kind (a case adjudicated in a New York court in 1968) it was found that a broker working out of a "blue chip" house churned a widow's account to the tune of 1,200 to 1,400 transactions in 200 different common stocks and 9,000 (!) transactions involving various commodities, for a gross trading volume of $100 million!

From 1939, starting with $2,000, the woman's account was run up by 1955 to $65,000. In that sixteen-year period there were only thirty-two sell orders and forty-one purchase orders with not more than five sales in one year and in most years less than five sales or none whatever.

The churning began in 1957 and continued through 1964. By the time she instituted suit, the value of her account had dropped from $533,161 to $251,237. More than 50 percent of her funds had disappeared. She paid $91,000 in commissions on her stocks and $98,000 for commissions on commodities. She also paid the house interest of $43,000 on money advanced on margin, including a one-half percent service fee to the brokerage firm.

The judge found that the income potential of her account was "vastly impaired" and that her funds "were grossly and unfairly traded for no reason other than profit to the broker and the house." The widow was awarded a judgment of $232,000 to cover commissions and interest and $143,000 in damages. A Federal appeals court in 1970 upheld the verdict.

This broker operated his churning mill out of one of the major Wall Street houses, a house with thousands of clients, over a period of six years and ten months. In all that time, where was the internal supervision of house officials? There wasn't any. The house was content to benefit from the massive commissions. Where was NYSE supervision? Why didn't the Exchange expel this member firm after the judge's verdict? If those every-Friday daily reports, suggested earlier, were being made on all transactions within all houses, the supernatural trading would have been quickly spotted.

In May, 1970, the SEC did bring fraud charges against four brokerage firms in New York, New Jersey and Massachusetts. The firms and three of their brokers had all allegedly violated antifraud laws by issuing fictitious quotations in two stocks. The SEC said the houses "did not exercise reasonable supervision to prevent violations."

But the SEC did not say what action, if any, was taken to make restitution to clients who were flim-flammed.

I know of one case where a deal was made in a large West Coast branch of a Wall Street firm which allowed a broker to accept $1 under the table for every share he sold of a Canadian outfit whose stock was trading in the 9–10 range. This broker sold enough shares to run the price of the stock up several points before it inevitably nosedived. The broker made frequent trips to Canada where he was paid off. On top of that he was making the normal commission from selling the stock to his clients who had faith and trust in him.

Where was management to kick this broker's butt out of the house for selling a huge amount of an issue it couldn't help but know was, to put it mildly, an extremely questionable investment?

These types of Wall Street crimes are anything but new. In some variation or other such offenses have been committed since the origin of the stock market. It is unnecessary to catalogue further examples—the cases could run dictionary-thick. It is necessary to point out, however, that Wall Street could have eliminated most of these fraudulent practices long ago with proper internal security bulwarked by effective NYSE and SEC action. This isn't a bank president embezzling $1 million on Friday afternoon and not being discovered until Monday, by which time he is in South America. These are complex crimes, manipulated over long periods. A system of checkpoints to nip these violations could be set up all along the way. Swift retribution in the form of court prosecution of culprits and expulsion from the Exchange should be inflicted without a moment's hesitation. If the houses really knew they would be expelled and prosecuted for their own or brokers' lawbreaking, they'd soon enough become choir boys.

This would be a matter of course if Wall Street was truly efficient, truly had the interests of clients at heart, was truly concerned with something more than an ethic of profit at any price, was truly concerned about the constant erosion of its image in the public mind.

What *is* relatively new along Wall Street is the soaring increases in securities thefts, a not inconsiderable $50 million worth in 1969 alone.

U.S. Attorney Robert M. Morgenthau said this total was a 50 percent increase over the previous year, and that his office had leads on cases involving $20 million worth of the stolen securities. The theft of securities, Morgenthau said, "impedes the liquidity of the market and threatens the solidity of brokerage houses." Interestingly, Morgenthau pointed out that most of the thefts were committed by young people who were offered "inducement bribes and blackmail." Wall Street owes higher salaries to its employees simply on the basis of humanity and fairness. I am not excusing and hold no brief for any illegal act— whether committed by a rich house, a managing partner, a broker or a high-school boy or girl working at some clerical job on the Street. But it's worthy of discussion and arguable that if Wall Street raised its disgracefully low wage scales perhaps fewer young people would be tempted. This thought is enforced by a comment on the securities-theft increase made by Will Wilson, New York Assistant Attorney General. "The heart of the problem is in letting employees get in the hands of [Mafia] loan sharks."

I went to a loan shark myself in time of need, albeit not Mafia-connected. By good luck, fear or whatever, I never came to the point where I had to steal to pay back my loan. But what basically honest man with his back against a financial wall can predict whether he will act irrationally and do something foolish to get his hands on some money for himself or his family? No matter what they are paid, there will always be a certain number of lawbreakers (Wall Street partners and brokers among them), but at least some of the people who labor in the Street sweatshops might not get involved with loan sharks if they were taking home a realistic paycheck.

The Street should reassess its pay scales both on the basis of equity and self-interest.

Wilson also said that reduction of thefts could be accomplished by keeping physical handling of securities to a minimum.

Yet again Wall Street is paying the price of third-rate management. It hired breathing bodies without checking their backgrounds, which only resulted in the Scylla and Charybdis of a paper pileup and a greater theft of the paper.

A study by New York Attorney General Louis J. Lefkowitz disclosed that 1½ percent of those employed in the securities industry had an arrest record. Lefkowitz said that compared to a

4 percent average arrest record found in other industries. Instead of quaking with alarm, working out reforms and new security precautions, the New York and American exchanges stupidly responded in a joint statement by saying that they were "gratified by the unusually low percentage."

I submit 1½ percent is too high a ratio in a business handling billions of dollars of accessible and negotiable securities.

Lefkowitz based his figures on a study he made of the fingerprint records of all Wall Street employees, partners to messenger boys. Fingerprinting was made compulsory in September, 1969. The fingerprint study uncovered the fact that 361 Wall Street workers had criminal records. Fourteen of them were principal officers of big houses. The fingerprint check also resulted in fifty-four resignations or dismissals.

But there are many others on Wall Street in every echelon who have committed or are contemplating larceny. And you can take the word of FBI Director J. Edgar Hoover for that. Hoover, in a March 1970, interview in *Nation's Business,* said his agency had under investigation thirty-one cases involving $30 million worth of stolen securities.

"These are just the cases which have come to our attention in one manner or another," he said. "There is no way to be certain that all such thefts have been detected."

Hoover confirmed that Mafia hoods were involved in some of the cases and that financial centers in New York, Boston and Los Angeles had all been victimized.

Continued the FBI chief:

"There seems to be little doubt that this problem has been aggravated by basic weaknesses in our financial community. In most cases, corruption of employees is a necessary element. These stocks and bonds are not simply left lying about. The question the industry must answer is whether its security measures are adequate. . . .

"When a customer buys or sells securities, he has the right to expect his transaction to be handled quickly and his purchase to be delivered in a reasonable time.

"As you know, banks dealing in cash transactions require

their tellers to 'prove out' at the end of each day, and an accounting procedure of this type would certainly go a long way
in preventing large-scale thefts in the brokerage houses.

". . . More frequent outside audits on a staggered basis,
whether complete or of a spot-check type, would be [another]
preventative step.

". . . This is a relatively new situation aggravated partly by
the fact that our financial industry has never really had to cope
with these thefts before and was not geared to protect itself. I
think one of the most effective deterrents is education, both of
the personnel in the brokerage houses and in our banking industry. Once these institutions become fully aware that criminal enterprise is capable of taking from them millions of dollars,
I am sure they will take positive steps to invoke protective procedures."

TWELVE

MORE TROUBLE WITH BROKERS

Whatever can go wrong, will go wrong.

MURPHY'S LAW

"If you know so much, why aren't *you* rich?"

That's a zinger a client, being asked to risk his money, might rightfully ask the broker asking him to risk it. Sitting across the desk from an investor or huckstering him frantically over the phone, the broker obviously isn't spending the season in Cannes or at a Princess Grace party. He isn't in deep consultation with Aristotle Onassis or any other Belshazzar-rich potentate.

He's functioning as a salesman. As playwright Arthur Miller said of Willie Loman, "He's a man way out there in the blue riding on a smile and a shoeshine."

But by implication or declaration, the broker palms himself off to clients as all-wise, all-knowing. To be sure, he may hedge a bit, leaving himself an out in case the stocks he ramrods clients into don't perform, which they often don't.

The client with money to invest in the market has accumulated his funds as a professional or skilled practitioner at whatever it is he does. He is an expert at his own thing. He naturally expects his broker to be an expert at his thing. And since Wall Street is a popular synonym for money, the client often takes it for granted that the man who is selling him stocks is not only chockablock with expertise, but wealthy.

However, his broker is seldom either expert or wealthy.

Yet the broker must appear as an expert to the client, else he couldn't sell him. And so he comes to the investor as a Caesar of common stocks. Only the laurel wreath is missing. He comes to the client as a man who can read the hieroglyphics of high finance; the unraveler of the megalithic Stonehenge-like mysteries of the market; code-breaker of Wall Street's charts and graphs, fundamentals, averages, blue chips and all the rest of the jargon.

175

The broker speaks with confidence and assurance. He gives financial bone and body to the stuff of which dreams are made. He is offering the pot of gold at the end of the rainbow.

And why shouldn't he?

Here's the broker sitting in the light at the end of a long tunnel. In the client's mind he is the superbly bred, brilliantly trained end-product of Wall Street. Behind him is the mighty apparatus of a vast, expensively maintained house forever beating its own drum about its orchestra of services to investors. Strange then that the drumbeat so often ends in a cadenced death march for clients.

It is perfectly and eminently sensible for the investor to assume that his broker is rich. The client, of course, is too polite or timid to ask his broker directly for an account of his assets. That simply isn't done. But the broker, after all, is on the inside. He is among the first to hear of new developments within a company. He knows everybody. Everybody knows him. He understands Wall Street, and when he recommends a stock he presumably knows what he's talking about.

Thus many clients assume that in his privileged position the broker is making killing after killing through his own investments in the market. If only I were a broker, clients sigh, and privy to all that sure-fire, can't-miss research and inside information, had all those contacts, I'd have my mortgage money in the market. The broker is in the catbird seat, and if only he would put me into the same stocks he's in, I'd be rich, too. Right?

Wrong.

Less than one percent of the nation's brokers are millionaires. And of this percentage, most have made their money primarily as salesmen, not as investors. For most big brokers, the money is in commissions from big clients and institutions. Why should they worry about risking their own money in stocks they're selling to clients?

Some of these millionaire brokers, operating like the owners of Las Vegas casinos, do go into the market, but only when the dice are loaded—when they have what is tantamount to illegal insider information. This species of broker, like a canny casino owner, knows gamblers always die broke. For the casino owner and such brokers the money is in a fixed game and the percentage that naturally accrues to the house.

But there is a slim percentage of brokers with discretionary income—I'm one of them—who will take the same risks they offer clients. In my own case, I buy into every situation in which I place my clients.

The smell of money is overpowering on Wall Street, and most brokers despite their lack of knowledge would be the first to trade in the market, if they had the money to buy stocks.

"The man who watches the ticker tape and sells you stocks and bonds, is, at an early stage of his business life, getting $10,-000 a year," said writer Leonard Sloane in a 1960 *Cosmopolitan* article that gave a rundown of what men in various professions were earning a decade ago. "But as the broker's clientele grows older and more prosperous, his income grows with them, and earnings of $50,000 to $60,000 are not rare."

Clients do grow older, but the supposition that they inevitably grow "more prosperous" is wishful thinking. By 1960 or present-day standards, I consider commissions of $50,000 to $60,000 a small income for a broker. If he really knew the business, he would be doing much better.

E. F. Hutton said in 1966 that the average income of all its account executives was $18,300, and that 25 percent of its brokers earned more than $20,000 a year.

Any broker who doesn't earn at least $100,000 a year is telling me that he is not performing at full potential. Any broker who earns only up to $20,000 a year is performing substandardly for his clients and himself, even though that amount of commission edges him into the topmost income level in America.

Many on Wall Street consider the turning point an income of $150,000—they mark this man as a successful broker.

In my estimation, a broker hasn't truly become successful until he hits the $200,000 to $300,000 range.

The top-flight broker is doing at least half a million in commissions a year.

What's the difference between the $60,000-a-year broker and

the $500,000-plus broker? Hard work, ethical salesmanship and performance for all his clients, large and small.

The broker operating out of most large houses is almost always limited in income because the house ordinarily discourages him from investigating his own situations. He must rely on research to supply him with recommendations, and these recommendations are generally ghastly. So the broker loses client after client. He must continually scrounge for new ones instead of having satisfied clients who give him repeat business. The clients of a good, successful, top-performing broker soon enough bring in relatives and friends to open accounts. The rest of his clients are quickly gathered by word of mouth.

Since the handicapped broker can't perform with the tools handed him by research, his foundation in the business is precarious, and whatever his average level of income through the years, it is always in jeopardy. Each year he has to scrounge a little harder to earn what he earned the previous year. This understandably makes most brokers quite insecure. The system of brokers who are only salesmen operating only with the aid of a know-nothing research department compounds the problems of the securities industry. The broker worries and suffers. The house is unhappy when profits fall off. But in the end it is the client who usually reaps more disaster than anybody else.

There are brokers who will read these lines and want to lynch me. They will aver that I'm a phony who hit it lucky in bull markets when everybody made money and I copped out in the 1969–1970 bear market by sitting tight for the most part, although sitting tight was the only possible action a responsible broker could take in behalf of his clients in such a cloudy atmosphere. Many other realistic brokers and managers of some of the biggest institutions also sat it out. Mutual funds, insurance firms and pension trusts, which account for almost two-thirds of all Wall Street's trading volume, "are known to be holding a large percentage of their assets in cash waiting for a strategic moment to move in and buy," said a *Life* magazine survey of the market on June 5, 1970.

"One thing I've learned, you can't play every hand. The poker player who plays every hand gets killed," declared broker Meyer Berman of Scheinman, Hochstin & Trotta in *Newsweek* on June 8, 1970. Berman had performed very effectively in the reigning bear market for his clients by selling short. The magazine's financial analyst, Clem Morgello, added: "Strand & Co., which has also done well during the bear market, agrees that you can't play them all. Strand runs four private funds worth a total of about $40 million. A year ago, it decided that it didn't like the looks of the market and that a 'retreat to cash' was the best way to preserve its capital."

There are brokers who will say they too have visited companies and talked with management—but it has done them no good. These men have come away empty-handed because they haven't acquired the necessary skills to ask the right questions and the more rarefied skill of evaluating a given body of information in concert with all the variables of the market. But it isn't all that difficult—any broker or investor who has enough passion and intelligence can do what I've done. I'm no genius, I won't make the history books for discovering anything comparable to $E=mc^2$, although I have found an equation that works extremely well in the market.

What success I've had wasn't achieved because my hair is brown or because I had a run of good luck. No one can luck out year after year in situation after situation. The only reason for my success is that my approach works, and it works better than any other method around. It isn't necessary for me to be my own advocate. The best test of a broker's success or failure is to ask his clients how much money they have earned or lost.

I must, however, play advocate for another moment in discussing the story that appeared about me in the *Times*.

The reaction to it was massive, and two distinct camps formed.

Virtually no one in the business thought it was complimentary to me or to the profession. I was called every name under the sun. Some brokers didn't even believe the article was truthful. And then there were those among my colleagues who reacted to the story as a personal affront. Perhaps they thought they would lose their clients to me; perhaps they thought I was an apostate. I don't really know what they thought, and I don't really care.

The public, however, had a distinctly different point of view. Uncounted letters and phone calls came in, unanimous in praise. There wasn't a single detractor, a single hate letter. Instead, people in their letters and calls poured out horror stories of their own experiences with brokers, and one woman, several months after the story appeared, turned up at my office, the crumpled article and $1,200 in hand. She asked me if I would handle her account, which I was delighted to do.

Almost certainly the same dichotomous reaction will result from this book, which has not been written to trumpet my own achievements or brag about my net worth. But the considerable time involved in preparing these pages is my attempt to repay the industry (read: clients) for its generosity to me.

It is to show the individual that he has no obligation to pour his money into a Wall Street establishment that disdains him, into a stock market snakepit.

It is to show that there are brokers who will move heaven and earth to protect a client's money, try to make him richer, guaranteeing nothing except that the odds are overwhelmingly on the client's side when he works with a broker who doesn't give a damn about the old rules, the old thinking of the establishment and the old methods.

This is a book for the man who should be the king of Wall Street—the client.

But the client, large and small, has become the peasant of the Street. He sits below the salt, occasionally fed a crumb or two, while most brokers stand in line to kiss the rear ends of the institutional moneymen.

It is certainly not the meek who have inherited the bloody ground of Wall Street. It is the mighty. But if the client en masse ever begins to awaken to what is being done to him, all the mighty are due for Samson haircuts.

This is also a far-from-perfect peek at the inside of a decidedly far-from-perfect industry, which should be investigated to death by Congress, then hopefully to rise rejuvenated and with honor.

So I simply don't give a damn about any name any member of Wall Street's private club cares to throw my way.

It is past time that the real hogs had a look at the slaughterhouse. Millions of investors have been gutted to bone and gristle for too long and too often.

The partners and princes of Wall Street deserve the clobbering they have taken and the clobberings they are going to take in the future. A deserved plague on most of their houses.

Even a thundering bull market won't cure the cancers of chaos canyon. The houses, once the pickings are ripe again, are destined to repeat all their mistakes.

In a bear market, business is bad for everybody. During the longest downswing since the 1930s, in excess of $335 billion worth of values was wiped away in the 1969–1970 decline, Wall Street suffered an overall drop of 33 percent in commission income. This was hardly surprising with so few buyers around.

But what should have surprised and shocked anyone in or out of the market was the little-realized fact that these alleged epicenters of knowledge took a huge beating in their own portfolios.

No one toted the complete dollar loss, but considering the tremendous positions many houses take in stocks for their own accounts, the beating was unquestionably stratospheric. Millions piled on millions went down the drain.

Losing money fist over hand in the market meant further deterioration of the cash position of brokerages. Profits from their own investment portfolios customarily are applied for working capital.

Here is yet another gargantuan illustration that the last thing Wall Street knows anything about is the very stocks it sells. And while it was urging clients to buy, buy, buy instead of advising them to hold back, the portfolios of the houses were being murdered.

All the insiders, when the blue chips were down, knew nothing.

All the hustling, high-flying brokers knew nothing.

All the ivory-tower research men knew nothing.

Wall Street couldn't win at its own game, not even playing

with its own dice. Yet the houses kept rapping out ceaseless buy recommendations to clients.

How in good conscience could they do it?

Because there are few who have good consciences on Wall Street. Besides, the show—in good or bad markets—must go on, and for the show to go on the entire system must try to keep rolling, which means clients must continue to be pitched to by commission-hungry brokers, brokers who are commission hungry in good markets and desperate for commissions in bad markets.

Contrary to popular belief, most individual brokers don't have a great deal of money invested in the market themselves. Like almost everybody else, brokers spend just about everything they make. In fact, most brokers spend more than they make. With the exception of those born wealthy or those who've been extremely successful, I don't know a single broker who has any money to speak of in the market, and that's the case whether the market is bullish or bearish.

As a group, brokers are very status conscious. Although they live on commissions in a twisting, turning industry with tremendous insecurities, they buy a bigger house before they're ready, they buy a bigger car before they're ready, they buy every big-ticket item in the merchandising marketplace before they're ready. They speculate on their own future income as carelessly as they gun clients into speculations. Most brokers are veritable compulsive gamblers, seldom deterred at playing Russian roulette with their own futures, much less the futures of their clients.

Brokers live in a self-created climate of never-a-rainy-day.

And so it came as no shock to me, as it must have to most readers, when the Los Angeles *Times* on May 23, 1970, apprised its readers of what seemed to be an unbelievable story— a thirty-seven–year–old manager of a local office of a Wall Street house who had averaged *$100,000* in salary and commissions for the previous three years *was collecting $65 a week in unemployment insurance!*

Reporter Robert E. Dallos peppered his story with the dismal facts. "Thousands of other stock brokers . . . are victims of a stock market that has been sliding for many months. . . . The market has been so bad, in fact, that the little investor isn't doing much trading. . . . As a result, customer's men, who depend exclusively on commissions on the trading they generate, aren't able to earn enough to eat. Large numbers are drawing against future commissions."

Thirty brokers in one large house in New York had average monthly take-home paychecks of $347. That was said to be high. The majority were averaging between $200 and $300.

"Even those brokers who are holding on have drastically changed their standard of high living," commented Dallos, relating the details of a broker who not long before had purchased a luxurious three-story townhouse and whose income had dwindled considerably. "All of a sudden," the broker said, "my standard of living reached the poverty level."

Bache vice-president Stanley A. Rasch, who is in charge of personnel and training for that big house, said manpower turnover among brokers had doubled.

Twenty percent of all the brokers in the nation had left the business.

Few will ever brave Wall Street again, nor should they. If they had been more than salesmen, there would have been no need to leave the business.

Brokers turned up in the most unlikely occupations. One was driving a New York taxicab. A moonlighting Boston broker was playing guitar in a cabaret. Five in northern California turned farmers. Several were pumping gas.

In Washington, D.C., there was a run on the Australian embassy. A spokesman for the embassy diplomatically refused to give figures, but acknowledged that a sizable number of brokers were joining the emigration of Americans to Australia.

The depression in brokers' employment wasn't entirely the fault of the brokers.

It was Wall Street's harvest-worker psychology in full bloom. Had these men been on a salary-commission-bonus formula (the salary should be at minimum $1,000 to $1,500 a month), a broker could ride out a bear market with enough money to afford him some dignity.

With that arrangement there wouldn't have been brokers driving hacks, pumping gas, fleeing to Australia.

The broker who swears allegiance to a Wall Street house in time of boom will usually discover he is worshipping at a fickle shrine as soon as the boom turns to bust.

A salary floor, fortified by additional income from commissions and bonuses in good years, would do much to relieve so much of the tension and turnover within the houses.

"The stockbroker has a private culture," said David North, who is in charge of a recruiting firm for high-priced executives. "He was making so much money in the trading heyday, he wasn't living in reality. His image of himself is so distorted, it's even difficult to advise him about employment. Finally the salary astronaut is coming in for a landing."

One broker who had seen his commission income of $175,000 in 1969 tail off to only $7,000 in the first quarter of 1970, wanted a job as a company president. Minimum salary requirement: $100,000 a year. When reality did set in, the former broker was willing to settle for $25,000. There was no indication he was employable at even that salary.

I've been through too many rough days of my own to enjoy the searing spectacle of other brokers taking it on the chin.

Aside from the dreadful way they are treated by the houses and all the obstacles put in their path, these brokers couldn't make it because they never learned the first law of the stock market jungle—survival.

And survival means not only conserving personal capital against a rainy day, but serving clients well when all is sunshine and tranquility.

Sure, it's rough on the man who went from $175,000 down to $7,000. But what about his clients? How much had they suffered? How much wallpaper were they holding?

Two brokers who left the business made the most cogent comments of all. These were two honest men who never had a chance in the Wall Street whirl. Said a broker from Arizona: "If you're concerned about your customers but still have six kids to feed as I do, there erupts a deep-seated conflict. It became difficult to convince myself and to convince my customers. How could I satisfy myself and how could I satisfy my customers? There was a moral conflict."

Of his new occupation, he said, "It's not difficult to sell IBM machines. You know you are selling a good product." Of his old occupation, he said, "Not so with stocks."

And a former New Jersey broker, selling steel after thirteen months in the business, declared, "We were all heroes in the bull market. But I found out one thing from my experience. No stockbroker—be he a greenhorn like myself or the president of the firm—knows what he's talking about."

The deepest tragedy of all is that a large number of the 20 percent of brokers forced out by the bear market could have made it if they'd had a salary and if they had been correctly trained and allowed to function the way they should function, as a combination broker-researcher.

Without such a revolution on Wall Street, no broker is safe. Neither is any client.

Which brings us to the point where we may now evaluate the evaluators, the analyst-aristocrat, Wall Street's new fair-haired boys—the chosen few who, like Moses, have been selected to lead clients through the wilderness of the stock market.

THIRTEEN

THE TROUBLE WITH ANALYSTS

> *research n. 1. diligent and systematic inquiry or investigation into a subject in order to discover or revise facts, theories, applications . . .—v.t. 4. to make an extensive investigation into:* to research a matter thoroughly . . . *—Syn. 1. scrutiny, study. See investigation. 4. study, inquire, examine, scrutinize.*

> *THE RANDOM HOUSE DICTIONARY OF THE ENGLISH LANGUAGE*

> *I have no mystic faith in the people. I have in the individual. He seems to me a divine achievement and I mistrust any view which belittles him.*

> *E. M. FORSTER*

> *I tell our clients to talk to each analyst out there like he was a beautiful, buxom girl he was trying to seduce.*

> *ROBERT MCLAREN*

"Few investors ever have direct contact with the man most responsible for the advice they base their investment decisions upon, the financial analyst," said a recent story in *California Business*. "Despite their involvement in the movement of billions of dollars yearly, these researchers remain rather mysterious figures."

The organizational setup inside the brokerage houses is cock-eyed. The brokers who actually sell stock to clients do not, except in very rare instances, do their own research. The broker is relegated to the status of a parrot—and what he parrots comes out of the research cage.

The new gods of the securities industry, a trend that accelerated in the 1960s, are the research analysts, the analysts seeking the new gods among the more than 825,000 American com-

panies that issue stocks, bonds and other investment paper, not
to mention the thousands of new corporations formed each year
and the virtually limitless number of foreign companies, some
of which are becoming increasingly alluring as investments
for U.S. shareholders.

From this incredible reservoir of choice, the analyst is called
upon to pick the winners, to select stocks that will swim rather
than sink. He is even expected to pick stocks that will swim
against the tide in a bear market.

And so the analyst has the most formidable of responsibilities.

He is Wall Street's bread and butter, the prophet who shells
the broker with ammunition. Without research, God only knows
what most brokers would sell clients.

The analyst is the most important man in the Wall Street
pyramid. Everything depends on his performance. No longer
does Wall Street fly by the seat of its pants regarding stock
recommendations to customers, or so the impression is given to
the public.

The analyst is Wall Street's new king, wizard, panacea, be-
nevolent dictator, seer. He is presented to the public as the man
who will solve all the problems of clients, lead them to the happy
hunting ground of profit.

One good analyst can make the reputation of a house.

A bad one can destroy the credibility of a house (although
usually only temporarily, since most investors have short
memories).

An analyst writes reports—sometimes long, seemingly endless reports—on companies. Sometimes he writes only a page
or so, or a paragraph or a single sentence.

Whether long reports or a brief machine-gun clatter of words,
what he writes can echo around the world with the ultimate result that thousands of investors either go down the tube or earn
money. It is the analyst's hand that is on the doomsday button.
On his say-so those billions of dollars are committed to the
market.

Who then are these "rather mysterious figures"?

In the first place, there's nothing mysterious about them.
They are anonymous, not mysterious, because the client under

the outdated procedures of the houses must normally deal with the broker rather than the analyst.

According to a questionnaire survey conducted by Don Howard Personnel, Inc., analysts as a group are well-educated. Some 93.5 percent hold a college degree; 51.2 percent have a master's, another 5 percent a doctorate. The degrees generally are in business and economics.

Education, however, is not by itself a passport to performance.

The survey also revealed that the average salary of a junior analyst twenty-five years of age or under is $10,670. As he moves into the senior-analyst category, his compensation is bucked another $7,000 in the twenty-five to twenty-nine age bracket. An increase of $15,000 is added when he reaches the thirty to thirty-four age span.

These conclusions also were drawn: The average analyst at forty-one earned $27,500. He had held his job with his house for 8.1 years, "a highly stable employment pattern," said Carl Michaels, a vice-president of the firm that conducted the study.

Michaels also called the average analyst's pay hikes "startling" and attributed them to "the general expansion of services in recent years, producing a great demand for analysts."

The first fallacy concerning analysts is the seemingly large amount of money they earn. A top salary of $32,210 is peanuts for a man on whom so much depends.

A first-rate analyst with a reputation for picking winners could increase his income at least ten-fold if he was a broker. If he's that good, what sense does it make for him to hand his reports to some broker sitting at a desk who will read his stuff to a client over the phone? Why should a broker profit from the analyst's brainwork and talent?

A good analyst should be a two-faceted man—both researcher and broker.

But few function in such a dual capacity. Not only are they prevented from doing so by the rigor-mortis rules in the majority of houses, but they opt for that "highly stable employment pattern."

In short, they prefer security. And they prefer it because as a group their performance has been abysmal.

Many of the top-drawer analysts have been kidnapped for a ransom of much higher salaries by the harried, confused mutual fund managers. These institutions tend to plunk out more for a good man than will the average retail house. This refusal of most houses to remain competitive in salaries with the institutions works against the best interests of the individual clients whose welfare is supposedly the Magna Carta of Wall Street. (Incidentally, in that survey, 72 percent of the analysts responding admitted they had reservations about the advice available to small investors as opposed to that given large investors.)

No matter how handsomely he believes he is being paid, the gifted analyst can earn far more by giving his recommendations directly to clients as a broker.

Suggest this to most analysts and they will freeze in bewilderment. Many would turn catatonic.

The profession of analyst is considered more an art than a science. It *is* an art to a large degree, although there could be a great many more scientific yardsticks applied in assessing a company than is customary. Because making a judgment about a company is supposedly an inexact discipline, and one which the bulk of analysts haven't conquered, the average analyst settles for his paycheck.

As with brokers, you can shake most analysts upside down and find they haven't got a dime in the market themselves. Few will bet a plugged nickel on their own horses.

Their record, and they know it, justifies their reluctance and hesitation to risk any money on their own recommendations. But, of course, clients are urged to bet *their* bankrolls on stocks the analysts won't touch.

There are those bright, fleet-footed, fleet-minded, gifted, unmitigatedly brilliant men who have been right most of the time. They picked Xerox, Polaroid and dozens of other successful situations at the right moment, and the clients who followed their advice did very well.

But most analysts bring about as much flair, drive, imagina-

tion and curiosity to their jobs as the average Federal bureau-
crat. What the bulk of analysts pump out amounts for the most
part to routine, dull, "safe" investment advice. Normally this
"research" isn't going to hurt clients badly, but neither is it going to earn them a great deal of money.

Almost every house, large or small, now has a research department, and do they ever let the investing public know it—
know it in terms that imply that if a client steps through the
doors of that house he is going to be handed a report on a company that can't help but make him money, a report so valuable
it should be chiseled in stone.

Declares the world's largest brokerage: "Merrill Lynch has
the biggest Research Department of any brokerage firm—a staff
of 300, including specialists and analysts covering all major industries. You get our factual reports and buy–sell suggestions
on every stock on the New York Stock Exchange, plus thousands of others. Free."

I cannot fathom—nor should the investor be asked to believe
—how 300 men can assess "every stock on the New York Stock
Exchange, plus thousands of others."

Considering the travel, the legwork, the conferences, the time
that must be spent with the management of each company, the
time that must be spent discarding acres of situations that seem
promising at first blush and then fail to bloom under investigation, considering all the other factors involved, how can 300
men or 3,000 give a sound judgment on every situation around?

It's clearly impossible.

The good analyst works like a good private investigator. He
patiently and doggedly amasses his evidence. He can work on
very few situations simultaneously. But the few, if properly researched and evaluated, can make clients beam with pleasure
as they watch these situations appreciate.

Quantity is not a substitute for quality in the field of research-
analysis.

Although virtually every house has its research department,
many of the smaller firms cut corners. They hire a recent college graduate and confer on him the knighthood of junior

analyst. Like a beginning broker, the beginning analyst should serve a long apprenticeship under a seasoned man. But it is unusual to find a good, seasoned analyst working in a small house. If he were any good, he wouldn't be there. Good or bad, however, a man with experience commands more money. So the house saves a little money and gives the totally unqualified youngster the job. Soon he's handing down recommendations to brokers who in turn convince clients to invest hundreds of thousands of dollars, sometimes millions. And all this movement of cash flows from the advice of a kid who isn't earning $10,000 a year and who in any case has no research experience beyond locating a phone number in the yellow pages.

This kind of hit-and-run driving is fatal for clients of such houses.

In that Don Howard survey, the responding analysts were about evenly divided on the question of whether some form of registration should be required for members of their profession —46 percent favored such a move, 42 percent opposed it (the opposition clinging to the argument that analysis is art rather than science, which makes it difficult to outline specifications).

A great number of researchers come to their calling with noble motives. They elect to prepare themselves by the standards of the Institute of Chartered Financial Analysts, which demands a great deal of special preparation before the last of three qualifying examinations can be taken. A minimum of five years of experience is required before an analyst can be chartered. (Thirty-five percent of those participating in the survey were so chartered.)

The five years of experience, the qualifying examinations and being chartered should be rock-bottom standards for the profession. It would at least avoid babes in the woods rifling out a lot of junk advice to trusting investors. It would upgrade the profession as a whole and save the public millions.

It would also help if every member firm of the NYSE (and those who aren't) demanded the same minimum preparation before permitting any analyst to write a report on his own.

Until that unlikely utopia is reached, most investors have the same chance of scoring a touchdown as a one-legged football player. Assaulted by bad research, investors are in the position of heart patients getting faulty cardiograms.

Among analysts, the Street needs more Beethovens. Slickness, superficiality, catering to the lowest common denominator of public taste, the ingrained prejudices, faulty predispositions and lack of sophistication of most investors is no substitute for hard, thorough work by an analyst who at least tries to touch all eighty-eight keys of a corporate piano before writing his report.

Wall Street has sold the public *God Bless America*. The Street has given the impression that it's downright unpatriotic for an American not to invest in the free-enterprise system by buying stocks. All this has been a smokescreen for bleeding investors white.

The analyst, to do his job the way it should be done, must at least make an assault at excellence. He should seek to create a symphony of profit for clients instead of a quickly forgotten hit-parade tune.

What passes for research in most houses is shocking. I've seen house after house (and mutual fund after mutual fund) where the analyst in charge had no real approach to research whatever. In one house, the chief analyst's main qualification was that he was the son-in-law of a senior partner.

Most research men—and this is the fundamental weakness of most of them—stay nailed to their desks. Instead of being peripatetic, getting out in the field and asking the questions that should be asked and making the necessary judgments, they are paraplegics. The only difference is that they sit in swivel chairs rather than wheelchairs. The analyst who isn't moving around, learning and growing and constantly sharpening his skills, isn't worth the price of his swivel chair.

An analyst is going to come up empty if the only well he goes to is the brackish water of financial publications, stockholders' meetings, corporate press conferences and those long, martini-drenched, second-grade roast beef luncheons where some self-serving company officer tries (often very successfully) to con a few hundred analysts into believing his firm is doing just great. Everybody comes away with the same routine information, and thus everybody comes away with nothing that is going to do much, if anything, for the client.

Analysts who are lazy, who completely misjudge a situation or who have the wool pulled over their eyes by management, can do and have done enormous damage to clients countless times.

Into the vast pond of the system as it now operates goes the analyst's unpolished pebble of a research report. In a big house a couple of hundred brokers take his report as gospel, and thousands of clients are sucked in. Millions on the line. Big commission income for the house and brokers. That regular paycheck for the analyst.

And where does all of it leave all the clients? Bombed out, that's where.

The clients are Wall Street's cannon fodder. The Street's generals count on an unending stream of expendable infantrymen. They've sold shirtsleeve capitalism successfully and watched gleefully as the statistics come in showing ever more people getting into the market, particularly when the averages are running high.

This house-analyst-broker pyramid is a game of take the money and run. And no one on Wall Street even bothers to hold a memorial service for the clients who've been sacrificed.

The majority of houses, the best as well as the worst, even cop out on their own research. Consider the man who walks into Merrill Lynch after reading one of its reports on a particular situation. He likes what he's read, and he's hot to buy.

Does this house stand behind its own research without qualification?

No.

Does it argue the case for its recommendation without timidity, with passionate conviction that comes from knowing a situation intimately?

No.

Will it, in the final analysis, sell a client any stock he wants if he chooses to make a last-minute switch into an issue that could be a dog?

Yes.

The evidence is contained in Merrill Lynch's own market philosophy, in one of its slick-paper pamphlets, "What Everybody Ought to Know About This Stock and Bond Business. Some Plain Talk About a Simple Business That Often Sounds Complicated."

"When you invest, you can tell your broker just as little or as much as you want to about your money problems, but whatever you tell him will be held in strict confidence. And the more you tell him, the better he will be able to help you.

"Frankly, we hope you will want to tell us enough so that we can help you work out an investment program that will best fit your needs.

"Does that mean that we will tell you how to invest your money? This is a point we want to make absolutely clear, for it involves a fundamental Merrill Lynch principle. Certainly, we'll try to help you if you want us to—if you *ask* us what we would do in your situation. But we have instructed our representatives not to impose opinions or recommendations on any customer. What you buy or sell is your own business. We don't want to be accused of trying to make up your mind for you."

But a good broker should do precisely that—he *should* make up the mind of his client, not by sledgehammering him into a stock but by convincing him with detailed knowledge that he knows precisely what he is talking about, that he knows the situation he is recommending like Thoreau knew Walden Pond.

Not trying to make up the mind of an investor is indeed a cop-out, practiced not only by Merrill Lynch but by virtually every broker in every house on the Street.

"Merrill Lynch spends millions of dollars a year in preparing and distributing to investors factual information about securities," the pamphlet continues.

What good does it do to spend those millions and then leave the choice to the investor? Again—I'm not talking about browbeating an investor into a stock. There are all too many clients who absolutely insist on buying into a company, even if you can prove to them it's a terrible situation and that they are destined to lose their money.

But those millions spent on gathering research should count

for something at the moment of decision. A broker shouldn't abdicate and lose his enthusiasm for a well-researched situation that the analyst has assured him is going to make money.

The average investor, by temperament and emotion, lack of time, ignorance and other failings usually isn't qualified to make up his own mind.

A doctor can't be expected to know the situation at GM at any given moment.

A lawyer probably has not been spending his days watching every jiggle and joggle of IBM.

A waiter who's been saving his tips and brings $1,000 or so to one of the houses that will deign to take his order generally hasn't any idea where his hard-earned money should go.

If it comes down to the investor finally making his own decision, Wall Street might as well fire all its analysts and save those millions spent on gathering research.

If a house won't stand firmly behind its own recommendations, it has cancelled out the money it has spent to acquire information, it has negated its responsibility to the client, it has admitted it hasn't the courage of its convictions, it has acknowledged a lack of expertise in the very area where it claims expertise.

In my own case, I do not put clients into a situation I know is bad. I don't want the responsibility of aiding and abetting a client to lose his money going in. When I run into this kind of client, who thinks he knows more than I do, I ask him to take his business elsewhere.

But since all my recommendations are researched as well as I can research them, I very seldom have this difficulty. I go down the line 100 percent on any situation I recommend.

Most analysts live in a safe, protected world. Since they do not come into direct contact with the public, they don't get those frightened, confused, angry or cursing phone calls that inevitably come to the broker when a stock doesn't perform as promised.

Thus few analysts develop a genuine sense of responsibility to the client. If everything the analyst recommends performs poorly, he may get some flak from the partners or the few brokers in a house who are unafraid to make waves. But the analyst has a built-in cop-out, too. He can recommend, but only God can guarantee.

What perhaps angers me more than anything else about those analysts who perform rottenly is their hauteur when it comes to recommending a stock priced under 5. If it's selling that low, they reason, it can't be any good. They won't even take the time to investigate the situation.

On any day of the week, I can tick off dozens of companies selling at 40 or above that are worthless and are going to collapse. I can also tick off situations at 2, 3 and 4 which in due course will perform brilliantly. At McDonnell it was policy for a time not to pay a broker a commission on any stock he sold under 5, even if the client bought $100,000 worth. Figure that one out.

It's easy enough for an analyst in the reports he writes to nitpick his way through one giant corporation or another or a well-established company—though these issues in a bull market won't perform in spectacular fashion, and in a bear climate will be zonked like everything else.

The big money for the client ordinarily isn't in the established corporate colossi. The big money is in uncovering small, unknown companies run by brilliant men, and having clients ride with these men who are creating tomorrow's real blue chips.

Everybody started small and unsung, even the companies generated by Mr. Bell and Mr. Ford and Mr. Du Pont.

You won't find many analysts thinking that way.

In one house in which I worked early in my career, I was at a meeting in which a senior partner recommended a stock that never again saw the price at which the brokers subsequently sold it to clients. At the meeting, there wasn't a broker or analyst who got up and said, "Mr. Senior Partner, you don't know what the hell you're talking about." It wasn't solely because they would be talking back to the boss. The reason essentially was that the brokers and analysts present knew as little as the partner recommending the particular stock. It never even occurred to anyone to say, "Let's check it out before we put our clients into it."

As fast as high-speed presses can run, the big houses grind out lists of analyst-recommended stocks, the ten best, the twenty best, the fifty best.

It's all a very solemn procedure: God handing Moses the Ten Commandments on Sinai.

But if an investor really wants to evaluate the quality of research from the big houses, he should take the trouble to go back five years and check what his profits and losses would have been had he bought all those "best" stocks. Even forgetting the 1969–1970 bear market, which shot almost everything down, no investor who purchased any or all of these stocks that were supposed to perform brilliantly saw any performance comparable to what he would have seen had he been in one or several of the buried treasure situations in which I specialize.

McDonnell used to issue such a list—its "Top Twenty." Some performed passably, buoyed by the momentum of a bull market; many drifted off, prices never again to return to their buying levels. Many were shudderingly bad recommendations, notably Automatic Sprinkler, which ended up in 1968—not long after McDonnell's recommendation—as the fourth worst stock of the year!

Analysts are charged not only with seeking out new companies but constantly reassessing previous recommendations. What performed for example in 1967, a good market year, did not necessarily perform in 1968, which was also an up year. Every stock must be looked at as a kaleidoscope, its patterns and forms constantly shifting.

For a long while many of the twenty-five worst-performing stocks of 1968 were dear to the hearts of many analysts. At some point they had written glowing accounts of the futures of all these companies. But few followed through and warned the brokers in their houses to get clients out in time—if, in fact, any of the analysts were actually capable of foreseeing the factors that would drive the prices down.

How many clients are still nursing these issues, still watching and waiting for these stocks to perform? Some were tagged as the most glamourous situations available as late as 1967 and into 1968.

By mid-September, 1968, the twenty-five worst stocks and their downswings were:

Stock	Percentage Decline
1. Freeport Sulphur	38.37
2. Instrument Systems	33.41
3. Allied Products CV	33.18
4. Automatic Sprinkler	24.45
5. Collins Radio	22.74
6. Allegheny Ludlum St.	22.70
7. Sprague Electric	21.91
8. Commercial Solvents	21.25
9. Stokely Van Camp	20.45
10. Texas Gulf Sulphur	19.94
11. Vornado	19.44
12. Hazeltine	19.13
13. Beckman Instrument	18.14
14. Pan Am Sulphur	17.67
15. Merritt Chapman & Scott	17.37
16. Adams Millis	17.20
17. Brown Co.	16.88
18. United Aircraft	16.67
19. Amsted Industries	16.67
20. Reading Co. Pfd.	16.48
21. Boeing	16.42
22. Dictaphone	16.10
23. Ling-Temco-Vought	16.00
24. American Hoist & Derrick	15.06
25. Dorr Oliver	14.66

Many on that list were highly speculative, but several were well-established firms whose kaleidoscopes had greatly shifted.

So swiftly can the picture change for any stock that what an issue did the previous year guarantees nothing the next year. I have long argued this to clients who were touted into stocks through the analyst-broker funnel on the basis that they had high performance the previous year. Good analysts and brokers are aware of this danger, and constantly alert to it. Says James L. Phillips, of Vance, Sanders & Co., a Boston investment firm, "Past performance is one of the least reliable guides to future performance."

In 1968 Anaconda ranked as the second best performing

stock on the Big Board. But by July, 1969, the stock ranked as number thirty, and this before the worst of the bear market.

The thirty top-ranking stocks on the basis of performance in 1968 flip-flopped all over the place in the seven months to July, 1969.

The list:

Stock	Percentage Change	Rank, 1968	Rank, July, 1969
Johns-Manville	−18.6	1	24
Anaconda	−55.0	2	30
Woolworth	+14.1	3	1
Owens-Illinois	−5.6	4	11
International Paper	+6.0	5	4
American Tobacco	−8.6	6	15
General Foods	−5.2	7	10
Standard Oil of New Jersey	−7.3	8	13
Standard Oil of California	−9.9	9	17
American Can	−17.7	10	22
Sears, Roebuck	+10.2	11	2
U.S. Steel	−11.4	12	20
AT&T	−0.7	13	6
International Harvester	−23.2	14	25
duPont	−24.0	15	26
Goodyear Tire	−6.3	16	12
Texaco	−18.3	17	23
Chrysler	−31.0	18	29
Eastman Kodak	+4.8	19	5
General Electric	−10.8	20	18
Westinghouse Electric	−13.6	21	21
General Motors	−8.4	22	14
Bethlehem Steel	−3.6	23	9
Proctor & Gamble	+9.8	24	3
Union Carbide	−1.9	25	8
Swift	−9.2	26	16
Aluminum Co.	−1.4	27	7
Allied Chemical	−25.3	28	27
International Nickel	−10.9	29	19
United Aircraft	−28.1	30	28

Many investors read about people fortunate enough to become millionaires in one stock, and that is what the eternal quest is all about, Jason looking for the Golden Fleece. Instead, the average investor is getting a golden fleecing.

No one is going to become a millionaire or make a great deal of money by following the recommendations of the overwhelming majority of analysts who work for most brokerage firms and mutual funds.

More often than not, it is suicidal to depend on the judgments of these men.

Most analysts are experts only after the fact. They can give dozens of reasons why their recommendations didn't perform, but few have the skill to pick the new winners on anything approaching a consistent basis.

And so, let the buyer beware.

Since I riveted the bolts of my own operation into place, I have never relied on outside research to find good situations for my clients. I don't have that kind of courage or faith. I do my own research and sleep well every night.

To further mess up an already terribly fouled-up situation, paid drum beaters, a very questionable breed of financial public relations men, have now infiltrated the market in force. In the *Wall Street Journal* of March 13, 1970, staff reporter Jonathan R. Laing documented a new Mayday for the investor.

He thoroughly researched the researchers and uncovered the alarming influence that for-hire public relations men had gained over analysts. That this should be allowed to happen and go unpoliced is unforgivable.

The long story showed that everything short of under-the-table payoffs, booze and girls was utilized to influence analysts. And it is entirely possible that even those ancient and reliable tools of the public relations trade were also being used to get to some analysts. This, however, in the absence of evidence, is a guess. But I'd put a lot of my own money on my guesswork.

These public relations operators "spend full time courting the men whose recommendations are most likely to move the stock market. They are not always scrupulous in their ways," wrote Laing.

Bert Gross, chairman of Hill & Knowlton, Inc., one of the largest of the nation's PR firms, admitted candidly, "To say that the purpose of financial PR is to get the price of a client's stock up is to put it rather crassly, but that's what it amounts to."

Individual corporations hire these boosters to spark interest in their companies. The specious reasoning is that in the welter of so many issues floating around, their firms may be overlooked by the analysts. The hard fact is, however, that a good situation will always be uncovered, or should be if analysts are doing their job effectively and thoroughly. There are never that many good situations around, and the good ones surface sooner or later if anybody out there is realistically and honestly looking for them with a hard, practiced eye.

A financial PR man is naturally going to write an extremely favorable report for the firm that is paying him. And, of course, this is what happens.

On request, the PR firms, continued Laing, "will imprint free of charge the names of brokerage firms on the reports they write on clients, so that the broker can distribute them to his customers. This practice persists even though it was criticized as misleading by a 1963 SEC study of security market practices."

The dangers to clients from this kind of puffery are manifold —overestimating earnings, overemphasizing the positive factors of a company to the neglect of the negative, booming stocks that probably will fail dreadfully over the long term, removing the analyst's objectivity.

The PR men have their approach down to a science.

"The public relations men at some firms not only tell their clients whom to talk to but also what to say and how to dress while saying it," Laing added. "At Robert Taplinger Associates, a New York financial PR firm, younger executives of client companies are encouraged to dress in mod style when talking to analysts 'because that's the kind of go-go image the Street buys these days,' according to Robert McLaren, Taplinger's president. Older executives are advised to wear 'dark suits and sincere ties.' Also, a Taplinger man who used to work in television decides whether an executive should put on face makeup for appearances before analysts.

"Executives' remarks are gone over thoroughly to make sure 'they sound right,' Mr. McLaren says. The speaker is advised to make earnings forecasts 'that he can live with.' Confession to a bit of negative news also helps, Mr. McLaren advises, because 'it closes a company's credibility gap.' "

And that's when McLaren declared: *"I tell our clients to talk to each analyst out there like he was a beautiful, buxom girl he was trying to seduce."*

Public relations men should be barred and barred absolutely from any relationship with analysts. It is bad enough that the analyst is generally poorly equipped to make judgments on stocks. But the analyst who relies on a paid flack whose knowledge of the market can be put on the head of a pin is only doing further damage to his profession and the public.

Wall Street's *ménage à trois* is running roughshod over investors. It has come to the classic point where the house-analyst-broker triumvirate constitutes a process that knows the price of everything but the value of nothing.

FOURTEEN

"WHAT! YOU STILL DON'T OWN ANY MUTUAL FUNDS?"

The public has shown extraordinary willingness to believe there are financial geniuses in the hundreds, each heading a mutual fund.

JOHN KENNETH GALBRAITH

A quickly told ten-minute drama from the Theater of the Absurd:

Time: September, 1968.

Scene: A dilapidated building.

Cast: A wild-eyed, middle-aged man sitting behind an incredibly disordered desk. Two other men, both nondescript, hover at the brink of the desk.

As I open the door to the dingy three-room office, after a ride in a creaking elevator, the wild-eyed man and his acolytes are laughing and yelling maniacally.

All is bedlam.

The screaming phones go unanswered.

The office is in total disarray.

Unopened boxes are strewn everywhere.

Checks for God knows how many hundreds of thousands —maybe millions—of dollars are lying carelessly on the floor.

After a moment or two the laughter dies and the man with the wild eyes notices me. He begins to pepper me with an incomprehensible stream of conversation, none of which has anything to do with the reason for my visit.

As far as I can discern, and I can discern very little, the man is attempting to explain to me his philosophy of life.

What he is saying is complete gibberish.

The minutes travel swiftly. Dumbfounded, I move out the door, down the groaning elevator, into the street.

I have an overpowering desire to stop the first person I see, to talk to someone in possession of his faculties so that I can reassure myself I am still sane.

This episode took place not in some Gothic backwater home for the demented, but in the heart of Wall Street.

That litter of checks on the floor represented real, not play, money.

The wild-eyed man was known to have an income well in excess of $250,000 a year.

How did he earn this huge amount of money?

By running a mutual fund.

He was in sole charge of an important fund with thousands of investors.

On some days about *$1 million a day* streamed into the dilapidated building housing the dingy office!

I had gone to meet the man after receiving a phone call from him in which he said he was interested in what I was doing, in discussing with me whether his fund might buy into some of my situations.

After regaining control of my senses, I was appalled, which is a totally inadequate word to describe my feelings about this confrontation with lunacy.

I would as soon do business with this man as with a known criminal.

I couldn't free my mind from those unattended checks, checks from people who perhaps didn't have money to buy groceries, yet had sent money they could ill afford to lose to this idiot who should have been in an institution, not running one.

The man and his fund are still in business. And although his fund has been shorn of more than 50% of its asset value as of this writing and the SEC has stepped into the picture, money continues to arrive in his office from all over the country faster than he can bank it.

Mutual funds (economist Galbraith calls them "the counterpart of the old investment trusts") have done an incredibly clever job of brainwashing the shirtsleeve investor.

Although big investors of all types (colleges, pension funds, profit-sharing plans, hospitals, churches, libraries, fraternal organizations, banks, insurance companies and corporations) have become increasingly larger buyers, most shareholders in mutual funds are individuals with incomes no higher than $11,-000 a year.

The thrust of the industry has been unmistakably aimed at the small investor. And some 10.3 million small investors have poured the lion's share of cash into the funds, which in toto shuffle about $55 billion a year through the market. Moreover, the outlook for the funds is overwhelmingly bullish—some Wall Street observers envision the industry handling $175 billion a year within the next decade. One fund-watcher goes so far as to predict that 65–75 percent of the total population will hold securities through mutual fund ownership in the years ahead.

Investors have been lured into mutual funds by every conceivable device.

They have been promised the moon and the planets—riches, diversification in a large group of "safe" stocks and brilliant management.

None of these promises have been kept.

"You can become part owner in a portfolio of more than 120 U.S. corporations for $20 a month," advertises the nation's largest fund, Minneapolis-based Investors Diversified Services, which buttresses its mass media pitch with a force of 4,000 salesmen. IDS alone in the six mutual funds under its tent handles about $6 billion annually.

Brokerage houses buy generous amounts of newspaper space to push funds. Typical is Walston & Co., which "invites investors and prospective investors to a FREE lecture on WHAT MUTUAL FUNDS COULD MEAN TO YOU." And Paine, Webber, "The Stockbrokers to Know Invite You to be their guest at a free lecture on 'FINANCIAL PLANNING AND MUTUAL FUNDS.' "

But the ads that score a record in sophistry are those underwritten by the Investment Company Institute, the powerful public relations arm and trade organization of the richest funds.

Their advertising approach consists of the juxtaposition of the line, "What! You still don't own any mutual funds?" with official U. S. Labor Department statistics that chart the ferocious rise in the cost of all goods and services—property taxes up 30 percent since 1963, medical care up 57 percent over the last ten years, children's shoes up 41 percent, the cost of a college education up 70 percent since 1959, food prices up 20 percent in the last ten years, public transportation costs up 39 percent, car insurance rates up 48 percent and home ownership costs up 29 percent over a ten-year period.

The clear implication is that these zooming increases can be met by investing in mutual funds.

No realistic, thinking person could possibly believe it, yet it's obvious that millions do. The ads are pure pap, adroitly written. They convey a misleading relationship between the runaway cost-of-living and what buying into a fund will do for an investor. "To beat inflation, it takes more than fixed-dollar reserves, essential as they are," the copy continues. "Isn't it time you seriously considered mutual funds?"

A great many people *have* been seriously considering mutual funds, especially men and organizations who have the capability of organizing new ones. They know a good thing when they see it—the funds are an enormously profitable enterprise for those who run them (hence their mushroom proliferation). Profit for people who buy into the funds is quite another matter.

The mutuals have become an all-pervasive juggernaut. Everywhere the public turns there's a fund salesman on hand. Sears, Roebuck, with its own fund, sells shares through its retail outlets. Banks and other financial institutions are going into the fund business. At least one huge mutual plans to peddle its shares through supermarkets.

The ubiquity is amazing. Said *Changing Times* in January, 1970: "Deducting pay for mutual funds, already in effect in several places . . . may turn out to be the hottest idea since the funds were invented. Fund promoters claim that for a minimum of $5 a week, anybody can contract to buy in if he belongs to a group using a payroll deduction plan. . . . Expect a big push on these plans this year."

Classes in public high schools are held every weekday somewhere in the country so that mutual fund messiahs can spread their gospel. The classes are usually taught by a local broker or fund salesman, not by an objective observer—say, an economics professor—and certainly not by a critic of mutual funds such as myself. According to one evangelist-instructor, "I believe the classes offered in mutual analysis and their use in estate planning are pertinent to the financial success of every person, regardless of age."

Notes Yale Hirsch, author of *The 1969 Manual of Mutual Funds,* "To win the trust and confidence of prospective shareholders, many mutual funds choose impressive names and trademarks for themselves. And so, we see a mighty lion striding across the television screen, four hands in the traditional clasp of faith, and such inspiring symbols as Minutemen, pyramids, balanced scales, knights in armor, sailing vessels and castles.

"A number of funds like to be identified with our national origins and have chosen such names as Concord, Lexington, Pilgrim and Puritan, or Liberty, Independence and Freedom."

"It is our attempt in this publication to take you from Wall Street to Main Street," says a pamphlet distributed free to all comers, *An Informative Guide to Mutual Funds.* "We shall not endeavor to make security analysts out of you but to show you the value of the Mutual Fund Investment Company Industry and how it can assist you in planning your financial future."

How nice, how cozy, how wonderful, how generous of Wall Street inviting Main Street to share the wealth.

But what is Wall Street really sharing with Main Street?

Does the man on Main Street, that $11,000-a-year breadwinner, have a chance to come out ahead?

The truth is that mutual funds are bad news from whatever angle they are viewed.

Shirt-sleeve capitalists had best roll up their sleeves and take a good look at what they are buying when they stash money in a fund, take a good look at the fine print and past performance.

By the end of 1969 there were more than 600 mutuals. At least 80 percent were "load" funds—which charge hefty commissions going in. These outfits have fast-talking salesmen with fast pencils who'd sign up anybody—a man on welfare, on his deathbed, if he was radioactive or living in a cave. Widows and orphans too. And all would-be investors get the same song and dance, wild claims of future profits in face-to-face contact that even the nerviest of the funds wouldn't dare put in their ads. The "no-load" funds that do not charge any commission to buy in must be sought out by the investor.

So with a slick-talking mutual salesman on virtually every street corner, it is not surprising that the load funds control the business. They have 92 percent of all the money invested in mutuals, and at least nine out of every ten Americans who are fund shareholders.

The moment anybody goes into a load fund he is an immediate loser, he is bucking terrible odds.

The load can vary from 6 to 9½ percent. The man who invests $1,000 in a fund that charges 8½ percent, which is the average for the industry, has already seen his investment shaved by $85. He has paid $1,000 for his shares, but is getting only $915 worth. The commission clout is actually higher—the $85 sales charge translates into 9.3 percent.

Most of this tribute goes to the salesman.

Nowhere is it ordained that an 8½ percent commission should be charged. Why shouldn't a fund, which would be helpless without the investor's money, pay all or part of the freight for the salesman, or at least reduce that high commission? Why should the man on Main Street pay that much for the dubious privilege of being put into a dubious investment? He is taking far more risk than the man who buys a good stock from a competent broker at a much lower commission rate and with a much higher chance for appreciation.

As elsewhere on Wall Street, the small investor takes it on the chin in mutual funds.

While the man with $1,000 to invest pays a commission of 9.3 percent, the man or institution with $25,000 to invest in the same fund pays a much lower 6 percent, the $50,000 investor a still lower 4 percent.

The first commission charge is only the beginning of the erosion of the small investor's nestegg.

The man on Main Street has not only not been told he is paying his salesman's commission, but he isn't told that the next

commission bite further dilutes the overall value of the fund he
has just purchased.

The men running the fund have a contract that pays them
one percent of the net asset value of the fund.

The salesman doesn't tell the guy on Main Street that he is
helping some guy on Wall Street become a millionaire, whether
the Wall Street fund manager performs or not.

What the salesman tells the small investor is that his money
is going to be guided and increased by a bunch of financial
whiz kids.

But, almost without exception, the men who manage the
funds are dreadful. They're essentially promoters who are too
busy promoting and worrying about getting more and more
money into the fund, thus driving up their own cut. Even if
they had the capability of investing all the money they control
in a sound, safe and profitable manner—virtually impossible
by the very nature of the market—they would have scant time
to attend to that part of the operation, the part that should be
foremost in their minds.

I have met very few mutual fund management men who could
make it on my staff as an assistant deal man.

And not one of these fund managers that I have met or
heard about ever made big money on his own until he stumbled
into the mutual fund mother lode. The madman story at the beginning of this chapter is a perfect illustration, a fuzzy-brained
creep with *no* previous market experience handling millions.
The only miracle is that his fund isn't in bankruptcy, although
it is more than likely that that is where it will eventually land.

A surprising number of funds, incredibly, are one-man operations.

But no one man, even if he's a super-genius, can possibly
run a money-coining mutual mill by himself. He hasn't the time,
to say nothing of the ability to make even a feint in the direction of researching his situations. So he ignores doing his own
research, the seminal factor of the market, and buys stocks that
to him are virtually unknown quantities. These operators
haven't a clue to what the market is all about (it is all about
honest, thorough, intelligent research, a point I think has been

made repeatedly, but which can't be repeated often enough because almost everyone ignores it). And so on this tenuous talent does a considerable portion of Main Street's investment rise or fall in mutual funds.

In a society and system that commonly and correctly awards wealth to the achiever, the mutual fund manager has beaten the game, bludgeoned out of existence the ethic that preaches a man should earn his fortune by working hard and mastering his craft. Within that ethic lies the strength of the free-enterprise system, but Wall Street doesn't operate under free enterprise. It always has been, and it remains, a game for insiders who don't want to take a chance at open, honest competition. The mutual funds are the lineal descendants of the old trusts, pools and monopolies, and should be hit with the same restrictive legislation that the government used to curb those earlier-day "free-enterprise" amalgamations of capital and power.

The mutual managers—with their solid one percent of the fund's entire kitty—are risking absolutely nothing, while shareholders are risking every cent of their investment. If the majority of these management men had their income tied to quality performance, they'd starve to death.

The third dilution of the Main Street man's investment comes through a scam that amounts to outright thievery.

The salesman boosts those financial whiz kids running the fund, but also fails to mention that their brilliance must be enhanced by bringing in an advisory service.

In theory, hiring an advisory service composed of experts who know the market (if such a conglomerate of financial brainpower exists) sounds very convincing. These experts will put the fund's money to work profitably.

But then why is there a need for an outside advisory service when the fund in the beginning was sold on the basis of genius money management?

The answer lies in the fact that the "outside" advisory service is composed of insiders. And the thievery lies in the fact that all these advisory services include the same men who are the fund's managers and a few of their selected friends. The SEC permits

60 percent of a fund's directors to be associated with an advisory service. This regulation should be trampled into oblivion. All it does is allow management to bleed another one-half percent of the fund's total assets. That's the high flat fee the advisory outfit receives for its highly questionable advice.

Almost all the big funds operate this way, and it involves big money. In a fund worth $500 million, the one-half percent flat fee comes to $2.5 million a year. And again, these advisers need achieve nothing. So having no real incentive because of their guaranteed fee, they don't bestir themselves to achieve much.

I'd once again be an anonymous broker somewhere or standing in an unemployment line in a year or so if all I did was wing clients into stocks on hunches, tips, inadequate or no research, and then take my commissions, hoping the stocks somehow would perform. Without knowing my situations like a pathologist knows anatomy, I would, as do most brokers, mutual fund managers and their advisers, lose money for clients or make very little money for clients in proportion to the risks they are taking and the time involved waiting for appreciation—five years, ten years, or more.

People are in the market, or should be, for appreciation as soon as possible. I'm always skeptical of the client who says he's content to wait ten years for a profit.

Everybody on Wall Street has the responsibility to do his best to perform, to try harder. In the case of the mutuals the best way to force responsibility and performance would be a system in which management-adviser income was directly tied to the net increase in the value of the fund. When this happens, the boom in mutual funds will be over. Few of these geniuses could cut it without their guarantees. It is manifestly unfair for the men at the top who run the mutuals to continue to prosper in a bad year while their shareholders are taking a beating.

"Mutual funds just do not go out to buy advisory and underwriting services on the open market on the best terms they can get. They are generally tied to their advisers," said SEC Chairman Budge in testimony before a House Commerce Subcommittee considering regulation of the fund industry. "The arms-length bargaining element in the ordinary business relationship is completely lacking here."

A 9.3 percent commission going in.

One percent for management fees.

One-half percent for an advisory service.

It adds up to nearly 11 percent, within sight of the usury laws in many states. On top of all this, the fund pays brokerage commissions when it buys a stock. The fund also deducts the brokerage fee before computing the profit, if any, to the individual shareholder.

Even in the best fund, it usually will take the luckiest investor at least two years to break even.

The no-load fund unquestionably offers a much better deal for the investor who insists on being in mutuals. But not entirely disclosed in the prospectuses of the no-loads is a 1½ percent management fee plus a 1 percent fee when shares are sold. (The loads do not normally charge an exit fee.)

Through laziness, ignorance and lack of salesmen in supermarkets and department stores, the Main Street man for the most part is unaware he can get into a no-load at a much lower premium. Brokers in the Wall Street houses get no commission for selling no-loads, so, of course, they do not sell them, much less call a client's attention to the fact that he has an alternative. "No-loads are taboo, we don't even mention them," a broker in one of the Street's biggest houses told me. This is standard in all houses.

The would-be no-load buyer has a good deal of difficulty finding them. He can visit a local library, most of which have financial publications that list the no-loads. Some of the no-loads are beginning to advertise, but it's mostly through chancy word of mouth that investors discover no-loads. However, enough investors discovered them in 1969 so that sales of no-loads shot up 20 percent, the first year these funds crossed the $1 billion sales mark. By the end of 1969 the number of no-loads had grown from 63 to 116, and their champions say they are the fastest-growing segment of the fund business. The spokesmen for the no-loads predict at minimum that 20 million Americans will be in mutuals by 1979, and more and more will choose the commission-free funds.

And so they should—since they generally perform as well or better than the loads.

This has been pointed out by a number of other observers, and the record proves it.

"To justify taking the investor's money, the load fund should promise performance not just comparable with a no-load's but *better*, so much better as to compensate for the commission loss," said writer Michael Laurence in a careful study of the funds published in *Playboy*. "Until a few years ago, fund salesmen— and even the prestigious statistical services such as Wiesenberger —tried to imply that load funds, despite their steep commissions, generally outperform no-loads. This is simply not true, and most likely never was."

Columnist Sylvia Porter: "The long-term records of the no-load funds compare favorably with those of the load funds. The lack of a sales charge has nothing to do with the calibre of the fund's management. In fact, of the 20 best performers in the first six of 1969's awful months, six were no-load funds."

Primarily because they don't exact the brutal commissions, the no-loads usually make more money for shareholders. In 1968 four of the top five performers among the funds were no-loads. From 1967 to 1969, Neuwirth Fund, a no-load, was *the* best performer of all the mutuals.

The big ads for the funds imply, and the salesmen for the funds tell potential investors, that mutuals are a "new" concept for making money.

Not true.

Funds were popular in nineteenth-century England. They have been a significant force on Wall Street for the last twenty-five years.

But what has been new in the fund picture since the 1960s is the emergence of the go-go funds, the so-called performance funds.

The go-go's are the complete antithesis and a total perversion of the mutual fund's original concept: that the investor went into a fund for the long haul, and that he was spreading his risk

over many, many well-known and conservatively managed companies. Through the years, assuming a constantly growing economy and a rising market, the fund owner would prosper.

That's still the fundamental reason most people are attracted
to mutuals.

But when the go-go's tore into Wall Street, the rulebook was
discarded. The result was a speculative spree that did as much
as anything else to create the 1969–1970 bear market. Equally
as bad, the go-go's were guilty of fraud against their own shareholders, who had received a pledge of caution, conservatism,
common sense.

What they got instead was stingingly described by Sylvia
Porter in May, 1970. "By violently changing their make-up,
objectives and activities in the late 1960s in ways that profoundly
conflict with their original function, they have DOUBLE-
CROSSED us all. I could not anticipate—nor could you—
that respected, trusted professional managers of money would
act more emotionally and erratically than the wildest individual
gambler in penny stocks or horses. . . . In their insane race
for performance, the performance institutions have harmed us
all."

The go-go cult justified its approach with claims that shareholders would earn more money. But if the fund shareholder
wanted speculation he could buy anything on any of the exchanges or over-the-counter without the fancy management
fees, fees that added up to a walloping $190 million for all
funds in 1969.

In the red-hot market atmosphere of 1967, a number of the
go-go's lucked in. "Wonder boys" blossomed like wildflowers
all over Wall Street. These whizziest of the whiz kids thought
they knew it all. They had contempt not only for their shareholders but for competitive investment and value-oriented mutuals. Bragged one of the breed that soon came to be known as
gunslingers: "By the time a conventional fund buys an airline
ticket, visits the company and makes a committee decision to
buy a stock, it's time to sell. And go short."

The gunslingers shot their investors into Wall Street's boot hill, stocks that for all intents and purposes were dead at the time of purchase.

To catch a winner, some funds churned their portfolios 400 percent or more a year. Illinois Commissioner of Securities Thomas Hawekotte said he was alarmed to the point where he hoped that such fund managers would be screened more carefully before being allowed to operate in his state.

By their own buying power, the go-go managers created only artificial, temporary performance. When they got caught in the 1969–1970 downswing, they found that they couldn't move millions through the market effectively as in-and-out traders.

One example of hundreds that could be cited of the power —and stupidity—of the gunslingers was the action in Memorex, a San Francisco area computer equipment company. In 1966 Memorex was selling at 11. As a darling of the go-go's, it rose to 95⅛ in October, 1969. On October 30 gunslinger buying alone—64,800 shares—pushed the price to 150½. In 1969 the stock had a high of 173⅞. In 1970 the price seesawed wildly, from a low of 44½ to a high of 166¾.

Memorex had never paid a dividend, was selling around forty times earnings. It is a tremendously high-voltage, volatile stock. If professional traders or individual investors want to fool with this kind of dynamite, that's their business, but what right has any mutual fund to play with Main Street's money in this fashion?

What the go-go's bought seldom had any relationship to value. And that's what brought about their downfall. From January 1, 1969, to May 7, 1970, the go-go's outperformed even the shaky Dow Jones averages on the downside. The Dow was off 23.4 percent for that period, the go-go's 30.1. But that's only the average. Some go-go's were off a staggering 50 to 60 percent.

The go-go's never bothered to build research departments. They held research in contempt. Knowing a company, its marketing abilities, even what it produces, didn't concern the wonder boys. The manager of one go-go, handling hundreds of millions of dollars, readily admitted that neither he nor anyone

on his staff ever visited any of the companies his mutual purchased.

Trading the market—trying to outguess it—is a sure way of
going broke. I never try to trade the market. I'm not smart
enough. I always look for individual companies, not stocks.
These *wunderkinds* weren't smart enough either. And in the
end they outsmarted themselves. Many ended up on the street
looking for jobs. But what they did to their clients in their "insane race for performance" is unmentionable. What they did to
the market as a whole is disgraceful. Trading 200,000 and 300,-
000 share blocks as if they were 200 and 300 share blocks in a
few days instead of over a year or two, they were responsible
for much of the sawtooth fluctuations of the market and much
of its downward slide (a guilt shared in equal measure by some
of the biggest Wall Street brokerage houses, also caught with
vast holdings of speculative securities that proved in the bear
market to be unmarketable or salable only at large losses).

Like the vaunted blue chips, mutual funds of all types proved
to be a gigantic sieve through which investors' money was
drained. All the claims of the funds—inflation-hedge, safety in
diversification and knowledgeable management—proved to be
myths.

Of 470 funds charted by the Arthur Lipper Corporation for
the period from January 1, 1969, to May 7, 1970, four had
plunged over 60 percent; thirty-two tumbled from 50 to 60 percent; sixty-eight dropped 40 to 50 percent.

There were increases in value in the shares of only four funds!
The funds proved as vulnerable, more vulnerable, than many
stocks.

Fund shareholders joined stock owners in the misery of the
declining market, although mutual investors had paid more
dearly for the privilege of losing. About the only people who
made money through the bear market were those who sat it out
with their cash drawing interest in Treasury paper, banks or
savings and loans. These were the investors who would have the
liquidity to buy once the market turned around.

Despite their beating at the hands of these incredibly inept
money managers, Americans continue to shore up the funds

with ever greater gifts of cash. The myth of the mutuals dies exceedingly hard.

The process moves into motion a chain-reaction disaster.

According to a NYSE survey, the individual investor is playing a declining role in the market. Clients buying and selling for their own accounts are now responsible for less than 40 percent of the value of shares traded. Ten years ago, individuals purchased nearly 53 percent of share volume on all the exchanges, and about 44 percent of all shares on the Big Board.

Institutional buying, primarily by the mutuals, has given the funds a stranglehold on the market, with potentially titanic consequences.

Ralph Saul, then president of the American Exchange, said warningly and worriedly: "The institutional phenomenon could significantly alter the public marketplace. It is not prudent to assume that fair and orderly markets, liquidity, broad public distribution and adequate regulation are expectations that will always be met. Individuals who formerly made their own investment decisions are delegating these decisions to institutions. Aggressively trading blocks of thousands of shares as though they were 100 shares disrupts the marketplace, reduces public floats and the flow of individual public orders."

Saul added, "The pressure to continually perform in a short time span has resulted in some money managers acting like traders in the marketplace rather than fiduciaries. Pressures on corporate executives to perform rather than to produce may have serious implications for our markets. Prior to the pursuit of performance, institutions carefully acquired or disposed of their holding in order not to disrupt the market. Now, some managers acquire or dispose of large blocks in a matter of hours. The emphasis has moved from conservation of capital and returning income, on one hand, to market performance on the other.

"The individual shareowner, for whose protection the securities laws and the administration of those laws were created, is delegating his role to professionals, who in exercising their fiduciary responsibility, become a powerful factor in the market system but are assigned no responsibility to the system."

Without government-enforced regulations, it is extremely unlikely that the mutual funds will show any responsibility. The funds are pressing for their own seats on the exchanges, which would in time drive most brokerages virtually out of business and compel investors into enforced purchase of mutual fund shares, which is the worst thing they can buy.

To stave off this disaster, I would recommend that no fund be permitted by law to purchase a seat on the exchange.

I would recommend further legislation so tough that no fund be allowed to accumulate capital of more than $50 million. Anything over that can't work effectively in the market. No fund can trade $100 million or more without negatively disturbing the entire stability of the market, much less know what they are buying.

Legislative proposals to limit and severely curtail the commissions of the load funds has been bouncing around Congress since 1967. That year, Senator Thomas J. McIntyre, Democrat from New Hampshire, gave a graphic demonstration of the performance of the funds. Ten years before, he had thrown darts at a list of NYSE stocks. Investing a hypothetical $10,000, the senator said his dart-selected stocks were worth $25,300, a better performance, he said, than many funds run by alleged professionals!

Fundscope magazine figures that if a person invested $10,000 in the average reporting fund on January 1, 1960, and reinvested all capital gains and dividends, he would have had $21,-225 on December 31, 1969. Unquestionably there would have been less gain had he held through the 1970 bear market. This arithmetic also means that investors would not have been able to extract any capital or dividends to meet the rising inflationary costs in food, clothing, shelter and so on.

Of course, no one buys the "average reporting fund." That $10,000, depending on which fund the investor was in for ten years, would have inched up only to $11,475 (a terrible clobbering when measured against the cost-of-living rise) in one of the worst-performing mutuals. In one of the best-performing mutuals (assuming he was fortunate enough to be in such a fund and willing to wait a decade for appreciation), his investment would have jumped to $51,344. The figures are for the end of 1969, and do not take into account the downslide still in effect through 1970.

Before anyone invests in a fund, however, three more critical factors should be considered.

1. The mutual fund investor is punished in both bull and bear markets. In a good market, funds of all types tend to increase in price much more slowly than the Dow Jones, and the Dow Jones should never be the performance barometer for the investor concerned with exciting growth of capital.

2. Despite the Investment Company Institute's anything-but-subtle implications, the overwhelming majority of funds are not even protection against inflation, much less a reasonable risk in the search for appreciation. By far the best chance a client has to stay ahead of inflation is through appreciation in good stocks recommended by good brokers at the right time. I usually take new clients who have mutuals in their portfolios out of them, substituting situations I know will perform.

3. Every investor who has any money earmarked for the market should never forget: A first-rate special situation stock will outperform, and outperform tremendously, not only the Dow Jones but any fund alive.

FIFTEEN

YESTERDAY, TODAY AND TOMORROW

History is the torch that is meant to illuminate the past to guard us against the repetition of our mistakes of other days.

CLAUDE G. BOWERS

Frankly, if I had any money I'd be buying stocks right now.

RICHARD NIXON

After the worst of times, it was now the best of times.

The war had receded from memory, the nation was flexing its muscles under the leadership of a popular President surrounded by some of the most gifted men ever to serve in any government anywhere in the world.

The nation's leaders, as far as fiscal policy was concerned, had only to worry about relatively minor interest payments on the public debt and arrange comparatively small loans from abroad to help fuel the country's breakneck expansion.

In all, the United States was in excellent financial health, its future unlimited.

Both urban and agricultural America were prospering. Employment was high in the humming factories. Farmers could sell all they could raise. Construction boomed. Inflation was under control. Foreign trade flourished. Hundreds of new companies blossomed.

And Wall Street, beneficiary of tremendous volume with attendantly high commission income, was riding high, wide and handsome on the crest of a long bull market.

The national optimism could be cut with a carving knife, optimism that was reflected in galloping stock prices.

Everyone who had money was in the market—and it seemed that everyone did have money, farmer to financier. The President himself, his Cabinet (including his Secretary of the Treasury) were buying stocks. It was rumored that the Treasury

Secretary was profiting from insider information—he was a declared friend of business and in his hands rested many of the economic decisions which would make the market flourish or founder.

It was known beyond rumor that many men highly placed in the government were profiting from insider information, notably the Assistant Secretary of the Treasury. These men did little to hide their machinations. In a position to hear good news before the general populace, they bought certain stocks heavily, then sold after the man in the street heard the good news and shoved prices up through hectic buying. As insiders, they pocketed enormous gains.

But what matter?

Everyone had made money on Wall Street. There was more than enough wealth for all, and all were certain prosperity would never end, that prices were destined to continue their rise by supernatural decree.

New issues were quickly oversubscribed, and clamor for shares outran supply. Shares in one bank issue, for example, were gobbled up in an hour, oversubscribed by 20 percent. The price zoomed from 25 to 185 in a few months.

The inns and taverns and restaurants intersecting Wall Street bulged with men drunk on dreams of fantastic profits. Workers from the brokerage houses ate their lunches in the courtyard of venerable Trinity Church, the beautiful brownstone Episcopal beachhead at the foot of Wall Street. The clerks, messengers and bookkeepers, however, spent their time talking more of Mammon than God.

Wall Street was the pivot of the nation, and judging by immediate past performance every man assumed he had a right to realistically dream of making killing after killing in the market.

But the seven-year up market reached a climax. Stocks could not be expected to remain forever tumescent, although it was nearly impossible to find a man who realized this fact of Wall Street life. There was always one more killing to be made, always one more profit sweep to be gathered in. The market thus degenerated into an orgy of speculation, investors buying paper rather than stocks with fundamental values. Paper representing companies in land and foreign trade was extremely popular. Shares in banks were at a premium. And there was big buying in bonds and widespread speculation in currency and commodities.

A few men raised cautious, warning voices, proclaiming that the market had passed the point of speculation, which was bad and dangerous enough. Now it was a market strictly for gamblers.

Hardly anyone listened or believed. The Wall Street watering holes were as full of money-intoxicated men as ever.

The mania for stocks was so compulsive that men borrowed at high interest rates to purchase shares at a set price, expecting to turn a profit in as little as two weeks when their shares rose, at which time they would sell, take the appreciation and repay their loans.

The madness volleyed to the point where daily volume was so high that the houses could barely handle the trading.

Then the bubble exploded.

Prices settled, inched off, finally turned downward in a steep dive.

The gamblers couldn't cover their loans. The Assistant Secretary of the Treasury was plunged overnight into more than $3 million in debt. He went to jail when he couldn't meet his obligations.

Two dozen brokerage firms failed.

Yesterday's millionaires were today's paupers.

The banks tightened up on money. The government tightened up on credit.

Little money was to be had at any rate of interest.

Bankruptcy was the sour anthem being played in the ledgers of countless companies and individual investors.

Finally, when the worst was over, prices eventually settled. But the paper millionaires never recovered. Those who had bought value at realistic prices prospered in time.

The history books call this episode the Panic of 1972.

President George Washington and his band of brilliant nation-builders had suffered losses through their speculations in the market. Treasury Secretary Alexander Hamilton's name has never been completely cleared of suspicion he acted on insider knowledge, although there were then no rules other than moral strictures against acting on such information. The Assistant Secretary of the Treasury who went to debtors' prison was a man named William Duer, a hustling insider, a long-forgotten loser who even with all the intimate knowledge he had of government economic policy failed to realize he couldn't expect to profit indefinitely. The most influential man to raise his voice against the tide of speculation was Thomas Jefferson, who had he not set himself the more important task of helping to guide an infant confederation of thirteen colonies, would have made an excellent broker. Jefferson had urged his countrymen to buy solid investments in stocks that would grow, companies engaged in enterprises basic to the well-being of the nation. He deplored paper gamblers such as Duer.

The 1792 panic proved that even many of the legendary Founding Fathers were not immune to the mania for speculation and gambling. The greatest collection of massed minds to come together in one period of history could be severely singed in the market. They fired the shot heard round the world, fought, bled and sacrificed through an earthshaking Revolution, wrote an unparalleled Constitution and forged an unmatched democracy.

But when it came to Wall Street, all their brilliance and talent wasn't enough. When it came to making money in the market they allowed greed and gossamer to overtake reason and logic.

So was it then.

So is it today.

Time and experience haven't changed the orientation of the speculator. Time and experience haven't changed human nature. Down through the years of the American economy, the most amazing and unique accumulation of riches in all human experience, there have been and are legions who troop to Wall Street and bet the earnings of a lifetime and mortgage their futures through borrowing in the hope of getting rich quick.

Getting rich quick in Wall Street is as emblematic of the American Dream as the stars and stripes.

There are those, of course, who've been rewarded with swift riches in the market. Most of these favored people have been uncommonly lucky or operated as insiders.

But the majority who have come to Wall Street with trust and hope, ready to invest $1 million or $1,000, have not made it, contrary to all the burnished propaganda of the history books and the NYSE.

The stories of the lucky and the manipulators are the ones that are heard, read and remembered. These are the tales that bring millions into the market and perpetuate the illusion of Wall Street as a financial Camelot.

Yesterday and today, the vast bulk of investors in the last analysis have not prospered substantially, if at all, from Wall Street.

Yesterday and today, Wall Street chalks up far more losers than winners.

As for tomorrow, it's highly unlikely that the ratio of losers to winners will change dramatically. More are going to continue to lose instead of win.

Risk is inherent in the market. Not everyone can come out a winner. But the odds and opportunities for coming out ahead could be realigned. Wall Street needn't be a slot machine with an occasional jackpot only for the lucky few or for those who have rigged the tumblers.

The odds for coming out ahead could be shortened by the member firms of the NYSE and ASE if, above all else, responsibility to clients instead of avarice was the reigning motive of Wall Street.

Since that is not about to happen in the forseeable future, the client will have to fend for himself—or find a broker who will give him an honest chance at a profit.

One of the results of the Panic of 1792 was the establishment of the NYSE, charged, among other things, with keeping an orderly market so that panic could never recur.

The idea that a group of men banded together in a tight little club, a group of men traditionally short on principle and who have functioned profitably as no more than glorified auctioneers, could maintain order in the market has not proved out in 180 years of financial tumult.

Historically the NYSE, as every other exchange in America and throughout the world, has been primarily a go-between for buyers and sellers, its profits accruing from a charge for each transaction. Along Wall Street, some houses have for years specialized solely in investment banking. Others fortify their retail order business by participating in underwritings, a lavishly rewarding field that serves the important function in the economy of raising fresh capital to finance new enterprises or to refinance older companies.

There have been brazen attempts by many, such as the House of Morgan (now, incidentally, a limp shadow of what it once was), to dominate the American economic landscape. In past eras buccaneers were sometimes successful in cornering certain industries or commodities, but the enormously diverse and complex American treasurehouse has always been too vast for any cabal of financial titans or any one man, one bank, one brokerage to control the national wealth. There are effective government regulations and enough SEC enforcement to prevent at least the most blatant attempts at massive manipulation. The newest threat of control, at least in the market, comes from the monster mutual fund industry, which hopefully will have its wings clipped in time through its own performance ineptitude, investor disenchantment and tougher regulations—probably a combination of all three factors.

Contrary to what many think, Wall Street has never really ruled the American economy. Wall Street doesn't even really understand the nature of the American economy. Essentially, the Street has been and remains an echo chamber, reflecting the national investment mood and the national financial condition. Wall Street has not been a pace-setter, but a follower of the collective mood of optimism or pessimism in vogue during any particular period.

The mighty of the Street are above all salesmen, hawkers, barkers, pitchmen. The last thing they can be called is innovative or prophetic.

This has been true since the first panic in colonial America, which occurred in 1785, seven years before the selloff of 1792.

The generations of geniuses, for all their apparent power at the summit of Wall Street, have followed and served, not led or ruled. They have proven totally ineffective in anticipating, much less coping with, what economists variously call a panic, crisis, crash, depression, erosion, recession.

Down through the years bear markets have stalked America with varying degrees of economic paralysis for the nation and pain for clients.

About all Wall Street could do during these crises was whistle in the dark, issuing bullish statements that stock prices were bound to rise. Its indefatigable surface optimism has always been linked to the categorical imperative of selling stocks and earning commissions, no matter what stocks it sold, no matter how many investors were led to destruction.

After 1792, bear markets occurred in 1785, 1808, 1819, 1825, 1837, 1847, 1860, 1865-69, 1873, 1878, 1884, 1889, 1898, 1903, 1920, 1929-32, 1937, 1940, 1945, 1955, 1962, 1963, 1966 and 1969-1970.

Boom and bust in the national economy and therefore in the echo-chamber stock market are built into the American system, inherent and endemic. But it is also true that the economy in general can perform quite well while Wall Street (and investors) suffer a depression. This was illustrated through the 1969–1970 period, with the national economy in a definite downslide but nowhere near the downslide that engulfed Wall Street. When such a mix occurs, it is only common sense to stay out of the market until the propitious moment arrives to get back in, when the intelligent analyst or broker estimates the bottom has been touched.

Every bad market occurs for a constellation of reasons, depending on prevailing conditions at a given time. But the one tie that brings all down markets together, the one critical common denominator, is that a point is reached when value is ignored in favor of speculation, the manifest-destiny psychology that stock prices will never react negatively as well as positively.

The belief persists among American investors that the stock market—sooner or later—will increase their wealth.

In the long haul this has been true. Stock prices have reflected the continued growth of the country. However, not all investors have profited, immediately or ultimately, from the overall historical surge of the economy.

It has always boiled down to choice and timing. What stock was bought? When was it bought? At what price? When was it sold? At what price was it sold?

In the answers to those questions lies the difference between profit and loss.

There are stocks that can be held 1,000 years and will never see their purchase price again. There is always a time to sell, always a time to buy, always a time to hold.

Gamblers and speculators in the end get burned every time. Those who buy real growth and value are the ones who eventually reap rewards. But even knowing and accepting this, the investor still is in potential quicksand. He must find and correctly evaluate growth and value himself or search out a broker who can do it for him.

Doom-sayers in every bear market have been ready to write the country off, consign the economy and future growth to limbo.

In every case they have been wrong.

As a bull market inevitably turns into a bear market, a bear market inevitably turns into a bull market, so far do the strengths of the American economy outweigh its weaknesses.

On December 3, 1968, the Dow averages were at 985.21. By May, 1970, the drop was so severe that the Dow was off 29 percent. Statisticians set themselves the grim job of comparing the 1929 disaster to 1969–1970, emerging with the conclusion that on a per capita basis each of America's 26 million shareholders had paper losses of almost $10,000 since late 1968. The downswing in effect canceled most of the profits accrued in the bullish decade of the 1960s.

Not much had changed since the speculative spree of 1792. Few bothered to learn from history, history "that is meant to illuminate the past to guard us against the repetition of our mistakes of other days."

Eighteen decades of experience had taught the gamblers and speculators nothing.

The 1969–1970 bear market was yet another payoff for yet another speculative jag. Prices had run to the point where investors were mesmerized by brokers into buying stocks selling at thirty, forty, sixty times their price-earnings ratios. There was enough water in most of these stocks to float the Spanish Armada.

Analysts were recommending, brokers were selling and investors were buying, an insane triple play, again a chain reaction detonated by Wall Street's necessity to sell whatever could be sold.

Billions thus were poured into calamitous situations.

The NYSE became an outpost for trading in Chinese money.

At three o'clock in the morning, bored, tired, impatient gamblers in the Vegas casinos with a need for action, spin out their chips sans any realization that the chips represent real money. The same thing occurs during a speculative binge in the market. Money loses its value as money, and millions toss it into anything brokers tell them is going to jump in price, when with five minutes of reflection even the most naive of investors should realize that buying stocks selling at staggering multipliers makes as much sense as climbing a mountain with leather-soled shoes.

Many communities throughout America and in Britain have written into law a three-day grace period for people who buy merchandise from slick door-to-door salesmen. The cooling-off period has saved millions from acting in haste, allowing their emotions and natural predilections for acquisition to subside, allowing rationality to surface, allowing them a chance to ask themselves, "Do I really need this refrigerator, freezer or aluminum siding?"

It wouldn't be entirely ridiculous if the government wrote a statute giving an investor the same option of a three-day cooling-off period, permitting him to change his mind after measuring and thinking through his snap decision. Such a requirement would play temporary havoc with the market as now constituted, but in the long run it would stabilize stocks and reduce speculation. It would keep a lot of people out of trouble and do much to turn a nation of market gamblers into a nation of more cautious investors. No client need be immediately hustled into a stock by a broker who doesn't give a damn about him, who is already figuring his commission instead of how the stock will perform. There are very few instances where the client will lose much, if anything, by postponing his buy order for at least three days. Lightning buys are for professional traders, not the average client who should be going for capital gains.

A three-day rule will be adopted by NYSE member firms on the same day the thermometer hits 120 degrees above zero in Antarctica.

Chinese money was also poured into the cliché blue chips the Wall Street houses continued booming to clients in the midst of the bear market. The houses were stressing "quality" at a time when profits of the corporate giants were off considerably, at their lowest since July, August and September of 1967, a net after-tax slide from $8.4 billion to $6.9 billion during the first quarter of 1969. The average profit dip was 18 percent among the biggest corporations in the world. Some firms were off 6 percent; others, such as automobile, airplane, metal-working machine and furniture industries, were down 25 percent.

And so if the sinews of the American economy, the blue chips, couldn't be trusted to survive in a bear market, what could be trusted?

Virtually nothing.

The slide in profits of the large firms also helped contribute to the down market in both a real and psychological sense.

Other complicating factors of the bear market were the cost of the Vietnam war, the move into Cambodia and the additional psychological uneasiness induced by the lingering, unresolved Indochina situation.

Rampant inflation and a sense of gloom at rising unemployment statistics gave America the worst of two possible economic worlds, a higher cost of living when more people were out of work. This hardly bolstered confidence.

The choking squeeze on credit was a further body blow to the market. When the Democrats gave way to a GOP Administration in January, 1969, the Republicans found they couldn't cope with inherited financial burdens. Inflation couldn't be tamed, so the Nixon strategy became one of putting strong clamps on money. Credit dried up quickly, more quickly than anyone thought possible. People couldn't borrow as readily from banks, even at higher interest rates. When investors can't borrow, they generally stop buying stocks. Then it went much further. Investors began selling stocks out of portfolios, even at a loss, to reduce some of their previous loans.

The bear market was feeding on itself.

It is not an accident that the word "depression"—a term borrowed from the psychologist's argot—is used to describe a hemorrhaging economy. Depression was what most investors felt, and when investors are depressed, they buy fewer and fewer stocks.

A bear market usually turns bullish at the point when hysteria is at its wildest and hope is at its nadir. Then come the thumping rises in the averages, record volume, mileposts established in the list of new highs. Across the board almost everything goes up. Five-minute traders and in and outers make a lot of quick money, only to lose it later when they finally guess wrong. Ultimately, the speculative orgy overtakes the market and it turns bearish again.

The whole process is doomed to be repeated endlessly in the future.

Investors smart enough to hold their financial firepower in reserve during a bad market should seek out on their own, or have their brokers pin down, companies whose earnings are in an upward trend. These are the first stocks to turn around when a bear market seques into a bull market. Such stocks are going to react and react fast, and even in a bad market the proportionate loss in basically sound situations will be less than in companies that are dead or stagnant. Companies that have earnings down from previous years are not going to keep rising in prices.

A really smart, responsible broker goes into a period of almost complete inaction in a bad market. A responsible broker, when he estimates the market has seen its bottom, then begins recommending stocks that are absolute bargains, bargains in the true sense of the word, and this generally excludes the traditional blue chips, whose major play occurred in some cases ten or twenty years ago.

The new winners are going to be companies whose major play has yet to come, even though most investors are not yet familiar with the names of these stocks. This is how the watchful broker should earn his bread and fulfill his responsibility to clients.

To believe the statistics of the National Industrial Conference Board, the future of America is boundless in terms of increased population, salaries and disposable income. Take-home paychecks will have increased unbelievably. Average family income in 1969–1970 was $8,330, to be augmented by 1980 to $13,800. There will be 95 million in the working force, and a fantastic $350 billion will be spent on luxuries compared to $50 billion allotted to such spending during the 1950s.

Other soothsayers see the average family income rising to $19,000 in the next ten years, and with inflation half of what it was from 1960 to 1970.

A $2 trillion national economy is in sight.

The handful of bloated brokerage firms that will probably be around in 1980 are certain to benefit. New investors will flood into the market. Unfortunately, the bulk of them may still be hypnotized by the false allure of mutual funds.

Wall Street will muddle through as ever, and as ever will continue picking up commissions while the picking is good.

Everyone who comes into the market—60 million shareholders are anticipated by 1980—will have the undying dream of striking it rich.

It will happen for very few.

The market will remain a place for insiders, the one percent who always come out. The year 1982 may be the same as 1792.

SEC strictures against insiders are violated every day on Wall Street, and unless the SEC really gets to the core of this continuing swindle, the public will continue to suffer. The average investor has nowhere near the same chance to profit while there are brokers and other insiders with a pipeline to the mutual funds, men who know in advance what the funds are going to buy, know beforehand about a piece of good news in a company that will send its stock soaring.

The only chance for the individual investor to come out will be with a research-oriented broker, who will make him an honest insider. The broker who has gone to the considerable trouble of digging out the facts that will make the price of a particular company rise, and spreads the situation around to all his clients, is the best one to show how important money will be made in the future.

An everlasting enigma to me is that people keep showering money into a very sick Wall Street establishment. It's no accident, given the low quality of management, that the Wall Street houses took a proportionately worse beating during the 1969–1970 bear market than the rest of the economy.

The NYSE, instead of its current membership of old men or men who think in old-fashioned ways, needs to recruit men of my generation or the generation behind me, men who really care about the future of the securities industry, men who feel that their overriding responsibility is to the client, not the partners of NYSE member firms.

If the analyst is to survive on Wall Street, his standards and methods of operation must be vastly improved.

Ideally, the broker's function should be changed completely so that he is no longer a salesman but is a broker-researcher. To those who cry that a broker doesn't have time to research companies, I answer that he doesn't have time not to.

The good situations are always there waiting to be found.

The growing reliance of investors on tip sheets is a sad development. These outfits are nothing but tout operations. They appeal to the lazy and the get-rich-quick dreamers. A stock service will recommend a given issue and it will rise on the sheer force of the subscribers buying the stock. But the rise usually is short-lived. The price settles back and then turns downward. The subscriber has paid for the privilege of being a loser.

If an investor must have a stack of "research" or tip material to fan through, any brokerage house will give him a shopping bag full—free. Their stuff is no better or worse than what subscribers pay for tip sheets.

At the outset I emphasized that there is no secret to what I am doing, what I have done. Brokers who follow my example are those who will achieve the twin objectives of earning tremendous money for themselves and their clients.

It makes no difference if a broker lives in Lincoln, Nebraska, or Miami or Minneapolis or Anchorage. If he's going to put his clients into Occidental Petroleum, he can find out the true situation at Occidental before he risks a dime of a client's money.

Above and beyond everything else, a client should remember how tough it was in the first place for him to earn the money he is investing in the market.

It is madness to commit that money to the first broker he meets, a broker who probably operates under a NYSE shingle, but that shingle doesn't carry the integrity of a caduceus.

I travel at least 300,000 miles a year, my associates another 750,000 miles. It takes that kind of effort to search out the right situations.

When I call a client with recommendations, I've paid my dues, done my homework. I cannot and do not give him 100 percent certitude that he is going to profit. But I know that what I'm recommending are the very best situations I have been able to find in a systematic, questing, objective way.

There is no substitute for knowing a company, for knowing a company's management, for knowing what a company is likely to earn, how it stacks up against its competition—and how all this information should be evaluated for the benefit of the client.

Any individual investor ready to put money into the market can—as some do—operate as his own broker. It's possible if the individual has the time and the ability to develop the skills to search out his situations. Since few investors are in that position, since they are otherwise occupied, it becomes a matter of the client finding the right broker.

How?

First of all, don't buy anything from a broker who solicits on the telephone. The broker should be confronted in his office when the first purchase is made.

Approach a broker with the same care any sensible person would use in evaluating a surgeon who is to operate on his brain.

Settle for nothing but the best.

Settle for nothing but a first-class track record.

Settle for nothing less than proven past performance.

When the broker is confronted face-to-face, the first tip-off as to whether he's a good or bad broker is if he pulls out a sheet from house research, telling you what another man thinks of a particular company. The client has no way of knowing how good or bad the assessment of that other man is. If the broker solemnly reads excerpts from a report prepared by an analyst, say, "Thank you very much"—then walk out. If the broker says, "You ought to buy this because it's had a lot of action on the tape," say, "Thank you very much"—and walk out.

If a broker says he's made a careful personal study of the company he's recommending, then it's time to begin listening. Utilizing that as a starting point, ask the broker if he's been to the plant, conferred with management; ask him for an evaluation; put the burden on him of proving he knows what he's talking about.

Make certain that a broker is personally involved in the stock he's talking up, personally involved in that he has the stock in his own account or has investigated it himself.

That will largely determine the caliber of the man asking a client to commit his hard-earned money.

If a client doesn't do these things, he may as well blow his money at the racetrack or Vegas. At least he'll get some sunshine and kicks.

A client should never be anxious. He should hesitate, think. He shouldn't be gulled by the better-get-in-now pressure, this is a chance of a lifetime, it's this minute or never.

There are going to be spectacular winners as long as America has a growth economy, which will be a very long time indeed. But an investor has more lives than a cat. There's a chance of a lifetime every month in the market, if the client's broker is capable of uncovering it.

The great new winners—the stocks that in the future will move from 8 to 240—will always be there. There will always be another Monogram.

A man operating as a broker-researcher is the only catalyst who can guide a client to profit. These men are comparatively rare, but with diligent research they can be found by investors.

If a client can't find such a man, he shouldn't invest in the market.

On April 28, 1970, President Nixon made his now-famous declaration that if he had any money he'd be buying stocks.

Less than a month after his statement, the market was down a horrendous 59.08 points. Three days later, on May 25, the Dow fell to 641.36, off 20.81 points, the biggest one-day drop since President Kennedy's assassination, when it plunged 21.16.

For Mr. Nixon, as for every investor, it all narrows down, once the decision has been made to *risk* money in the market, to three questions:

When should I buy?

What should I buy?

And, transcendently, from what broker am I going to buy? Which broker am I going to heed before I entrust money I can't afford to lose?

Millonaire or otherwise, I have never met a man who thought he could afford to lose the price of a good dinner.

Wall Street is anything but a philanthropic institution.

A broker is giving a client nothing if he is not giving the best of which he is capable.

And the best must always be the finest of the wheat.